"Professor Sanders is one of the most sophisticated and historically sensitive contemporary theologians. In this volume he brings his considerable acumen to bear on the relation between the doctrine of the Trinity and the scope and content of salvation. The result is a tour de force that demonstrates the fecundity of trinitarian theology for the church and the Christian life. An impressive achievement."

— **Oliver D. Crisp**
University of St. Andrews

"To paraphrase Kant: the Trinity without salvation is empty, an intimidating abstraction; salvation without the Trinity is blind, an inexpressible experience. Sanders here strikes the perfect balance between the triune God of the gospel and the gospel of the triune God, offering a compelling argument for both their proper distinction and their proper relation. Thanks to this *Fountain of Salvation,* my cup of theology runneth over. I can't wait to assign this refreshing cup of cold water to my students."

— **Kevin J. Vanhoozer**
Trinity Evangelical Divinity School

"In *Fountain of Salvation*, Fred Sanders offers a wonderful introduction to the Trinity as the object of Christian worship and as a belief inseparable from and indeed structuring the doctrine of salvation. He then leads us clearly, interestingly, and dependably through recent theological debates on this fundamental Christian belief, always showing us where (and where not) those debates really do enable Christians to grow in knowledge of the Triune life. Across Christian traditions Sanders's argument should resonate and inspire."

— **Lewis Ayres**
Durham University

"In *Fountain of Salvation*, Fred Sanders continues, interrogates, and extends the modern program of reflecting on the being of the triune God in light of the history of salvation. Ever on guard against reducing the being of God to his works, Sanders analyzes topics as diverse as atonement, church, Christian life, and theological education through the bifocal lens of Trinity and salvation. The result is a work of subtle judgment and profound insight, exactly what one would expect from our most gifted theologian of the Trinity."

— **Scott R. Swain**
Reformed Theological Seminary, Orlando

T0287006

"In this characteristically insightful work, Fred Sanders illumines the deep and inextricable connections between the doctrine of the Trinity and the doctrine of salvation. Treading a difficult path through the theological temptations and perils on either side, he sets out a sound programmatic agenda for constructive Trinitarian thinking today. Deeply rooted in Scripture and widely informed by tradition, this volume is a welcome and salutary addition to the shelves of both theologians and pastors."

— **Paul T. Nimmo**
University of Aberdeen

FOUNTAIN OF SALVATION

Trinity and Soteriology

Fred Sanders

WILLIAM B. EERDMANS PUBLISHING COMPANY
GRAND RAPIDS, MICHIGAN

Wm. B. Eerdmans Publishing Co.
4035 Park East Court SE, Grand Rapids, Michigan 49546
www.eerdmans.com

27 26 25 24 23 22 21   2 3 4 5 6 7

ISBN 978-0-8028-7810-6

Library of Congress Cataloging-in-Publication Data

Names: Sanders, Fred (Fred R.), author.
Title: Fountain of salvation : trinity & soteriology / Fred Sanders.
Description: Grand Rapids, Michigan : William B. Eerdmans Publishing Com-
    pany, [2021] | Includes bibliographical references and index. | Summary:
    "A soteriology expounded through the lens of trinitarian theology"—
    Provided by publisher.
Identifiers: LCCN 2021009211 | ISBN 9780802878106 (paperback)
Subjects: LCSH: Trinity. | Salvation—Christianity.
Classification: LCC BT111.3 .S274 2021 | DDC 234—dc23
LC record available at https://lccn.loc.gov/2021009211

To my mom

Contents

Behold, God is my salvation;

...

With joy you will draw water from the fountain of salvation.

—Isaiah 12:2–3 (author's translation)

The Gospel of God

CALVIN FAMOUSLY OPENS his *Institutes* with the observation that all true and sound wisdom consists in knowledge of God and knowledge of the self. But "which one precedes and brings forth the other is not easy to discern,"[1] on account of how many bonds hold them together, and the way these two knowledges mutually presuppose each other. There seems to be no proper place to start. Calvin proposes this difficulty to his readers as if it is a puzzle to be solved, but he only does so as a rhetorical strategy to draw us into the circle of the exposition of Christian wisdom. In fact, as his ensuing discussion makes clear, it does not matter which subject is treated first, so long as the two come together in the decisive encounter between God and humanity which alone can give us theological insight into both.[2] He invites us to consider the problem of how these two matters are related to each other just so he can engage our minds simultaneously in the contemplation of them both.

With slight adjustments, we can say that the same complex relationship obtains between the doctrine of the Trinity (as knowledge of God) and the Christian doctrine of salvation (which stands here as knowledge of self). The two arise together from the scriptural testimony, because the Bible consistently speaks of salvation and of God together. In particular, the revelation of the triunity of God is tightly bundled with the fulfillment of God's promises in the gospel, and it is the Father's sending of the Son and the Holy Spirit that accomplishes at the same time the revelation of God as Trinity and the particular salvation accomplished by these three as one.

1. Calvin, *Institutes of the Christian Religion* 1:1, McNeill/Battles 1:35.
2. In this carefully structured exordium, Calvin invites us to ponder this relation first in one direction (1.1.1) and then in the other (1.1.2). He then displays, from a half-dozen biblical examples, the "dread and wonder" by which we are "stricken and overcome" when the self recognizes its place in the presence of God (1.1.3). Calvin then reverses his initial sequence, moving into a longer discussion of the knowledge of God (1.2.1), which he handles first because it fits "the order of right teaching."

The Triune God and Salvation

This book is concerned with exploring and specifying precisely that relation between the Trinity and salvation. The presupposition of everything in the following chapters is that a great deal is at stake for theology and the Christian life in grasping this relation correctly. If the two doctrines are only connected loosely, both suffer. The doctrine of the Trinity, presented without reference to soteriology, begins to seem altogether irrelevant, floating away into a conceptual stratosphere as something that may be true but cannot be significant. The doctrine of salvation meanwhile, treated in isolation from the doctrine of the immanent Trinity, sinks down to the level of mere history and experience, losing its transcendent reference. Therefore these doctrinal complexes must be connected. On the other hand, if they are drawn together too tightly, human salvation begins to seem inherent to the divine reality itself, as if God has no other business but to save, no other being than being savior. The godness of God is in danger, in this case, of being eclipsed by the dynamics of salvation. The more classical, lofty, or austere a doctrine of the triune God is, the more it seems immune from being dissolved into soteriology. Christian theology ought to be an exercise in knowing God precisely as the God of salvation. But we have not confessed the God of salvation at all if we have not confessed God's perfection and self-sufficiency apart from any considerations about salvation. As Karl Barth asked, "What would 'God for us' mean if it were not said against the background of 'God in Himself?'"[3] Ivor Davidson draws attention to both elements of this polarity when he describes "the boundaries of speech about reconciliation" as being "marked out by the marvel of its *positum*: '*This is the God who is known—by us!*'"[4] More expansively, Davidson argues that this polarity is necessarily constitutive of the theological task of soteriology: "Soteriology's particular but spacious remit is to retell the grand sweep of this divine economy as announced in Scripture: to identify the source, occurrence and consequences of salvation by speaking of the nature of the one who lets us know him as he really is."[5]

In the comings and goings of recent academic theology, it is roughly fair to say that a great deal of theological excitement was generated by a recovery

3. Karl Barth, *Church Dogmatics*, 1/1, trans. G. W. Bromiley, 2nd ed. (Edinburgh: T&T Clark, 1975), 171 (hereafter: *CD*).

4. Ivor J. Davidson, "Introduction: God of Salvation," in *God of Salvation: Soteriology in Theological Perspective*, ed. Ivor J. Davidson and Murray A. Rae (Burlington, VT: Ashgate, 2011), 7.

5. Davidson, "Introduction," 7.

of the soteriological side of this equation in the late twentieth century, after which a kind of correction set in to recover the side of the equation devoted to God *in se*.[6] Certainly there are some contemporary theological projects oriented toward recovering a more classical theological emphasis on God's aseity and blessedness: Kevin Vanhoozer's *Remythologizing Theology*, James Dolezal's *All That Is in God*, Steve Duby's *God in Himself*, and, in their own distinctive ways, the large systematic projects of John Webster and Katherine Sonderegger.[7] Many of them are animated by a sense that the trinitarian excitement of the past half-century put the clear confession of God's aseity in jeopardy. None of them, however, could be credibly accused of unhooking the doctrine of God from the doctrine of salvation, or of pursuing trinitarianism nonsoteriologically. Conversely, the same sort of allowance must be made for the major practitioners of the earlier renaissance of economic trinitarianism. Theologians like Karl Rahner, Wolfhart Pannenberg, Jürgen Moltmann, and Robert Jenson may have re-centered the business of trinitarian theology radically onto the project of describing God's engagement with creaturely history, but they also signaled their intention to acknowledge the freedom of God. Catherine Mowry LaCugna's influential 1991 book *God for Us* was widely heralded both as the manifesto of a powerfully focused thinker and as one of the most characteristic products of the entire trinitarian revival. She begins her book with a recognition of both poles of the polarity we are considering:

> To be sure, the doctrine of the Trinity is more than the doctrine of salvation. Theology cannot be reduced to soteriology. Nor can trinitarian theology be purely functional; trinitarian theology is not merely a summary of our experience of God. It is this, but it also is a statement, however partial, about the mystery of God's eternal being. *Theologia* and *oikonomia* belong together;

6. For details, see especially chapters 9 and 10 below. See also Stephen R. Holmes, *The Quest for the Trinity: The Doctrine of God in Scripture, History, and Modernity* (Downers Grove, IL: IVP Academic, 2012), and Lincoln Harvey's remarks that "the renaissance project is now under attack and beats a retreat," in "Essays on the Trinity: Introduction," in *Essays on the Trinity*, ed. Lincoln Harvey (Eugene, OR: Cascade Books, 2018), 4.

7. Kevin J. Vanhoozer, *Remythologizing Theology: Divine Action, Passion, and Authorship* (Cambridge: Cambridge University Press, 2010); James Dolezal, *All That Is in God: Evangelical Theology and the Challenge of Classical Christian Theism* (Grand Rapids: Reformation Heritage Books, 2017); Steven J. Duby, *God In Himself: Scripture, Metaphysics, and the Task of Christian Theology* (Downers Grove, IL: IVP Academic, 2019); John Webster, particularly the essays in *God without Measure: Working Papers in Christian Theology*, vol. 1, *God and the Works of God* (London: Bloomsbury T&T Clark, 2016); Katherine Sonderegger, *Systematic Theology: The Doctrine of God* (Minneapolis: Augsburg Fortress, 2015).

we cannot presume to speak about either one to the exclusion of the other. A theology built entirely around *theologia* produces a nonexperiential, nonsoteriological, nonChristological, nonpneumatological metaphysics of the divine nature. A theology built entirely around *oikonomia* results in a skepticism about whether how God saves through Christ in the power of the Holy Spirit is essentially related to who or what God is.[8]

Of course the emphasis of *God for Us: The Trinity and Christian Life* fell decidedly on the practical side of the equation, enough so that many critics judged the book to be in danger of collapsing the immanent Trinity into the economic. LaCugna's next sentence immediately shows her disdain for focusing on "the inner workings of the 'immanent' Trinity" and her principled commitment to reconceiving the matrix of *theologia* and *oikonomia* as taking up "the question of how the trinitarian pattern of salvation history is to be correlated with the eternal being of God."[9] Nevertheless, it is worth recalling that even in such a book, at the height of the revival, one of the most accomplished and articulate advocates of a thoroughgoing soteriological trinitarian vision recognized the other pole of the polarity, and spoke in favor of "the mystery of God's eternal being" and "who or what God is."

The present book, *Fountain of Salvation*, approaches what LaCugna called the dual theme of *theologia* and *oikonomia* with a definite emphasis on *theologia*. The intent is, of course, to be perfectly, exquisitely balanced ("we cannot presume to speak about either one to the exclusion of the other"), and to do proper justice to both the triune God and the trinitarian gospel. What theologian could in good conscience intend otherwise? What reader could trust a writer who declared an intention to exclude either topic? Nevertheless, all theological programs proceed from some construal of the main dangers to be guarded against, and some attraction to the emphasis that is required under present circumstances. This book is no exception. So along with the intention to take the full measure of the claims of deity and the claims of salvation, I confess to being more concerned about the former. The concern is evident in every chapter, in different ways appropriate to the varieties of the themes explored.

8. Catherine Mowry LaCugna, *God for Us: The Trinity and Christian Life* (San Francisco: HarperSanFrancisco, 1991), 4.

9. LaCugna, *God for Us*, 4. A feisty critic of LaCugna's trinitarian theology, Paul Molnar argues at length that whatever her intentions, she does not in fact follow through on confessing divine freedom. Paul D. Molnar, *Divine Freedom and the Doctrine of the Immanent Trinity: In Dialogue with Karl Barth and Contemporary Theology*, 2nd ed. (London: Bloomsbury T&T Clark, 2017), 8-12, 263-64, 307-8, 434-35. These criticisms were already present in the first edition of Molnar's book, in 2002.

TRINITARIAN FOUNTAIN OF SALVATION

How near and how far apart from each other should the two doctrinal complexes be in an overall account of Christian doctrine? Stating it in this mechanical idiom already runs the risk of inviting answers in the form of emphases and proportions, perhaps even of experimentation or tinkering, as if the trick is to fit the two things together snugly but not too snugly. But the relation of God and salvation is not, in either the first instance or the final analysis, a problem to be solved. It is instead the nexus of theology, the blazing core of biblical revelation where the reality of God and the truth of the gospel are co-posited in dynamic unity. Salvation flows from its deep source in the triune God, who is the fountain of salvation. This phrase, fountain of salvation, goes back at least to a Latin hymn from the sixth century that praises God as *fons salutis Trinitas*. As one English translation renders the lines, "Blest Trinity, salvation's spring, may every soul Thy praises sing."[10] The sense that the nature of salvation is only understood properly when it is traced back into its principle in the depth of God's being is evoked by Scripture's own way of speaking. The Old Testament bears witness to it in an intensely personal idiom, as for instance in Isaiah 12:2's confident boast, "Behold, God is my salvation; I will trust, and will not be afraid; for the LORD GOD is my strength and my song, and he has become my salvation." The connection here between God and salvation is direct: he is it. When Isaiah goes on to spell out an implication of salvation being in God, that is, that there is exuberant resourcefulness to be drawn from, then he uses our fontal image: "With joy you will draw water from the wells of salvation."

Theological interpreters have found much in this image from Isaiah 12. Scottish preacher Alexander MacLaren (1826–1910) points out that Isaiah is not referring to "the source of salvation as being a mere reservoir, still less as being a created or manufactured thing; but there lies in it the deep idea of a source from which the water wells up by its own inward energy."[11] That source, says MacLaren, is "GOD—GOD HIMSELF." And the fountain of salvation from which we draw a continuous supply of water is presented "as having its origin in His deep nature, as having its process in His own finished work, and as being in its essence the communication of Himself." Here the evangelical preacher truly warms to his subject, pointing out that if God is this way, in

10. Venantius Fortunatus (530–609), from the hymn *Vexilla regis*. Translation by Walter Kirkham Blount, from *The Office of the Holy Week* (Paris, 1670).

11. Alexander MacLaren, *The Book of Isaiah: Chapters I to XLVIII*, Expositions of Holy Scripture (London: Hodder and Stoughton, 1905), 66.

person the source of salvation, then we must expand the very idea of salvation correspondingly:

> If there is a man or a woman that thinks of salvation as if it were merely a shutting up of some material hell, or the dodging round a corner so as to escape some external consequence of transgression, let him and her hear this: the possession of God is salvation, that and nothing else. To have Him within me, that is to be saved; to have His life in His dear Son made the foundation of my life, to have my whole being penetrated and filled with God, that is the essence of the salvation that is in Jesus Christ. And because it comes unmotived, uncaused, self-originated, springing up from the depths of His own heart; because it is all effected by His own mighty work who has trodden the winepress alone, and, single-handed, has wrought the salvation of the race; and because its essence and heart is the communication of God Himself, and the bestowing upon us the participation in a divine nature, therefore the depth of the thought, *God Himself* is the well-fountain of salvation.[12]

MacLaren registers the personalist element in the prophetic word, and uses the imagery to reinforce the progression in the passage from "God is my salvation" through "the LORD GOD is my strength and my song, and he has become my salvation" to the conclusion: "With joy you will draw water from the wells of salvation."

Before MacLaren, Baptist theologian John Gill (1697–1771) had already connected the passage not just to the personal character of the God of salvation, but to that God as specifically triune. Gill notes the plural form of the key word: "out of the wells of salvation, or 'fountains;' as all the three Persons are." Cross-referencing for other water imagery in the canon of Scripture, Gill ingeniously connects all three persons to these plural wells:

> Jehovah the Father, as he is called "the fountain of living water", Jeremiah 2:13 so he is the fountain of salvation; it springs from him, from his everlasting love, his eternal purposes, his infinite wisdom, his sure and unalterable covenant, his free grace in the mission of his Son; and he himself is the God of grace, from whence it all comes, and every supply of it. The Spirit and his grace are called a "well of living water", John 4:14 and he also is a well of salvation; it is he that convinces men of their need of it, that brings

---

12. MacLaren, *Book of Isaiah*, 67–68.

near this salvation to them, and shows them their interest in it, and bears witness to it, and is the earnest and pledge of it; and he is the author of all that grace which makes them meet for it, and from whom are all the supplies of it by the way. But more especially Christ is meant, who is the "fountain of gardens, and well of living water", Sol 4:15 in whom salvation is, and in no other: the words may be rendered, "the wells" or "fountains of the Saviour," yea, of Jesus.[13]

The imagery runs deep in the history of Christian theology. Although Basil of Caesarea is not referring specifically to Isaiah 12, in his letter praising the theology of Gregory of Nazianzus he makes free use of the Bible's fountain imagery for God and salvation, and connects it to the life-giving teaching of trinitarian doctrine. He accuses teachers who deny the eternal Son and Spirit of being those who would

bewitch the sheep . . . that they may not drink from the pure water which springs up unto life everlasting, but may draw down upon themselves the saying of the Prophet: "They have forsaken me, the fountain of living water, and have digged to themselves cisterns, broken cisterns, that can hold no water." For, they should confess that the Father is God, the Son is God, and the Holy Spirit is God, as the divine Word teaches, and as they who have pondered it more deeply have taught.[14]

According to Christian teaching, salvation's source is God, and the manifestation of God as Father, Son, and Holy Spirit in the gospel is what opens up that fountain in its fullness and depth.

THE ARGUMENT OF THIS BOOK

The following chapters consider the relationship of Trinity and soteriology from a number of angles. The first two chapters describe the territory of Christian theology and explain how the doctrine of the Trinity gives shape to all the sub-doctrines of soteriology: the nature of revelation, the economy of salva-

13. John Gill, *An Exposition of The Books of the Prophets of the Old Testament*, vol. 1 (London: Mathews and Leigh, 1810), 76–77.

14. Basil of Caesarea, Letter 8, in *Saint Basil: Letters, Volume 1* (Washington, DC: Catholic University of America Press, 1951), 22–23. On page 22 he has already called Gregory of Nazianzus "a chosen instrument and a deep reservoir" of orthodox teaching.

tion, and the experience of salvation. Indeed, the real conceptual breakthrough to which readers are invited in these two chapters is coming to view those fields within soteriology as sub-doctrines of a fully elaborated doctrine of the Trinity. In the first chapter, "The Trinity as the Norm of Soteriology," we see the doctrine of the Trinity providing both the form and content of the doctrine of salvation. But then the second chapter, "The Doctrine of the Trinity and the Scope of God's Economy," simultaneously expands the theme and reverses it, describing the doctrine of the Trinity as itself a doctrine whose task and scope are in part determined by the triune God's self-communication in the economy of salvation. Chapter three, "Trinity and Atonement," prepares the reader for the theological turn from God's work in the *historia salutis* to the human reception of it in the *ordo salutis*, primarily by focusing on the doctrinal implications of the accomplishment of salvation in Christ. The strategy of this chapter is to state the two doctrines as expansively as possible (taking a clue from the way Adam Johnson describes the comprehensiveness of atonement theology) and then see if the doctrines coexist, overlap, or mutually subsume one another. In chapter four, "Trinity and Ecclesiology," we see the difference the triunity of the divine Savior makes to the ontology and mission of the church: *communio* ecclesiology and *missio Dei* theology both enter into the conversation, though what John Webster calls "trinitarian reduction" provides the best model. Chapters five through eight are the soteriological core of the book, in which I articulate an approach to God's saving work that trades on a tight coordination between the Son and the Holy Spirit, both in their historical sendings and their eternal origins from the Father. Chapter five sketches the trinitarian depth dynamic of the Christian life, and then chapters six and seven examine the Son's eternal generation and the Spirit's eternal procession respectively. Chapter eight, "Trinitarian Theology, Gospel Ministry, and Theological Education," gathers together the threads of these previous three chapters and applies them to the contemporary task of Christian ministry and theological work. Finally, because the modern revival of trinitarian theology was instructively, though often problematically, focused on the relation of Trinity and soteriology, chapters nine and ten examine the modern revival of interest in a soteriologically focused doctrine of the Trinity, and also engage the historical claims made during the modern trinitarian revival. The final chapter ends with a meditation on the way the doctrine of the Trinity benefits from the theological method of retrieval.

Readers will no doubt see that the order of the discussion follows, more or less, a sequence advocated by John Webster: first the immanent Trinity in its eternal relations of origin, and then the external works of the triune God in salvation, descending all the way into some of the details of salvation history, Christian experience, and spirituality. If it had been possible to adhere even more strictly to that sequence, I would have done so, to emphasize the same Websterian point. But in a book that is concerned to make that very point in every part of the argument, it was necessary to include some soteriological discussion in the sections on God's immanent triunity, and to include the upward glance at the perfection of God's own life right in the middle of the soteriology.

I have been preoccupied by the relation of Trinity and soteriology for several years now, and it is fair to say that three of my previous books have, in various ways, orbited around this theme. *The Image of the Immanent Trinity* was my early attempt to come to grips with the literature of the trinitarian revival by mapping the influence and implications of Karl Rahner's claim that the economic Trinity is the immanent Trinity and vice versa.[15] *The Deep Things of God*[16] was my most direct attempt to link Trinity and gospel in the popular Christian mind, both by arguing that the two belong together and by calling numerous witnesses from recent centuries who confessed as much. My concern there was to discipline evangelical theological language so that it followed the deep logic of the gospel, which of course I take to be trinitarian. *The Triune God*[17] was my constructive statement of the shape of the doctrine of the Trinity, with special attention to the processions-missions schema and to the biblical support for a classically formed doctrine of the Trinity. Obviously this is a theme that I find endlessly fascinating, and that I commend to the theological public as worth continued attention and refinement. Fortunately, this is no private obsession: many of the most interesting theologians at work in recent decades have continued to work on the issues that arise from this nexus of the doctrine of God and the doctrine of salvation. The chapters of this book were commissioned by a variety of editors, addressed to a range of different interlocutors, and shared in a number of venues where meaningful work on this aspect of trinitarian theology was under discussion. Together they constitute a sustained investigation of salvation as access to the Trinity, and the Trinity as the fountain of salvation.

The image on the cover is a detail from a fifth-century mosaic in Ravenna, Italy. The cross-shaped building known as the Mausoleum of Galla Placidia

15. *The Image of the Immanent Trinity: Rahner's Rule and the Theological Interpretation of Scripture*, Issues in Systematic Theology (New York: Lang), 2005.

16. *The Deep Things of God: How the Trinity Changes Everything*, 2nd ed. (Wheaton, IL: Crossway, 2010).

17. *The Triune God*, New Studies in Dogmatics (Grand Rapids: Zondervan, 2016).

is richly decorated inside with imagery of holiness and blessedness, including four sets of doves, like these, drinking from bowls of water. I chose this image for its inherent loveliness, its exquisite craftsmanship, its venerable antiquity, and its water imagery. I do recognize that what refreshes these little birds is more of a tiny tub than a great fountain, so I ask the viewer to use some sympathetic imagination. This is certainly not a book about a little bowl of blessing, but about God as salvation's endless, triune source. However, visually representing the relation between the boundless depths of divinity and the experienced reality of salvation raises insuperable problems, not least of scale. If the little birds of Ravenna's mosaics receive life and health and peace appropriate to their size, let this be our visual reminder that God supplies all our needs according to his riches in glory: not just *from* his riches, but *in proportion to* them.

The Trinity as the Norm for Soteriology

T HE CHURCH OF ST. SERVATIUS in Siegburg, Germany, has a treasure room full of medieval art and relics. Among the artifacts is a portable altar crafted around the year 1160 by the workshop of Eilbertus of Cologne. Eilbertus was a master craftsman of Romanesque metalwork and enamel decoration, a sturdy artistic medium that withstands the centuries with minimal fading or decay. The colors remain brilliant after nearly a millennium. But Eilbertus was also a skillful iconographer, whose fluency with the symbolism of Christian art equipped him to construct dense and elaborate visual arguments. Consider

Lid of a portable altar-box, the workshop of Eilbertus of Cologne, ca. 1160

*Altar-box lid,
detail, right border*

*Altar-box lid,
detail, left border*

the lid of the altar-box, shown here. Ranged in bands along the top and bottom of it are the twelve apostles of the Lord, labeled "*apostoli domini.*" Running down the right border are three ways of depicting Christ's victory over death: at the bottom is the post-resurrection appearance to Mary Magdalene in the garden, at the center is the empty tomb (*sepulcrum domini*) with sleeping soldiers and the three women seeking the Lord among the dead where he is not to be found, and at the top is the ascension, *ascensio Christi*. The event of the resurrection itself is not directly portrayed, of course, but Eilbertus juxtaposes three images of the resurrection's consequences: the presence of the Lord with his people, the absence of the Lord from the tomb, and the ascension of the Lord by which he is now both present to us (spiritually) and absent from us (bodily) until his return. If a picture is worth a thousand words, three pictures placed together in significant visual proximity are not increased simply by addition of ideas, but rather by a remarkable multiplication of meaning.

But it is the left border that showcases Eilbertus as the iconographic and doctrinal master that he was. In the middle is the crucifixion of Jesus, where the Son of God is flanked by his mother Mary and John the evangelist, as well as by the moon weeping and the sun hiding his face. At the foot of the cross, from the feet of the savior runs the blood of the crucified, and as it runs down the hill of the skull, it crosses a rectilinear panel border in which is inscribed *passio Christi*, the passion of Christ. The blood runs out of its own frame and into an adjoining visual space, a space in which Adam (clearly labeled *Adam*, which is Latin for . . . Adam) is rising from a sepulcher. Adam's arms are outstretched in a gesture of reception, but they also set up a powerful visual echo of the outstretched arms of Jesus. Adam's tomb and its lid are arranged perpendicular to each other so that Adam's body is framed by an understated cruciform shape of the same blue and green colored rectangles as Christ's. Eilbertus is making another visual argument here: where the two crosses cross, salvation takes place. Because the second Adam bends his head and looks down from his death, the first Adam raises his head and looks up from his. Eilbertus is offering an invitation here: above are the everlasting arms, outstretched but unbent, as linear and straight as panel borders or the beams of the cross, while below the salvation is received with appropriate passivity into the bent arms of the father of the race of humanity. Redemption is accomplished and applied, and at long last an answer is given to God's first interrogative: "Adam, where are you?"

But even this is not the peak or extent of Eilbertus's iconographic teaching. For that master stroke we have to look not below the cross but above it. In another pictorial space, framed by both a square and a circle, is God the Father flanked by angels. It doesn't look much like God the Father. It looks instead exactly like Jesus, right down to the cross inscribed in the halo. Pity the iconographer who has to represent the first person of the Trinity visually. As a general rule, the Father should not be portrayed: even in the churches that use icons in worship, stand-alone images of the Father are marginal, aberrant, noncanonical. Do you portray him as an elderly man with a flowing white beard, as if he were modeled on Moses or even perhaps Zeus? Eilbertus has taken the imperfect but safe route, and depicted the Father christomorphically: since Christ told his disciples "If you have seen me, you have seen the Father," it stands to reason that if an artist decides to show the Father, he should show him looking like what we have seen in the face of Jesus.

Representing God the Father visually is a problem not even Eilbertus can solve, and even though other options might be worse, this christomorphic Father is nevertheless a rather regrettable solution. But if you avert your eyes from that difficult figure, you will notice the dove of the Holy Spirit ascending from Christ on the cross. The dove imagery is of course not found at the end of the gospels ascending from Golgotha, but rather at the beginning of the gospels, descending at the Jordan, onto the scene of the baptism of Christ. Eilbertus has moved the symbol here to provide a visual cue for something like Hebrews 9:14, where we are told that "Christ . . . through the eternal Spirit offered himself without blemish to God." Just as the blood broke the bottom border, the dove breaks this upper border, crossing over from the Son to the Father. The dove also breaks the crucial word, the label that makes sense of it all: *trinitas*, Trinity.

It's a little word, but it changes everything. Simply by juxtaposing the death of Christ with a visual evocation of God in heaven, Eilbertus indicates that what happened once upon a time in Jerusalem, a thousand years before Romanesque enamels and two thousand years before the internet, is not simply an occurrence in world history but an event that breaks in from above, or behind, or beyond it, an event in which God has made himself known and taken decisive divine action. But by adding the word *Trinity*, the artist has turned scribe, and has proclaimed that what we see at the cross is in some manner a revelation of who God is. Here God did not just cause salvation from afar, but caused himself to be known as the Father, Son, and Holy Spirit. And here we cannot press Eilbertus any further, because the diction of enamel and the grammar of metalwork are not precise enough to say what we must go on to say. Eilbertus has reminded us of the essential movement that we must make, has set us on the path that faith seeking understanding must follow: from the history of salvation to the eternal life and unchanging character of God. But it is high time to come to terms with the precise meaning of that movement, and for that task we need not images depicting the truth, but words: first the form of sound doctrine given in the teaching of the apostles, then the interpretive assistance of classical doctrines, and finally the conceptual redescription that characterizes constructive systematic theology in the present. The craft and wisdom of Eilbertus frame the discussion, but we need to have the discussion.

In this chapter, I want to characterize not the doctrine of the Trinity itself but how it functions within systematic theology. The adjective in the phrase "trinitarian theology" is grammatically ambiguous, since it could indicate either a theology that is about the Trinity, or an overall theological system that is shaped and conditioned by the doctrine of the Trinity. The latter sense is what I intend to describe by exploring what the doctrine of the Trinity is for; what follows is an account of the dogmatic function of the doctrine of the Trinity in the overall structure of Christian theology and life. Under the guiding image of Eilbertus, we have already begun the task of considering the events of salvation history against the background of the eternal being of God; the doctrine of the Trinity poses the question of how salvation history is to be correlated with the divine being in itself, or to describe the connection between God and the economy of salvation.[1] As it does this, the doctrine of the Trinity provides five services that promote the health and balance of Christian theology as a whole. First, trinitarian theology summarizes the biblical story. Second, it articulates the content of divine self-revelation by specifying what has been revealed. Third, it orders doctrinal discourse. Fourth, trinitarian theology identifies God by the gospel. And fifth and cumulatively, it informs and norms soteriology.

---

1. This is the thesis I develop in chapter 2, below.

SUMMARIZING THE BIBLICAL STORY

The easiest angle of approach to the Trinity begins with a straightforward reading of the gospels as rather obviously the story of three special characters: Jesus Christ, the Father who sent him and who is constantly present in his conversation and actions, and then, rather less clearly, the Holy Spirit, who seems simultaneously to precede Christ, accompany Christ, and follow Christ. There are many other characters in the story, but these three stand out as the central agents on whom everything turns. And the actions of these three are concerted, coordinated, and sometimes conjoined so that sometimes they can scarcely be distinguished and at other times they stand in a kind of opposed relation to each other. As for the salvation they bring, it is not three salvations but one complex event happening in three ways, or (as it sometimes seems) one project undertaken by three agents. The epistles, each in their own way, all look back on and explain this threefold story, adding more layers of analysis and insight but not altering the fundamental shape of what happened in the life of Jesus.

We could summarize this threefold shape of the New Testament story in the formula "The Father sends the Son and the Holy Spirit." And though we can't take the time to develop it here, we would then have to extend the analysis to include the entire canon, to demonstrate that what happens in the New Testament is a continuation and fulfillment of what happened in the Old. To trace the storyline of Scripture, and especially of the Old Testament, as the God of Israel promising to be with his people in a Son of David who is the Son of God, and to pour out his Holy Spirit on all flesh in a surprising fulfillment of the promise to Abraham, is a task for a comprehensive biblical theology. But it can be undertaken while remaining in the mode of mere description, rather than moving to the more contentious field of systematic construction. In that case, giving a particular kind of interpretive priority to the New Testament because of its position at the end of a process of progressive revelation, the sentence "The Father sends the Son and the Holy Spirit" would be a summary of the entire Bible.

This particular threefold formula is not the only possible summary of the storyline of the Bible. Other themes in salvation history could be highlighted. Even other threefold patterns could be discerned: the triad of exodus, exile, and resurrection suggests itself. The themes of kingdom or covenant could be pushed to the foreground, or even substituted for the schema of Father, Son, and Holy Spirit. Much can be gained from investigations that give prominence to these other themes, but what I am describing here is how to read the salvation history witnessed in Scripture in such a way as to reach the doctrine of the Trinity. The reason we would want to read it that way as Christians is that only the trinitarian reading is actually attempting to read salvation history as the revelation of God's identity in a way that transcends salvation history; that reads it as showing not only what God does but who God is. The God behind the stories of kingdom or covenant, of exodus, exile, and resurrection, could remain personally undisclosed except insofar as his faithfulness to stand reliably behind his actions suggested something about him. The trinitarian reading of salvation history goes further: it construes the divine *oikonomia* (God's wise ordering of salvation history) to be simultaneously an *oikonomia* of rescue, redemption, and revelation, indeed self-revelation. Salvation history on the trinitarian reading is the locus in which God makes himself known, the theater not only of divine action but also of divine self-communication. A faithful God may stand behind other construals of salvation history, but on the trinitarian reading, God stands not behind but also in his actions, at least in the actions of sending the Son and the Holy Spirit.

There are numerous advantages to beginning in this way. In our age, many Christian readers have trouble seeing the doctrine of the Trinity in Scripture. They see a verse here and a verse there that may help prove the different parts of the doctrine (the deity of Christ, the unity of God, etc.), but they struggle to see the whole package put together in any one place. Granting that the doctrine is not compactly gathered into any one verse (not even Matthew 28:19 or 2 Corinthians 13:13 are quite as complete or as detailed as could be wished), it is quite beneficial to approach the doctrine in a bigger-than-one-verse way.

Follow the whole argument of Galatians 4, for example (in the fullness of time, God sent his Son, and has sent the Spirit of his Son into our hearts crying Abba Father), or 1 Corinthians 2 (in apostolic foolishness we have the mind of Christ, we have the Spirit who searches the deep things of God), or of Ephesians 1 (we are blessed with every spiritual blessing by the Father who chose us before the foundation of the world, gave redemption in the blood of the Beloved son, and sealed us with the Spirit of promise), or of the Gospel of John (the Word became flesh, talked endlessly about the Father who sent him, and then gave the Spirit), and the Trinitarian profile of God's self-revelation emerges clearly. We have to train our minds to think in bigger sections of Scripture than just a verse here and a verse there; the bigger the better.

To arrive at the biblical doctrine of the Trinity requires three very large mental steps. The first step is simply to read the whole Bible, to achieve some initial mastery of the long, main lines of the one story that is the Christian Bible. An interpreter needs to be able to think back and forth along the canon of

Scripture, with figures like Abraham and Moses and David and Cyrus standing in their proper places, and with categories like temple and sonship and holiness lighting up the various books as appropriate. This familiarity and fluency with all the constituent parts is the prerequisite for further steps.

The second step, though, advances beyond canonical mastery by understanding not just the shape of the biblical text but of God's economy. What is required here is to comprehend the entire Bible as the official, inspired report of the one central thing that God is doing for the world. God has ordered all of these words and events that are recorded in Scripture toward one end. Simply knowing the content of the entire Bible is inadequate, if that content is misinterpreted as a haphazard assemblage of divine stops and starts. These are not disparate Bible stories, but the written witness of the one grand movement in which God disposes all his works and words toward making himself known and present.

The third step is to recognize the economy as a revelation of who God is. This is the largest step of all. Once interpreters have mastered the contents of the Bible, and then understood that it presents to us God's well-ordered economy, they still need to come to see that God is making himself known to us in that economy. After all, it is theoretically possible for God to do great things in world history without really giving away his character or disclosing his identity in doing so. This final step on the way to the doctrine of the Trinity is the recognition that God behaved as Father, Son, and Spirit in the economy because he was revealing to us who he eternally is, in himself. The joint sending of the Son and the Holy Spirit was not merely another event in a series of divine actions. It was rather the revelation of God's own identity: the doctrine of the Trinity commits us to affirming that God put himself into the gospel.

This is, I claim, the right way to interpret the Bible, and it is also a rough summary of the traditional way the Bible has been interpreted classically, recognized by the church fathers and the Reformers. We could call it the Christian way. It yields the doctrine of the Trinity, not in scattered verses here and there that tell us of an esoteric teaching at the margins of the faith, but as the main point. The New Testament obviously features these three characters, the Father, the Son, and the Holy Spirit. Classically, Christian theology has traced these persons back to an eternal Trinity of God *in se*. Since this threefoldness belongs to what God actually is rather than only being something he freely does, it has been called the ontological Trinity, the essential Trinity, or the Trinity of being. Theologians have also called it the immanent Trinity, because "immanent" means "internal to" itself.

In summary, the most crucial conceptual step that must be taken is the move from the events of the economy of salvation to the eternal life of God. This is the crucial step, and it is a step taken with the fewest explicit and concise expressions: verses. Because of the uniquely integral character of the doctrine of the Trinity, it resists being formulated bit by bit from fragmentary elements of evidence. The atomistic approach can never accomplish or ground the necessary transposition of the biblical evidence from the salvation-history level to the transcendent level of the immanent Trinity. Such a transposition requires first the ability to perceive all of the economic evidence at once, including the intricately structured relations among the three persons. As a coherent body of evidence, then, that economic information can be rightly interpreted as a revelation of God's own life. To make the jump from economy to Trinity, the interpreter must perceive the meaningful form of a threefold divine life circulating around the work of Christ. What psychologists of perception call a gestalt, a recognizably unified coherent form, is what the trinitarian interpreter must identify in the economy. This triune form, once recognized, can then be understood as enacting, among us, the contours of God's own triune life. God is among us what he is in himself: Father, Son, and Holy Spirit.

ARTICULATING THE CONTENT OF DIVINE SELF-REVELATION

Summarizing the biblical story requires an ascent of thought from the economy to the divine being; this is the distinctive movement of thought that makes possible the doctrine of the Trinity. For the sake of clarity, the question that needs to be posed more explicitly is the question of how much the economic Trinity reveals about God's eternal and essential being. As nineteenth-century Congregationalist theologian R. W. Dale said, the most important question in trinitarian theology is "whether in the Incarnation of our Lord and in the 'coming' of the Spirit and His permanent activity in the Church and in the world there is a revelation of the inner and eternal life of God."[2] In other words, "have we the right to assume that the historic manifestation of God to our race discloses anything of God's own eternal being?"[3] Dale answers yes, as all trinitarians, by definition, do. But trinitarian theologians have developed different opinions about what precisely is revealed. The decisions we make here are the master decisions, affecting everything we say about trinitarian theology's other tasks, expressing the material content of the whole doctrine. If we say the right things about divine self-revelation in salvation history, the

2. R. W. Dale, *Christian Doctrine: A Series of Discourses* (London: Hodder and Stoughton, 1894), 151.
3. Dale, *Christian Doctrine*, 151.

other tasks will fall more easily into place: doctrinal discourse will be better ordered, God will be identified by the gospel, and our soteriology will be properly informed and normed thereby.

So much good work is to be done at the level of describing salvation history holistically, that we might reasonably ask whether it is really necessary to transcend the economy and make claims about the God behind it. Even without angling for a trinitarian conclusion, the answer is yes. If Christian salvation is a real relationship with the true God, some such step is necessary. This is a point that Thomas Torrance made with great force and consistency throughout his work:

> the historical manifestations of God as Father, Son, and Holy Spirit have evangelical and theological significance only as they have a transhistorical and transfinite reference beyond to an ultimate ground in God himself. They cannot be Gospel if their reference breaks off at the finite boundaries of this world of space and time, for as such they would be empty of divine validity and saving significance—they would leave us trapped in some kind of historical positivism. The historical manifestations of the Trinity are Gospel, however, if they are grounded beyond history in the eternal personal distinctions between the Father, the Son, and the Holy Spirit inherent in the Godhead, that is, if the Fatherhood of the Father, the Sonship of the Son, and the Communion of the Spirit belong to the inner life of God and constitute his very Being.[4]

The fact that God makes himself known to us as Father, Son, and Holy Spirit because he is in himself Father, Son, and Holy Spirit is the occasion for wonder and praise, especially since God did not make this revelation to satisfy our curiosity about the divine, but in order to reconcile and redeem us. The revelation shows rather than tells. God the Father did not merely inform us that he had a Son and a Spirit; rather he sent them to be among us. And the Son and Spirit did not come to us only in order to transmit information, but to do the work of saving, with the information about their existence and their nature being a necessary accompaniment to their saving presence. Considered from this angle, the correspondence between who God is in himself and who he shows himself to be in the economy of salvation is something we receive with praise, raising our bent arms like Adam. Theology in this mode is doxology, the praise of God.

---

4. T. F. Torrance, *The Christian Doctrine of God: One Being Three Persons* (Edinburgh: T&T Clark, 1996), 6.

But considered as a reflective theological movement of thought from below to above, the relationship between the economy and the eternal life of God is an intellectual project whose closest analogues are observation, induction, and the formation of conceptual models. Here theology has to be rigorous, consistent, creative in articulating how the various elements of the biblical witness are to be integrated, and accountable to others. It is all well and good to assert, as Karl Barth does, that "to the involution and convolution of the three modes of being in the essence of God there corresponds exactly their involution and convolution in his work."[5] But the actual work begins when we describe *how* the particular involution and convolution seen in the economic relations among Jesus Christ, his Father, and their Spirit are to be construed as revealing the very life of God. Theology in this mode is not just doxology, but "the praise of God by crafting concepts to turn the mind to the divine splendor."[6]

When we ask, "What does the economy signify about God's eternal life?" we have, first, the challenge of how to draw such inferences, and second, the range of options that emerge in answering the question. First, the rules and restrictions on the inferences.

Not everything that God does is to be taken as revelatory of what he is. Some of what happens in the economy stays in the economy. Some obvious examples would be aspects of the incarnation that have to do with the Son's appropriating of a human nature: if Jesus has brown eyes, should we say that the eternal Son before the foundation of the world had this feature? No. There are other, non-biological aspects of salvation history having more to do with the nature of the humanity being saved than the character of the person doing the saving: metaphysical finitude, for example, characterizes not divinity but humanity. As we consider aspects of salvation history and what they reveal about the life of God in himself, we should bear in mind certain limitations.

A set of three limitations attaches to the notion of divine self-communication. First, divine self-revelation takes place under the form of some condescension from majesty, such that God in the incarnate Son and outpoured Spirit does not appear in his own proper glory but in a humbled form. As a result, second, it requires accommodation to human terms. As patristic discussion helped to clarify, even the term "sonship" is a term first

---

5. Karl Barth, *CD* 1/1, 374.

6. John Webster, "Life in and of Himself," in *God without Measure: Working Papers in Christian Theology*, vol. 1, *God and the Works of God* (London: Bloomsbury T&T Clark, 2016), 27.

learned from human relationships before God shows us that it applies analogically to a transcendent reality. The writings of Pseudo-Dionysius are a potent witness to the Christian theological tradition of understanding God's self-revelation as being simultaneously an unveiling of the truth about God and a veiling of the divine being behind revealed concepts and images. Calvin likewise describes God's speech as taking the form of divine "lisping," by which God speaks the truth about himself, but in a manner that is adjusted to be appropriate to our understanding. Calvin is also an eloquent advocate of the third restriction, which is divine reserve: God knows that some truths about divinity would not be beneficial or edifying for us, and so he withholds them from revelation. Anything that God does show or tell us, then, is selected from a larger pool of divine truth, things that are not shown or told according to God's inscrutable wisdom (Deut 29:29).

Another set of three limitations attaches to the fact that the incarnation is the central point of God's self-revelatory presence. First, incarnation means that God is present under conditions of createdness, since the eternal Son of God took to himself a true human nature that, considered in itself, is creaturely. This means that in the incarnation God appears under the sign of his opposite, or at least by taking a stand on the other side of the creator-creature distinction. Entailed by createdness, second, is the fact that what God makes known here is made known under conditions of temporality and multiplicity, whereby the God who does one continuous eternal act of faithful love must act out that same act repeatedly, in a temporally extended way, to continually manifest who he is in the schema of successive moments. Third, the incarnational focus of divine self-revelation means that the Son of God undertakes his mission as a participation in our fallen human plight, not for his own sake but "for us and for our salvation" as the Nicene Creeds says. This being the case, what we see in Christ is God being himself under conditions that are not his native sphere, so to speak.

Any particular observation we make about God's presence in the Son and the Spirit runs the risk of bouncing off these barriers. These barriers to inference are formidable, but none of them is sufficient to block all real knowledge. In fact, the trinitarian schema is uniquely well suited to pierce these barriers and apprehend personal knowledge of God. Consider, for example, the way trinitarianism accounts for how God becomes man: not by deity becoming humanity, nor by God showing up in his majesty and lordship to exert sovereignty in the flesh and demand the worship due him. Instead, on the trinitarian view, the Father sends the Son, and so the divine person of the Son can appear under the sign of his opposite (strength as weakness, lordship as obedience, etc.) while still making known the character of God. Austin Farrer puts it this way:

> God cannot live an identically godlike life in eternity and in a human story. But the divine Son can make an identical response to his Father, whether in the love of the blessed Trinity or in the fulfilment of an earthly ministry. All the conditions of action are different on the two levels; the filial response is one. Above, the appropriate response is a co-operation in sovereignty and an interchange of eternal joys. Then the Son gives back to the Father all that the Father is. Below, in the incarnate life, the appropriate response is an obedience to inspiration, a waiting for direction, an acceptance of suffering, a rectitude of choice, a resistance to temptation, a willingness to die. For such things are the stuff of our existence; and it was in this very stuff that Christ worked out the theme of heavenly sonship, proving himself on earth the very thing he was in heaven; that is, a continuous perfect act of filial love.[7]

As Farrer says, it is impossible to imagine how God would act if God were a creature. To put the matter that way is to force ourselves into an unresolved paradox: Would God act like the creator, or like a creature? What action could he take that would show him to be both? When the incarnate God walked on water, was he acting like the creator or the created? None of these questions are the kind of questions the New Testament puts before us. The New Testament is not making a series of statements about God (as such) behaving humanly, but about the Son behaving filially in human nature. This focus on filiality is Farrer's point. What the apostles want to show is that Jesus was the Son: He came, lived, taught, acted, died and rose again like the Son of God: the Son in particular, in person.

It was the eternal Son, whose personal characteristic is to belong to the Father and receive his identity from the Father, who took on human nature and dwelled among us. His life as a human being was a new event in history, but he lived out in his human life the exact same sonship that makes him who he is from all eternity as the second person of the Trinity, God the Son. So when he said he was the Son of God, and when he behaved like the Son of God, he was being himself and explaining himself in the new situation of the human existence he had been sent into the world to take up. Notice that Jesus does not merely act out sonship but also declares it and describes it. It

---

7. Austin Farrer, "Incarnation," in *The Brink of Mystery*, ed. Charles C. Conti (London: SPCK, 1976), 20.

would not be appropriate to give the impression that God's self-revelation is a pantomime routine, in which our job is to guess the right words from divine actions in history. No; Jesus as the incarnate Son is eloquent; he tells us he is the Son, and then behaves as such. God's self-revelation is not charades but show and tell. Our inference is never guessing form actions, but is always a matter of hermeneutics; that is, it is always irreducibly textually mediated.

Once we pose the question openly: What do the sendings of the Son and the Holy Spirit signify about the eternal life of God? we need to consider the range of possible inferences from the economy of salvation.

Consider the possible answers as ranged on a spectrum with the classic answer at the center: The sending of the Son signifies the eternal relation of generation from the Father, and the sending of the Spirit signifies the eternal relation of the breathing of the Spirit from the Father. Ranging to the left are more minimal positions, and to the right are more maximal positions.

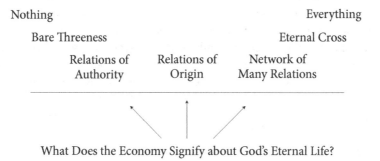

What Does the Economy Signify about God's Eternal Life?

To begin with a glance at the extreme minimalist side, we can see that it is possible to deny that the coming of the Son and Spirit reveal anything whatsoever about the being of God. God shows nothing in the economy; he does something, but shows nothing. The most illuminating light in which to consider unitarian theologies is as the entirely negative answer to the question of what the divine reveals about itself in the history of salvation. Heresies like monarchian modalism, in which the one unipersonal God behaves three ways in his actions toward us, are also best understood as minimalistic answers to our basic question.

But what about the maximalist answer? What if God reveals everything in the history of salvation? This equally radical view on the other end of the spectrum takes all divine action in history and eternalizes it. It is a hard view to maintain because it requires a total rethinking of metaphysics. So Hegel has been the leading spirit, and Anglo-American process theology a distant second, in developing this sort of view. The sendings of the Son and Spirit reveal God in this case, but so does everything that God does, because the divine nature is actualized fully and only in the history of salvation. In fact, on this view, it is hard to explain why the sendings of the Son and the Spirit should be considered as especially apt for the task of revealing God's historicized essence. As discrete events, the sendings of the Son and Spirit are merely things that take place within the more comprehensive field of history. As such, they ought to be considered as less determinative for the shape of history than the comprehensive starting point of the original creation, or the culminating ending point of the final consummation.

The extremes are full of instructive errors, but perhaps the most basic error they share is the assumption that the economy can be interpreted using a general principle of self-revelation. For our purposes, the extremes serve as a warning that our inference from the economy is not a general principle of God-world relatedness, but something we had to be told. Whatever riches of the knowledge of God are revealed in the history of salvation, to approach the history as if it were self-evidently God's self-revelation would run perilously close to positing a general principle about the God-world relationship, a general principle that would itself be underdetermined by revelation. Divine revelation is inalienably linked to intention on the part of the revealer, and "unfolds through deeds and words bound together by an inner dynamism," to use the words of Vatican II's *Dei verbum*.[8] Notice also that the two extremes both give rise to modalism. The nothing option gives us monarchian modalism in which one God does three things, whereas the everything option gives us dynamic modalism, in which the one God becomes three persons by self-actualizing along with creation.

Moving inward from the minimal answer is the position holding that what God has revealed in the economy is that there are three persons. This position refuses to specify further the identity of these three, and remains satisfied with bare threeness itself. Relations among the three need not be specified, and the three need not be distinguished from each other. They are, in other words, potentially anonymous and interchangeable, perhaps undistinguished from each other even in themselves, but certainly in their revelation to us. If one sends and the other is sent at the economic level, this is not grounded in any actual relational distinction among them at the level of the eternal or immanent

8. *Dei verbum*, §2, in *Decrees of the Ecumenical Councils*, vol. 2, ed. N. P. Tanner, SJ (Georgetown: Sheed & Ward, 1990), 972.

Trinity. Relationships of sending are considered to be not only below the line, but are considered as revealing nothing about what is above the line. Above the line is anonymous threeness, and below it is free divine action. "Sonship," on this view, can be considered a messianic or salvation-historical characteristic, not attaching to the eternal second person but only taken on as this one takes up his mission and enters the economy.

If the "bare threeness" position is too minimal, the three can be said to be related to each other through eternal relations of authority: the first person sends the second because in eternity they are distinguished by personal characteristics of headship and authority. A Father is ordered over a Son, which is why the Father sends the Son. Readers familiar with the controversial proposal that the Son is eternally, functionally subordinate to the Father will recognize his position as a deviation from the classical view.[9]

The central position on this spectrum is the classic one, maintaining that the missions in the economy of salvation are revelatory of eternal relations of origin. Classic trinitarianism teaches that the Son and the Spirit proceed from the Father by two eternal processions. The sending of the Son, on this view, reveals that Son was always from the Father in a deeper sense than just being sent from the Father: he is eternally begotten. Nicene theology safeguarded this confession by distinguishing between the Son's being begotten by the Father and the world's being created by the Father through the Son. Just as "a man by craft builds a house, but by nature begets a son," reasoned Athanasius, "God brings forth eternally a Son who has his own nature."[10] A parallel argument for the Spirit, that the Pentecostal outpouring is an extension of his eternal procession from the Father (with or without the *filioque*), completes the classic doctrine of the Trinity. On this view, the coming of the Son and the Spirit into our history is an extension of who they have always been. When the Father sends the Son into salvation history, he is extending the relationship of divine sonship from its home in the life of God, down into human history. The relationship of divine sonship has always existed, as part of the very definition of God, but it has existed only within the being of the Trinity. In sending of the Son to us, the Father chose for that line of filial relation to extend out into created reality and human history. Again, a parallel argument for the sending

9. For a thorough discussion of the proposal from a variety of viewpoints, see Keith Whitfield, ed., *Trinitarian Theology: Theological Models and Doctrinal Application* (Nashville: B&H Academic, 2019). For a clear account of how the eternal submission view differs from classical trinitarian theology, see D. Glenn Butner, *The Son Who Learned Obedience: A Theological Case against the Eternal Submission of the Son* (Eugene, OR: Pickwick, 2018).

10. Athanasius, *Contra Arianos* 3:62.

of the Holy Spirit completes the doctrine: at his outpouring, his eternal relationship with the Father and the Son begins to take place among us.

Moving from this classic central position toward the more maximal end of the spectrum, we could argue that relations of origin are not enough, and that the complex relationships that unfold among Father, Son, and Holy Spirit in salvation history must be the manifestations of a corresponding set of eternal relations in the eternal divine life. On this view, not only does mission reveal procession, but economic destinations ("I go to the Father") reveal eternal terminations, and temporal glorifications reveal eternal effusions (as when the Spirit rests on Jesus at his baptism, or when the light of the transfiguration illuminates him). Many of these relationships are more obviously reciprocal than relations of origin. The Son comes from the Father, but not vice versa. However, the Son and the Father mutually and reciprocally glorify each other. Aware that he is recommending an innovation, Wolfhart Pannenberg argues that "the nexus of relations between [the persons] is more complex than would appear from the older doctrine of relations of origin . . . each is a catalyst of many relations"; indeed, each person is constituted by a "richly structured nexus of relationship."[11] The crucial thing to note about this view is that it occupies a position from which classic trinitarianism seems too reserved in its affirmation about how much is revealed in the economy of salvation.

Further in the direction of a maximal interpretation of economic revelation is the view that what we have seen in the death of Christ does not stand in paradox to what God is in eternity, but instead stands as the revelation of the very being of God. On this view, Christ's subjection to the conditions of human life, and especially his suffering and death, manifest the truth that God as such suffers. A variety of modern theologies since Moltmann have been drawn to a trinitarian version of theopaschitism.[12] Again, for our purposes here it is only necessary to note how far this view is from the classical tradition in terms of its answer to the question of what is revealed in the economy: proponents of this view believe that more has been revealed than previous theologies have confessed.

This second task of the doctrine of the Trinity, the task of articulating the content of divine self-revelation, is where major doctrinal judgments are ren-

11. Wolfhart Pannenberg, *Systematic Theology*, vol. 1 (Grand Rapids: Eerdmans, 1991), 320.
12. Moltmann's *The Crucified God: The Cross of Christ as the Foundation and Criticism of Christian Theology* (Minneapolis: Fortress, 1974) was already quite far along the path of this sort of "trinitarian theology of the cross" (see 235–49), but *The Trinity and the Kingdom: The Doctrine of God* (Minneapolis: Fortress, 1981) has been most influential.

dered. At stake here is the utterly fundamental issue of how we understand God on the basis of self-revelation in word and act. Having surveyed the spectrum of options and indicated how they relate to each other and to the classic formulations of the doctrine, we are prepared for some briefer remarks on the three subordinate tasks of trinitarian theology: ordering doctrinal discourse, identifying the Christian God, and regulating soteriology.

Trinitarian Theology Orders Doctrinal Discourse

Trinitarian theology orders our doctrinal discourse simply by being such a vast doctrine. It is a field that encompasses many other fields of theology, most notably the doctrines of Christology and pneumatology. The health of a doctrine of the Trinity is a good indicator of the overall vigor and balance of a theological system. Christology and pneumatology are each doctrines comprehensive enough to be treated as central and definitive areas; and yet they require to be not only fully elaborated in their own right, but correlated with each other. The correlation of Christology and pneumatology with monotheism is not a bad description of the formal structure of trinitarian theology. Other sprawling doctrinal constellations or frameworks, such as the doctrine of revelation or the doctrine of salvation, likewise loom large in theology, and are likewise to be subsumed and placed in the matrix of a well-articulated doctrine of the Trinity.

Since theology is primarily about God and then secondarily about all things in relation to God, it stands to reason that the doctrine of God ought to occupy a determinative place in an overall doctrinal system. A theological system that takes its bearings from theology proper (that is, the doctrine of God) will be centered on, or dependent on, or (to vary the figure of speech again) located within the doctrine of God. When that doctrine of God is elaborated as a doctrine of the Trinity, the implications for the order of the entire system ought to be pronounced. John Webster has put this case sharply: "in an important sense there is only one Christian doctrine, the doctrine of the Holy Trinity in its inward and outward movements."[13] The implications for a rightly ordered theological system are that "whatever other topics are treated derive from the doctrine of God as *principium* and *finis*"; recognition of this is "crucial to questions of proportion and order in systematic theology. No other doctrinal

13. John Webster, "Principles of Systematic Theology," in *The Domain of the Word: Scripture and Theological Reason* (London: Bloomsbury T&T Clark, 2012), 145.

locus can eclipse the doctrine of the Trinity" in its role of shaping theology as a whole.[14] The doctrine of the triune God, in other words, shapes the entire outlook of theology and serves as the matrix for the placement and treatment of all other doctrinal loci.

There are many possible ways of describing the relation of the trinitarian matrix to the other doctrines of systematic theology, especially as it forms the background of Christian thought. I have come to prefer a kind of theological Cartesian plane, or the intersection of two axes. Because God has made himself present to us and known to us in the Son and the Spirit, the first axis runs from God's immanent life down to the economy, and the second runs between Son and Spirit. In other words, there is an immanent-economic axis crossed by a Christology-pneumatology axis.

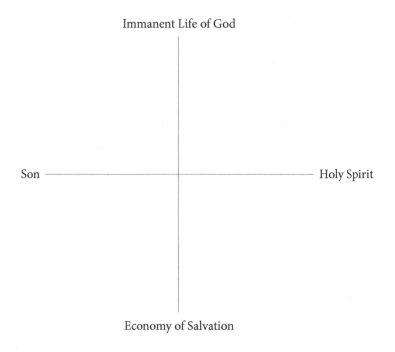

The resulting quadrants establish the field of trinitarian theology, but they do more: they display the way that trinitarian theology orders other doctrinal discourse. The theological dynamics that generate the doctrine of the Trinity are those of God's self-communicating presence on the one hand (vertical axis)

14. Webster, "Principles," 145.

and the two missions of the Son and the Holy Spirit on the other (horizontal axis). All Christian doctrines must in one way or another work themselves out in these same tensions, whether each doctrine is rendered in explicitly trinitarian terms or not. Because this way of schematizing the doctrine is an attempt to depict the theological structuring forces of trinitarianism rather than to signify the Trinity itself (as triangular diagrams inevitably suggest), it has some helpful peculiarities. Using these quadrants to describe the Trinity, we could talk about the immanent Son and the economic Son, or the immanent Holy Spirit and the economic Holy Spirit. This enables us to discuss the personal identity of the Son and the Holy Spirit at either end of the immanent-economic axis (that is, in the top two quadrants and in the bottom two quadrants, respectively).

Trinitarian Theology Identifies God by the Gospel

The task of ordering doctrinal discourse follows rather directly from the primary tasks of summarizing the Bible's storyline and then articulating the content of divine revelation. Taken together, these three tasks imply a fourth task, one that is so normative and critical that it must be accomplished simultaneously with them. The doctrine of the Trinity serves to identify God by the gospel, or to specify the identity of the God of Christian faith. It does so primarily by insisting that God is the author of two central interventions into the course of human history, the incarnation of the Son and the outpouring of the Spirit. These two actions, considered not in isolation but as culminating events, mark God as a particular God. The God who sent a Son and a Holy Spirit, because he always already had a Son and a Holy Spirit to send, must be essentially different from a God who could not and did not self-communicate in this way.

To say this is to treat the doctrine of the Trinity as a kind of name of God, as Robert W. Jenson has argued: "Thus the phrase, 'Father, Son, and Holy Spirit' is simultaneously a very compressed telling of the total narrative by which Scripture identifies God and a personal name for the God so specified."[15] Kendall Soulen's book *The Divine Name(s) and the Holy Trinity* has championed and recovered the tetragrammaton, the actual revealed name of God, with such vigor that he has made it impossible to speak blithely about the trinitarian formula as the name of God, without at the same time recalling the tetra-

15. Robert W. Jenson, *Systematic Theology*, vol. 1 (New York: Oxford University Press, 1997), 46.

grammaton as the one un-superseded, unrelativized name.[16] But trinitarian doctrine continues to play its crucial role in identifying God by reference to the gospel. Lesslie Newbigin has argued that this function of trinitarianism comes to the fore especially in periods when Christian theology recalls that it cannot take the identity of its God for granted. Various periods of increased awareness of cultural diversity and pluralism have historically brought with them renewed attention to trinitarian theology: the fourth century, the sixteenth, and the late twentieth.[17]

TRINITARIAN THEOLOGY INFORMS AND NORMS SOTERIOLOGY

Finally, as the cumulative result of all these movements, trinitarian theology plays an indispensable role in orienting the doctrine of salvation. We have already said as much in indicating the trinitarian background of all Christian doctrines, and how they must all be placed on the field of trinitarian discourse. But this function of informing and norming soteriology requires special attention, because it moves us from Christian theology to the Christian life.

To say that the Trinity informs and norms soteriology is to say that the doctrine of the Trinity gives soteriology its shape and its material content, and that it dictates soteriology's parameters. The doctrine of salvation needs this sort of outside guidance if it is to maintain its balance between two besetting errors. The errors are of deficiency and excess, of not enough salvation on the one hand and too much salvation on the other. Trinitarian doctrine holds soteriology to the mean between them.

First, the error of deficiency: I have in mind a perennial tendency to minimize soteriology, to diminish it to something with no depth of ingression into the life of God. Soteriology anchored in the Trinity is an account of divine sonship that begins in the being of God by nature and is extended to creatures by grace. If soteriology is reduced from a relation of sonship to a relation of lordship and obedience, with forgiveness or sacraments as a way of patching up that relationship when it has been transgressed, then all the richness of the biblical language is flattened out or dumbed down. Christian sonship is then taken as merely metaphorical or analogous, and all the apostolic language of

16. R. Kendall Soulen, *The Divine Name(s) and the Holy Trinity* (Philadelphia: Westminster), 2011.

17. Lesslie Newbigin, *The Relevance of Trinitarian Doctrine for Today's Mission* (Edinburgh: Edinburgh House Press, 1963), 32.

temple, courtroom, and family are interpreted as poetic ways of saying that God chooses to forgive or reconcile. A depth is missing here, and it is against this kind of reduction that so many modern trinitarians are reacting, under the slogan of Karl Rahner that many believers are "almost mere monotheists."[18] This minimal soteriology could be underwritten by a unipersonal God; almost by a deistic God; certainly by Allah. Trinitarian theology summons Christian soteriology to go deeper.

But not too deep. For at the opposite extreme is the error of excess. I have in mind here a style of soteriology that obliterates all distinctions between divinity and humanity, leaping over every barrier, beginning with that between creator and creature. Think of the Rhineland mystics who boasted of being "Godded with God and Christed with Christ," but also of the way *theōsis*, or deification, is celebrated at the popular level, or the way schemes of ontological participation are championed in a variety of theologies.

When the doctrine of the Trinity is fulfilling its function of informing and norming soteriology, it rules out both extremes. John Calvin reminds us that "God, to keep us sober, speaks sparingly of his essence."[19] And yet the same Calvin, taking his norms from a trinitarian account of the adoption of believers by the Father in the only begotten Son by the Spirit of adoption, celebrates the depth and richness of the fellowship that is ours in Christ. God speaks sparingly of his essence, but lavishly of his Son and of our adopted sonship. A soteriology informed and normed by the doctrine of the Trinity equips us to recognize our intimacy with and our distinction from God in Christ. As Kevin Vanhoozer says, "Only the doctrine of the Trinity adequately accounts for how those who are not God come to share in the fellowship of the Father and the Son through the Spirit."[20] This too is one of the tasks of the doctrine of the Trinity in relation to soteriology, and it follows directly from the major and primary task of correlating the events of salvation history with the divine being in itself.

18. Karl Rahner, *The Trinity*, trans. Joseph Donceel (New York: Crossroad, 1997), 10.

19. Calvin, *Institutes* I:13.1, 121.

20. Kevin J. Vanhoozer, *The Drama of Doctrine: A Canonical-Linguistic Approach to Christian Theology* (Louisville: Westminster John Knox, 2005), 43-44.

The Doctrine of the Trinity and the Scope of God's Economy

ONCE IT HAS BECOME clear that the doctrine of the Trinity exerts formative pressure on the doctrine of salvation, it is tempting to move directly
from Trinity to soteriology. But in this case, too direct a route would be neither
safe nor fruitful. By a direct route, I mean the kind of approach that would
have to trade on correspondences between the threefoldness of God and some
observable triplicity in salvation. A move like this would inevitably be a feeble
and impressionistic gesture, because it would rely on the theologian's ingenuity
in picking out triadic correspondences between the immanent Trinity and the
experience of salvation.[1] As we have already seen, the crucial link between
the Trinity and soteriology is the economy of salvation, into which the triune
God has impressed a significant form. God's economy is the matrix of both
doctrines simultaneously, so that our theologizing about salvation and about
the triune God both arise from this context. This remains the case even when
we confess that the Trinity infinitely exceeds the economy. If God's transcendence of the economy requires us to confess that the doctrine of the Trinity
norms soteriology (as we argued in chapter 1), it is nevertheless also true that
soteriological concerns require us to approach the doctrine of the Trinity from
the angle of the economy of salvation. That is the approach this chapter follows,
and the position from which it presents the entire doctrine of the Trinity.

The doctrine of the Trinity stands out as more than a single doctrine within
Christian theology. The word *Trinity* denotes a field within which an extraor-

---

1. See Louis Dupré's critique of the superficial and merely "external resemblances" between God and the "threefold function" of the soul into which some facile interpretations of Augustine's theology degenerated. Louis Dupré, *The Common Life: The Origins of
Trinitarian Mysticism and its Development by Jan Ruusbroec* (New York: Crossroad, 1984),
1–19. Despite Dupré's over-reliance on an East-vs-West schema and a desire to see all good
developments reach their fruition in Ruusbroec, this brief book remains a powerful sketch
of trinitarian mysticism.

dinary range of dogmatic material must be comprehended, brought to expression, and integrated. Its most obvious constituent territories are those of Christology and pneumatology, but through these it also determines the comprehensive loci of revelation and soteriology, taking up the full scope of salvation history and providing the framework for the confession of God's gracious self-giving in the economy of salvation. Furthermore, the doctrine of the Trinity has as its characteristic feature that it takes up all of this material together, against the horizon of the eternal being of God *in se*, systematically posing the question of how salvation history is to be correlated with the divine being in itself. To characterize the doctrine of the Trinity in this way is already to charge it with its defining task: The task of the doctrine of the Trinity is to describe the connection between God and the economy of salvation.

More concretely, the doctrine of the Trinity asks about how the threefold act of God in history (the Father sending the Son and the Spirit) corresponds to the triune being of God in eternity. Trinitarianism did not originate from asking about this correspondence as if it were an open question, but on the basis of the primal Christian conviction that God is truly present to his people in Christ (Immanuel, God with us) and the Spirit. There is no prior, abstract principle in place dictating that God's salvific actions, whatever they might be, must be revelatory of the divine life itself. In the majestic freedom and condescension of God, it simply is the case that he has elected to open this triune divine depth for human knowledge and fellowship, by accomplishing salvation in this threefold way. The correspondence is grounded in God's determination to be our salvation in person, and his accompanying refusal to neglect, delegate, or even merely create human salvation. Positing himself as the source, means, and end of salvation, God makes himself present to us in salvation history in the same way as he exists in the uttermost depths of his own exalted being: as Father, Son, and Holy Spirit. The doctrine of the Trinity is "the change in the conception of God which followed, as it was necessitated by, the New Testament conception of Christ and His work."[2] On the basis of the gospel of God, Christian faith confesses the God of the gospel. When systematic theology takes up the doctrine of the Trinity, it is scrutinizing and conceptually clarifying this simultaneous confession of God and the gospel. The following chapter is a description of the doctrine of the Trinity from this evangelical perspective.

From the primary task of describing the connection between God and the economy of salvation, there is derived a secondary, critical task of the doc-

---

2. James Denney, *Studies in Theology* (London: Hodder and Stoughton, 1895), 70.

trine of the Trinity. The doctrine functions to identify God, or to specify the particular identity of the God who is the referent of all Christian discourse. "It is the business of the doctrine of the Trinity," Karl Barth said in 1932, "to answer the question who God is," and to distinguish "the Christian doctrine of God as Christian . . . in contrast to all other possible doctrines of God."[3] To say with all seriousness that this doctrine identifies God is to treat it as God's proper name, which is the direction in which Robert W. Jenson developed Barth's lead in his influential 1982 book *The Triune Identity*.[4] Thus "Father, Son, and Holy Spirit" names the Christian God, just as "Yahweh" and "Allah" name the divinities of Judaism and Islam (assuming for the moment that "Yahweh" points to a biblical monotheism disconnected from a constitutive Christology or pneumatology, as opposed to the New Testament construal of Yahweh via Christology and pneumatology).[5] This critical naming function derives from the task of describing God's connection to the economy of salvation, because it is neither as a set of syllables nor as a conventional label that "Father, Son, and Holy Spirit" does the work of naming, but as a condensed narrative providing "identifying descriptions" from God's history with his people. As Jenson would later put it in his *Systematic Theology*, "thus the phrase, 'Father, Son, and Holy Spirit' is simultaneously a very compressed telling of the total narrative by which Scripture identifies God and a personal name for the God so specified."[6] The Christian God is specified when Israel's monotheism is elaborated through a Christology and pneumatology so robust as to be constitutive of that monotheism. Where any of these elements are lacking, God-talk has not yet specified its referent well enough to single out the God who has revealed himself in the sending of the Son and the Spirit. When Lesslie Newbigin argued that one of the functions of the doctrine of the Trinity is to identify the Christian God, he also noted that the doctrine of the Trinity has usually seemed less urgent in

3. Karl Barth, *CD*, 1/1, 301.

4. Robert W. Jenson, *The Triune Identity: God according to the Gospel* (Philadelphia: Fortress Press, 1982).

5. Jenson's invocation of the Trinity as the divine name was early, vigorous, and influential. The maneuver was often, in earlier decades, closely connected with questions about gender-neutral language for God; see the essays gathered in Alvin F. Kimel Jr., ed., *Speaking the Christian God: The Holy Trinity and the Challenge of Feminism* (Grand Rapids: Eerdmans, 1992). Certain ways of talking about Trinity as the Christian name of God also raise questions about supersessionism. All of these issues are canvassed and taken up into a powerful constructive proposal in R. Kendall Soulen's *The Divine Name(s) and the Holy Trinity, Volume One: Distinguishing the Voices* (Louisville: Westminster John Knox, 2011).

6. Robert W. Jenson, *Systematic Theology*, vol. 1 (New York: Oxford University Press, 1997), 46.

historical periods when Christian theology thought it could take the identity of its God for granted, whereas epochs marked by a greater awareness of cultural diversity and doctrinal pluralism (the fourth, sixteenth, and late twentieth centuries, for example) have considered the identity of God as something that requires deliberate specification.[7]

THE PLACE AND FIELD OF TRINITARIANISM

Because the doctrinal territory being surveyed here is a field-encompassing field, it is a locus where basic decisions are made that have ramifications for all of theology. Even the doctrine's proper place within systematic theology is a matter of unusually sharp contention. There was a traditional scholastic sequence, deriving from Aquinas (who in this departed from Lombard), which first established the doctrine of the one God (his existence, essence, attributes, and operations), and then turned to the triunity of that God (processions, persons, missions).[8] A two-part doctrine of God thus preceded the doctrine of creation, at the beginning of the system. Modern theologians like Rahner have complained that the scholastic order brings with it the temptation to develop the doctrine of the one God in a "quite philosophical and abstract" manner that "refers hardly at all to salvation history," meanwhile locking the Trinity "in even more splendid isolation, with the ensuing danger that the religious mind finds it devoid of interest."[9] Rahner could also rightly acknowledge, however, that "if the treatise *De Deo Uno* is to be real theology and not mere metaphysics, it cannot speak of the one God and his nature without speaking of the God of history and of a historical experience of him, of the God of a possible revelation and self-communication. Hence it is already orientated to the treatise *De Deo Trino*, which deals with such a God in salvation-history."[10]

In Protestant theology, a similar traditional order[11] was overturned by Friedrich Schleiermacher, who postponed discrete consideration of the Trinity un-

7. Lesslie Newbigin, *The Relevance of Trinitarian Doctrine for Today's Mission* (London: Edinburgh House Press, 1963), 32.

8. Thomas Aquinas, *Summa Theologiae*, Part 1, questions 2–26, followed by questions 27–43.

9. Karl Rahner, *The Trinity* (New York: Herder and Herder), 17–18.

10. Karl Rahner, "Trinity in Theology," in *Encyclopedia of Theology: The Concise Sacramentum Mundi* (New York: Crossroad, 1986), 1767.

11. Richard A. Muller, *Post-Reformation Reformed Dogmatics: The Rise and Development*

til an appendix of his carefully structured *Glaubenslehre*, because the doctrine fell outside of the range of things that could be described scientifically within his method of exegeting the Christian consciousness of redemption. Barth somewhat puckishly inverted Schleiermacher's decision and set the doctrine at the very beginning of his *Church Dogmatics*, precisely where a prolegomena might be expected. As Robert W. Jenson observed, "it was Barth who taught postmodern theology that the doctrine of Trinity is there to be used: that it is not a puzzle but rather the framework within which theological puzzles can be solved. The *Kirchliche Dogmatik* is a parade of trinitarian solutions to questions that modern theology had answered in unitarian fashion."[12] For his part, Jenson crafted his own *Systematic Theology* with such an expansive account of the Trinity that it has room for his entire Christology, pneumatology, and atonement theology, reflecting his view that the identity of God is only rendered by the presentation of these economic events by which God identifies himself. On this plan, the doctrines of creation, the church, and eschatology could easily have been developed internal to the doctrine of the Trinity, "but organizing the work on the plausible principle that finally all Christian teaching in one way or another tells God's own story would of course have obliterated the point."[13]

Since the mere external sequencing of the doctrines is hardly a matter of great importance, consensus at the level of the table of contents is no goal worth seeking. The substantive concerns behind these questions of order, however, can be seen in the tension between two structural principles: On one hand, since systematic theology must presuppose Christology and pneumatology pervasively, it is best to deploy the doctrine of the Trinity immediately in order to allow it to shape the treatment of every doctrine. On the other hand, since the doctrine of the Trinity cannot be elaborated without rather detailed accounts of its sub-fields, it should be postponed until those doctrines (at the very least, the doctrines of Christ and the Spirit) are in place. All these elements mutually presuppose each other, and while systematic theology must strive to attest "the *circumincessio* in which all the treatises of dogmatic theology are in the nature of things involved"[14] it is not possible to say everything at once, at least for those who live and work "where a word has both a beginning and an ending."[15]

---

of Reformed Orthodoxy, ca. 1520 to ca. 1725, vol. 4, *The Triunity of God* (Grand Rapids: Baker Academic), 59–143.

12. Jenson, *Systematic Theology*, 1:154.

13. Jenson, *Systematic Theology*, 2:v.

14. Rahner, "Trinity in Theology," 1767.

15. Augustine, *Confessions* 9.10: "ubi verbum et incipitur et finitur." This was how Au-

Whenever the time comes, in a comprehensive systematic theology, to give an account of the doctrine of the Trinity, the connection between God and the economy of salvation must be described with adequate attention to both poles. In the history of the doctrine, a formidable array of conceptual categories has emerged to this end: mission, procession, person, nature, consubstantiality, relations of origin, perichoresis, psychological and social analogies, etc. Each of these categories continues to be important and illuminating in its proper place, but each has also proven capable of breaking free from its place and becoming an independent center of interest. Whether the free-floating element is the Cappadocian account of relations, the psychological models from the final books of Augustine's *De Trinitate*, or Aquinas's anatomizing of internal processions, there has been a recurring tendency for the conceptual apparatus, helpful in itself, to escape the orbit of the gospel and begin exerting an independent gravitational pull on later theology. For this reason, the history of the doctrine of the Trinity is punctuated by laments about the doctrine's apparent abstractness, irrelevance, and inscrutability—laments that are themselves expressions of the enduring Christian instinct to keep the trinitarian confession transparent to its biblical, experiential, and evangelical basis.

To establish good order among the elements, the doctrine of the Trinity must take its orientation from the dynamics of God's saving act. What vigorous trinitarian theology demands is a flexible and modest conceptual framework that retains enough vestiges of the biblical narrative to situate the conceptual elements. Much contemporary trinitarian theology operates within such a framework, though the framework itself is usually left implicit, and there is considerable difference of opinion about its precise borders. One possible explication of the framework is as follows. As noted earlier, the field of the doctrine of the Trinity can be plotted within the coordinates of two intersecting axes that trace the dynamics of God's self-giving. The defining axis runs from the immanent life of God to the outward acts of God in creation. The other axis connects the two trinitarian persons who are revealed by their personal presence in the missions of the economy, and is therefore an axis running between the Son and the Holy Spirit. The resulting field provides the context for situating the traditional conceptual apparatus of trinitarianism, highlighting certain elements while relegating others to the background. For instance, questions about how the three can be one, or about analogical aids to understanding, are temporarily suspended because they can arise mean-

gustine characterized the descent from the singular bliss of the intellectual vision of God back down to the prosaic world of ordinary thought and speech.

ingfully and concretely only after being situated within the field defined by these axes. More significantly, the suggested field indicates the presence and action of the first person of the Trinity only obliquely. "The invisible Father" is not mappable on these coordinates because of the unique, mediated way he comes to be present in the economy of salvation. Just as the hypostatic depth of God the Father is what brings forth the Son and Spirit *ad intra*, it is his love that grounds their missions in the economy. The massive attention that patristic authors gave to the Father-Son relationship is represented in modern theology by the immanent-economic axis, which was often the real point at issue in Arian controversies: Is the messianic Son also an eternal Son? The other advantages of this framework are that it frustrates the over-neatness of habitual geometries, resists the seductions of the magic number three, keeps the immanent and economic poles from collapsing into each other, draws special attention to the nexus between Christology and pneumatology, and postpones elaborate conceptual definitions long enough to cede priority to the substantial descriptive work that must precede them.

Re-centering Trinitarianism on the Economy of Salvation

All of what has been said above reflects the widespread consensus in contemporary theology that the doctrine of the Trinity must be developed in a way that is centered on the *oikonomia*, the history of salvation. A classic expression of this commitment emerged from the *Mysterium Salutis* group of Roman Catholic theologians who took up the task of carrying out the theological renewal called for by Vatican II. The subtitle of their multivolume work, published between 1965 and 1976, was *Grundriss heilsgeschichtlicher Dogmatik*, and as a foundation for a salvation-historical dogmatics the work attempted to recast all of Christian doctrine in terms of the key motif of salvation history. Salvation history was a category that had emerged from the *nouvelle théologie* of the early twentieth century as well as from dialogue with Protestant thought, and which subsequently informed the council. The assignment of setting the doctrine of the Trinity in the framework of the mystery of salvation fell to Karl Rahner, whose chapter for the series was entitled "The Triune God as the Transcendent Primal Ground of Salvation History."[16] This chapter was later published separately as his influential short book *The Trinity*. Of all the mysteries of faith, the teaching about God's essential triunity seemed to many theologians, from that

16. Johannes Feiner and Magnus Löhrer, eds., *Mysterium Salutis: Grundriss Heilsgeschichtlicher Dogmatik*, vol. 2 (Einsiedeln: Benziger Verlag, 1965–76), 317.

mid-century vantage point, to be the least promising for salvation-historical treatment. As Rahner later reflected, "Since St Augustine, the 'immanent' Trinity has been so much to the fore in theological discussion . . . and the 'economic' Trinity has been so obscured in Christology and *De Gratia* by the principle that all actions *ad extra* in God are common to all three persons or belong to God as one, that it is hard to see what Christian existence has to do with the Trinity in actual life."[17] When, in light of the mystery of salvation, Rahner located the Trinity as "the transcendent primal ground" of salvation history, he was articulating the consensus that marks the twentieth century's renewed interest in the doctrine: a resolute focusing of attention on the economy of salvation as the ground and criterion of all knowledge about the Trinity.

On the whole, this trend to an economic re-centering of trinitarian theology has been a beneficial and necessary corrective within the long history of the doctrine. Although the importance of such re-centering is often exaggerated by self-congratulatory contemporary theologies, there had indeed been a dangerous tendency in older works to construct the doctrine of the immanent Trinity from speculative or metaphysical arguments. Whenever the doctrine of the Trinity has been presented as a teaching about the inner life of God, and this inner life is filled out conceptually without sustained reference to God's self-revelation and self-giving in salvation history, the doctrine has gone adrift. It is true that God exists eternally as one being in three persons. The danger lies in stating this doctrine in a way that is opaque to its mode of revelation. In more daring versions of speculative theology, this abstraction takes the form of transcendental deductions from the concept of interpersonal love, or the structure of absolute subjectivity, or some other phenomenon sufficiently complex to entertain a threefold dialectic treatment. In conservative theologies of various kinds, a different kind of abstraction threatens to reduce knowledge of the Trinity to a merely verbal transfer of information, as if God transferred a set of propositions about his threefoldness in order to make it known for its own sake. Either way (through speculative expansion or propositional reduction), dislocated from God's saving acts the doctrine of the immanent Trinity becomes distracting, theologically non-functional, and nettlesome. Against such "exclusive concentration on the immanent Trinity" that has "brought the doctrine of the Trinity into disrepute among Catholics and Protestants alike, and has often led to its being dropped from the theological curriculum," David Coffey contends, "the proper study of the Trinity is the study of the economic Trinity."[18]

17. Rahner, "Trinity in Theology," 1765–66.
18. David Coffey, *Deus Trinitas: The Doctrine of the Triune God* (New York: Oxford University Press, 1999), 16.

On the other hand, merely to narrate the events of salvation history, that is, to tell the story of the Father's sending of the Son and Spirit, without allowing the claims of the narrative to push back into the eternal being of God, is to stall out at the level of the economy of salvation without actually saying anything about God himself. Soteriology then exhausts theology proper. However conceptually unstable the position may be, a great deal of trinitarian theology in the late twentieth century took as its starting point a strong interpretation of Karl Rahner's theological *Grundaxiom* that "the economic Trinity is the immanent Trinity, and vice versa."[19] Taken in its most radical sense, this axiom indicates not merely an epistemological focus on the economy of salvation, but (especially in the direction indicated by the vice versa) a denial that God in himself is triune apart from salvation history. Catherine Mowry LaCugna's *God for Us: The Trinity and Christian Life*, for example, inveighed against "the nonsoteriological doctrine of God," or any version of immanent trinitarian theology that claimed to be "an analysis of what is 'inside God'" rather than "a way of speaking about the structure or pattern of God's self-expression in salvation history."[20] Speaking programmatically, for LaCugna, "the fundamental issue in trinitarian theology is not the inner workings of the 'immanent' Trinity, but the question of how the trinitarian pattern of salvation history is to be correlated with the eternal being of God."[21] This way of framing trinitarianism includes both a salutary affirmation and an unfortunately polemical denial. The advent of "scare quotes" around the "immanent" Trinity, for example, is symptomatic.

Such reductionistically economic trinitarianism is equivalent to a denial of the immanent Trinity altogether, and leaves theology with nothing beyond structure, pattern, and history, with no way of referring to the God who takes his stand in that history. As Karl Barth had already asked in the 1930s, "What would 'God for us' mean if it were not said against the background of 'God in Himself?'"[22] Wolfhart Pannenberg's theological system depicts God as very closely engaged with history, but Pannenberg also warns that the priority of the immanent Trinity must be maintained:

> It is certainly true that the trinitarian God in the history of salvation is the same God as in His eternal life. But there is also a necessary distinction

19. Rahner, *The Trinity*, 22.
20. Catherine Mowry LaCugna, *God for Us: The Trinity and Christian Life* (San Francisco: HarperCollins, 1991), 225.
21. LaCugna, *God for Us*, 6.
22. Barth, *CD*, 1/1, 171.

that maintains the priority of the eternal communion of the triune God over that communion's explication in the history of salvation. Without that distinction, the reality of the one God tends to be dissolved into the process of the world.[23]

What Pannenberg describes in somewhat metaphysical terms can be stated more personally: without this distinction, the freedom of God is eclipsed. Paul D. Molnar has argued that "all Christian theologians realize that the purpose of a doctrine of the immanent Trinity is to recognize, uphold and respect God's freedom,"[24] and has shown how the distinction must be not simply asserted, but guarded with vigilance at strategic points such as *creatio ex nihilo*, the preexistence of Christ as *logos asarkos*, and the distinction between the Holy Spirit and the human spirit.

Notwithstanding the variety of "post-Rahnerian programmes to collapse the immanent Trinity into the economic" that flourished for a time,[25] the twentieth-century re-centering of the doctrine of the Trinity on the economy of salvation does not of itself entail denying the immanent Trinity nor assimilating *theologia* to *oikonomia* without remainder. The editors of *Mysterium Salutis* had already recognized this in the period just prior to the ecumenical revival of interest in trinitarian theology:

> without the depth dimension of *theologia*, all talk about the *oikonomia* and salvation history becomes admittedly flat and merely foreground. What Barth said of evangelical theology holds also for Catholic: "The subject of evangelical theology is God in the history of his acts."[26]

Such easy balance is characteristic of any elaboration of trinitarian theology that recalls that its criterion is the clear articulation of the gospel. Thus Thomas F. Torrance strikes the same equipoise when he says that the significance of the historical manifestation of the Trinity is its "transhistorical and

23. Wolfhart Pannenberg, "Books in Review: Robert W. Jenson, Systematic Theology: Volumes I & II," *First Things* 103 (May 2000): 51.

24. Paul D. Molnar, *Divine Freedom and the Doctrine of the Immanent Trinity: In Dialogue with Karl Barth and Contemporary Theology* (Edinburgh: T&T Clark, 2002), ix.

25. Colin Gunton, *Father, Son, & Holy Spirit: Toward a Fully Trinitarian Theology* (London: T&T Clark, 2003), 71.

26. Feiner and Löhrer, *Mysterium Salutis*, 1:30. The internal quotation, significantly, is from Karl Barth's *Evangelical Theology: An Introduction* (New York: Holt, Rinehart & Winston, 1963), 9.

transfinite reference beyond" to the eternal being of God. The relations made known in salvation history must be grounded in relations that "belong to the inner life of God and constitute his very being."[27]

If a speculative construction of the immanent Trinity is one possible abstraction from the serious business of trinitarian theology, the opposite abstraction is a speculative deconstruction of the immanent Trinity that reduces trinitarian theology to "some kind of historical positivism."

THE ECONOMIC-IMMANENT AXIS

Epistemic priority may rest with the economic Trinity, but ontic priority resides in the immanent. The two are bound together. Much depends, then, on the direction being followed by any particular theological treatment of the Trinity. Augustine's *De Trinitate*, for example, begins with the sendings of the Son and Spirit, asking how sender and sent can be equal in all ways. From here Augustine climbs to the eternal relations of origin revealed by the missions, and ends with an attempt to conceive of the one God's immanent triunity. The trinitarian treatise in Aquinas's *Summa Theologiae*, on the other hand, begins with the most fundamental logical distinction, the processions (Part 1, Question 27, Article 1: "Are there processions in God?"), and ends with missions (Part 1, Question 43, Article 1: "Is it suitable for a divine person to be sent?"). In whichever direction it moves, trinitarian theology must make the trip along the axis between God *in se* and God *pro nobis*, tracing God's covenant faithfulness as it is grounded in his character, and thus following what Barth called "the way of the knowledge of God."[28]

Considered as an actual movement of God's grace from above to below, the immanent-economic axis is the occasion for wonder and praise, the one event of divine self-giving than which nothing greater can be thought. Here theology inevitably approximates pure doxology. Considered as a reflective movement of thought from below to above, however, the economic-immanent axis is an intellectual project whose closest analogs are observation, induction, and the formation of conceptual models. Here theology confronts the demand that it be rigorous, consistent, and creative in articulating how the various elements of the biblical witness are to be integrated. As we have seen

27. Thomas F. Torrance, *The Christian Doctrine of God: One Being Three Persons* (Edinburgh: T&T Clark, 1996), 6.
28. Barth, *CD*, 2/1, 179.

before, it is one thing to assert, with Barth, that "to the involution and convolution [*Ineinander und Miteinander*] of the three modes of being in the essence of God there corresponds exactly their involution and convolution in his work."[29] It is another thing to describe how the particular involution and convolution seen in the economic relations among Jesus Christ, his Father, and their Spirit are to be construed as revealing the very life of God. It is no surprise that the thorniest problems of the doctrine of the Trinity tend to be located precisely here.

The notoriously difficult question of the *filioque*, for example, is mainly an extended discussion about the degree to which the economic missions are revelatory of the immanent processions. The pentecostal Spirit is obviously poured out on all flesh by both the Father and the exalted Son; they are the senders behind the advent of the Spirit. If it were axiomatic that every salvation-historical manifestation of a person of the Trinity is revelatory of a procession, then the Spirit would obviously be known to proceed, within the immanent Trinity, from the Father and also the Son: *filioque*. But there are good reasons to withhold assent from so immediate a deduction, and not simply the monopatrist or anti-filioquist reasons traditionally urged by the Eastern churches. More fundamentally, the direct deduction of trinitarian relations from the history of salvation is rendered unworkable by what Gary D. Badcock has called "the problem of economic diversity," which is a "diversity, not only of the possible trinitarian interpretations to which the economy of salvation is susceptible, but of the actual economic basis of trinitarian theology itself."[30]

Father, Son, and Spirit interact in so many ways in the economy of salvation that we are actually confronted with the material for multiple models that resist harmonizing. In the instance of the *filioque*, while the Word pours out the Spirit, the Spirit also brings about the incarnation of the Word. As Bruce D. Marshall summarizes, "Thus we can read off from the economy both that the Spirit originates from the Son, and that the Son originates from the Spirit. But these look like contradictories, so one of them has to be false."[31] Why do filioquists ignore the trinitarian implications of the spiritual conception of Christ, and the other triadic configurations? Why do monopatrists refuse to read back along the trajectory of the Son's sending of the Spirit? Without some

29. Barth, *CD*, 1/1, 374.

30. Gary D. Badcock, *Light of Truth and Fire of Love: A Theology of the Holy Spirit* (Grand Rapids: Eerdmans, 1997), 213; see 212-29.

31. Bruce D. Marshall, "The Trinity," in *The Blackwell Companion to Modern Theology*, ed. Gareth Jones (Oxford: Blackwell, 2004), 197.

criterion for deciding which economic relations are revelatory of God's own life, such problems are not resolvable, and divergent conclusions are bound to seem arbitrary.

If the excess of economic configurations seems at first to set a limit to coherent trinitarian constructs, the sheer abundance of relationships may also hold untapped possibilities. There are economic relations among Father, Son, and Spirit that are clearly witnessed in Scripture, but which have been underused in developing the doctrine of the immanent Trinity. Relatively early in the development of the doctrine of the Trinity, the Christian tradition recognized the privileged status of one set of relations as the foundation of trinitarian difference: relations of origin. The *filioque* disagreement is precisely over these primal relations, to the exclusion of the others. For example, it has not normally been considered relevant that John of Damascus described the Holy Spirit as "associated with the Word and making the operation of the Word manifest." The Spirit is "a substantial power found in its own individuating personality, proceeding from the Father, coming to rest in the Word and declaring Him."[32] Is John mobilizing these verbs and prepositions to describe the *oikonomia*, or does he allude to the Spirit's accompanying, manifesting, and resting on the Word within the immanent Trinity as well? If they are realities within the immanent Trinity, are they any less decisive than the relations of origin? In ecumenical dialogue over the *filioque*, Jürgen Moltmann has proposed distinguishing between two dimensions of God's life: the constitutional level of the processions, and the relational level at which all of these other pluriform and perichoretic relations take place. The two dimensions need not be thought of as temporally sequential nor ontologically ranked, merely as distinct.[33] Pannenberg likewise has argued that there is a "richly structured nexus of relationships" among the three, and that while the persons are indeed constituted by their relations to each other, "yet the persons cannot be reduced to individual relations" such as origin. "None of the other relations is merely incidental to the Son and Spirit in their relation to the Father. All have a place in the distinctiveness and fellowship of the trinitarian persons."[34] Robert W. Jenson, typically, makes the point more clearly but too drastically: "That the

32. John of Damascus, *An Exact Exposition of the Orthodox Faith* 1:7, in *Saint John of Damascus: Writings*, trans. Frederic H. Chase Jr. (New York: Fathers of the Church, 1958), 175.

33. Jürgen Moltmann, "Theological Proposals towards the Resolution of the *Filioque* Controversy," in *Spirit of God, Spirit of Christ: Ecumenical Reflections on the Filioque Controversy*, World Council of Churches Faith and Order Paper No. 103, ed. Lukas Vischer (London: SPCK), 164–73.

34. Wolfhart Pannenberg, *Systematic Theology*, vol. 1 (Grand Rapids: Eerdmans, 1991), 320.

Spirit rests upon the Son is not a phenomenon merely of the economic Trinity—there are in any case no such phenomena."[35]

The thorough privileging of the relations of origin has put a certain amount of pressure on trinitarianism, forcing the rest of the data to find recognition elsewhere, as for instance in Moltmann's somewhat idiosyncratic constitutive-relational distinction. The same pressure has also found release in established doctrinal traditions like the exploration of the divine energies in Eastern Orthodoxy, or the explication of eternal decrees and an immanent trinitarian covenant in Reformed thought. In their own ways, each of these traditions opens up zones where the manifold relations of the three persons can be confessed without causing confusion over the processions. Whatever their limits, they approach the insight that relational complexity in the *oikonomia* may faithfully enact the richness and multiplicity of the personal relations in the being of the one God. The sudden popularity of a strong version of social trinitarianism in the late twentieth century is probably most charitably understood as another of these attempts to trace the richness of the economic configurations to their transcendent ground in the divine being. Granted such a "richly structured nexus of relationships" among Father, Son, and Holy Spirit in the history of salvation, the immanent-trinitarian nexus must be equally rich and no less structured, even as we move upward along the axis from economic to immanent. This move alone, however, would not signal what is novel in contemporary social trinitarianism. The characteristic social-trinitarian move is to transpose the conceptual apparatus of personal distinction as well, positing in the immanent Trinity three distinct centers of consciousness, volition, and agency, which stand as persons over against each other with faculties of their own. At issue are some general questions of theological language, such as whether terms like "person" and "self" can be employed univocally at both ends of the axis. Equally important is the gap that appears here between an ancient valorizing of essence categories (with person categories relatively under-stocked), over against a modern elaboration of person categories (with an accompanying emptying out of essence categories). The strength of this recent social trinitarianism is this: Everyone is bound to be a social trinitarian at the economic level. Porting over all of the categories (person, mind, agent, will, faculties, etc.), however, as univocally true of the eternal divine persons, is probably an instinctive attempt to bridge the gap between the richly interpersonal economy (Jesus and his Father) and the sheer austerity of the relations of origin confessed by classic trinitarianism (paternity and filiality). Whatever

---

35. Jenson, *Systematic Theology*, 1:143.

that "richly structured nexus of relationships" is among Father, Son, and Spirit, it must be confessed to be love. Wherever relations of origin seem inadequate to bear that description, there will be a need to articulate the other relations in which Scripture sets before our eyes the love of the Father and the Son in the Spirit.

Fraught questions such as the *filioque* and the meaning of personhood are rooted, then, in the prior question of what criteria should guide trinitarian theology in interpreting the economy of salvation as revelatory of the divine life. Prior to that question, however, is a fundamental question of why Christian doctrine should regard the *oikonomia* as revelatory of *theologia* proper in the first place. Where does the initial cue come from that lets the interpreter know to start the project? Does the economy itself teach us to read the economy as an image or revelation of God's self? Walter Kasper has warned against behaving as if the Trinity is deducible from the history of salvation "by a kind of extrapolation." Reading evidence from the economy back into the immanent Trinity "was certainly not the path the early church followed in developing the doctrine of the Trinity in the form of confession and dogma."[36] Kasper points away from the welter of events that make up the economy and fixes our attention first on the primal ecclesial act of baptism in the triune name, a practice and formula that developed "from the risen Lord's commission regarding baptism," that is, the great commission passage, Matthew 28:19. "Knowledge of the trinitarian mystery was thus due directly to the revelation of the Word and not to a process of deduction."[37]

Whatever riches of the knowledge of God are revealed in the history of salvation, to approach the history as if it were self-evidently God's self-revelation would run perilously close to positing a general principle about the God-world relationship, a general principle that would itself be underdetermined by revelation. Divine revelation is inalienably linked to intention on the part of the revealer, and "unfolds through deeds and words bound together by an inner dynamism," to use again the words of Vatican II's *Dei verbum*.[38] Kasper's caution is a good reminder that theology should have a good conscience about behaving as if it were led by Scripture, even taking crucial guidance from the inspired text as containing, among other things, revealed propositions. Kasper's own theological work is an instance of a project that is well disposed

36. Walter Kasper, *The God of Jesus Christ* (New York: Crossroad, 1984), 276.

37. Kasper, *God of Jesus Christ*, 276.

38. *Dei verbum*, §2, in *Decrees of the Ecumenical Councils*, vol. 2, ed. N. P. Tanner, SJ (Georgetown: Sheed and Ward, 1990), 972.

toward revelation through history and committed to reading the signs of the Trinity in the history of salvation. He admits, however, that theology is in possession of a rudimentary doctrine of the immanent Trinity even before it turns to the task of exegeting salvation history under the guidance of an axiom that the economy is revelatory: "This axiom presupposes knowledge of the immanent Trinity and is meant to interpret and concretize the immanent Trinity in an appropriate way."[39] Carried out in conjunction with some amount of verbal revelation, reading the economy is not a self-initiated or self-norming project. As Bruce D. Marshall notes, "if we are to 'read' the economic data in a way which yields a coherent set of results regarding the relations of origin among the divine persons, we need guidance which the economic data do not themselves provide—perhaps from some sort of authoritative teaching about what makes each person the unique individual he is."[40] Any such authoritative teaching would of course have to be handled not as a sheer given, but scrutinized to see whether "an inner dynamism" between word and deed can be discerned. The main lines of the doctrine of the Trinity have been defined by a Christian tradition that at least thinks it does discern such a relation.

What is needed above all is a holistic approach that can assess all of the economic evidence in one massive movement of theological understanding. Because of the uniquely integral character of the doctrine of the Trinity, it cannot be formulated in a fragmentary way, one bit of evidence after another. Specifically, the fragmentary approach cannot of itself underwrite the necessary transposition of the biblical evidence from the salvation-history level to the transcendent, immanent-trinitarian level, a transposition that requires that all the evidence be reinterpreted simultaneously with its structuring patterns intact. Making the jump from economy to Trinity requires a kind of economy-wide gestalt perception, in which the involution and convolution of Father, Son, and Spirit around the life of Jesus are seen as one coherent pattern bearing a discernible, describable, threefold form. This triune form, once recognized, can then be understood as the projection onto human history of the form of God's triune life. Taken in isolation, none of the elements of the economy makes a particularly strong case for being read back into the immanent Trinity: not even the begetting of the Son or the procession of the Spirit. They must be perceived together integrally, together with the structures obtaining among them, in order to motivate and accomplish the jump to the immanent Trinity.

39. Kasper, *God of Jesus Christ*, 277.
40. Marshall, "The Trinity," 197.

This becomes a more urgent requirement the more trinitarian theology settles into its task of reflection on revelation that is always mediated by the text. Arguments about texts can quite readily degenerate into fragmentary observations and isolated proofs, to the detriment of the larger doctrinal outlines. This tendency has been exacerbated by the rise of a crucial dialogue partner for modern systematic theology: the discipline of historical-critical biblical research. The overall trend of modern biblical scholarship has been toward a severe attenuation of the traditional exegetical arguments by which the doctrine of the Trinity was crafted and by which it has been supported since patristic times. This is true not only of biblical criticism in its most corrosively skeptical expressions, which have often enough been explicitly anti-trinitarian in scope and motivation. Richard A. Muller has argued that what was occurring in the era after the Reformation, and is continuing today, is a massive "alteration of patterns of interpretation away from the patristic and medieval patterns that had initially yielded the doctrine of the Trinity and given it a vocabulary consistent with traditional philosophical usage."[41] To say that this brings us to a crisis is not to lament the contribution of critical biblical research: Who today would want to support the doctrine of the Trinity using the strangely agglomerated testimony of Proverbs 8 (translated, no less, with Wisdom saying, "God *created* me at the beginning of his ways"), the *comma johanneum*'s "three that bear witness in heaven," and an allegorical gloss on the Good Samaritan leaving two coins (the Son and the Spirit) with the innkeeper? The vocabulary and conceptual apparatus of trinitarianism need to be chastened and kept near to Scripture, and critical scholarship demands this. But the discipline also tends toward fragmentation and a kind of textual atomism, which make the trinitarian construal of Scripture impossible. Whatever weaknesses may have hobbled patristic and medieval interpretive practices, and however unusable some of those techniques may be for us, their great virtue was always their grasp of the overall meaning of Scripture. The doctrine of the Trinity is a large doctrine, and its formulation and defense have always required a certain ampleness of reflection on the revealed data. The way forward is to admit that, in Colin Gunton's words, "it must be acknowledged that there is some doubt as to whether Scripture supports the creedal confession directly or without great labour." For the justification of a crucial trinitarian doctrine like the Son's eternal generation, "prooftexting is not enough. . . . we must go beyond any

---

41. Richard A. Muller, *Post-Reformation Reformed Dogmatics: The Rise and Development of Reformed Orthodoxy, ca. 1520 to ca. 1725*, vol. 4, *The Triunity of God* (Grand Rapids: Baker Academic), 62.

single proof-text or texts and examine the broader context in which it must be understood, that of Scripture as a whole."[42] The doctrine of the Trinity is a conceptual foregrounding of the entire matrix of economic revelation. Only in this comprehensive context can the Christological monogenesis of John 1:18 be combined with the pneumatological *ekporeusis* of John 15:26 to produce a doctrine of the eternal Trinity. It is senseless to try to retain the result of the early church's holistic interpretation of Scripture (the doctrine of the Trinity) without cultivating, in a way appropriate for our own time, the interpretive practice that produced that result. The crucial interpretive practice, which as we have seen must inform both exegesis and doctrinal theology, is attention to the economy of salvation as a coherent whole.

REAL PRESENCES

The doctrine of the Trinity, centered on the history of salvation and inquiring systematically into the connection between that history and the God who takes his stand therein, is an account of the real, personal presence of the Son and the Spirit among us. The economy of salvation is actuated by the two kairotic missions, the Christological and the pneumatological (Gal 4:4–6). These two missions are mutually constitutive, or configured internally toward one another, such that it is hard to know whether it is best to go on describing them as two missions or as a single, twofold mission of the Son and the Spirit. Without the anointing Spirit, there is no *christos*, no anointed one. On the other hand, the Spirit is the "Spirit of Jesus Christ," the "Spirit of the Son," and comes decisively into the church through the ascended Christ on the basis of his accomplished work of incarnation, death, and resurrection. The outpouring of the Spirit seems to presuppose the work of Christ and to find its purpose in extending that work or applying it. The incarnation and atonement, on the other hand, seem to be ordered toward making the pentecostal indwelling possible. The Irenaean metaphor of the Father taking hold of the world through his two hands has become increasingly common, and a growing awareness of the interpenetration between Christology and pneumatology has opened new paths for theological exploration. All of this, however, is predicated on the fact that the second and third persons of the Trinity are confessed to have been actually sent out from their inalienable center in the divine life, to enter our existence in manners appropriate to each of them: hypostatic union on the one

42. Gunton, *Father, Son & Holy Spirit*, 63.

hand, and indwelling on the other. These missions, of course, are not categories of creation but of redemption, and we are bypassing the question of personal trinitarian presences in creation to pursue the decisive question of how the persons of the Trinity are present in redemption. To put it another way, we are asking how systematic theology in the various ecumenical traditions has developed the doctrine of grace in trinitarian terms.

By common consent, it was for us and our salvation that God has drawn very near in the Son and the Spirit. But the distinct theological traditions of the Christian churches have explicated this rather alarming nearness in various ways: through doctrines of appropriations, of energies, and of created grace. Each of these doctrines is attended with some ambiguity regarding the nearness that it permits. Appropriation, for example, is the ancient practice of attributing to one person of the Trinity a characteristic or action that is in fact common to the Trinity as a whole. The ancient creed appropriates the creation of heaven and earth to God the Father almighty, but this is not to be understood as proper or exclusive: the Son and Spirit are also the creator, are also the almighty. It is proper to refer creation to the first person of the Trinity because from the first person proceeds everything within the Godhead. The whole point of appropriation is to illuminate or illustrate the distinct features of each person, even in those undivided external acts of the Trinity where no distinct personal action is manifest.[43] However, the doctrine can easily function the other way, relegating every apparent trinitarian disclosure in history to being a function of the one God causing effects within creation, but sending signals that these effects are to be referred in name or understanding to one particular person of the Trinity. External actions appropriated to a trinitarian person are not real presences in the way incarnation and Pentecost are. A central task embraced by western theology, in fact, is explicating the missions of the Son and Spirit as being proper, not merely appropriated.

The theology of the Eastern churches does not use the doctrine of appropriations as thoroughly as Western theology, preferring to describe external actions of the Trinity as concerted rather than undivided. Instead, it has employed a conceptual distinction between the ineffable divine essence and the uncreated energies around that essence; the redeemed can participate in the latter but not in the former. The doctrine seems to have been crafted to explain how monks involved in hesychastic prayer were in fact communing with the true God, seeing uncreated light rather than created. Yet this doctrine, designed

43. See Gilles Emery, "The Personal Mode of Trinitarian Action in Saint Thomas Aquinas," *Thomist* 69, no. 1 (2005): 31–77.

to underwrite intimate contact with God, can also convert suddenly into its opposite and serve as an explanation of how Christian religious experience does not in fact strike home in the heart of God. In this case, much depends on whether the uncreated energies are thought of in entitative terms, or alternatively as divine actions. The more the energies are described in entitative terms, the more they seem to be buffers between God and the human person. When they are construed more dynamically along the lines of divine actions, it seems clearer that believers are immediately in the hands of God their redeemer.

Roman Catholic theology under the Thomist rubric (and this includes magisterial teachings such as those of Trent and Vatican I) has spoken of God's personal presence to believers in a way that includes the notion of created grace. According to this tradition, God does not directly and personally act on the created person without a created medium, but instead causes effects in the redeemed by the infusion of a gift that is distinct from himself. The point of the doctrine is not to deny God's personal agency, but to account for it in a way that recognizes the form of its reception by a creature and to preserve the kind of room for creaturely freedom that direct divine action on the soul would seem to obliterate. Sympathetically understood, as for instance it has been in dialogue with Eastern Orthodoxy,[44] created grace is not a substitute for uncreated grace (the personal presence of God, particularly of the Holy Spirit), but the means by which uncreated grace causes effects in the soul. On the other hand, once in place the doctrine has acted as an obstacle to a clear confession of differentiated trinitarian presence: the Spirit's indwelling is less proper to the third person and more proper to the Godhead, and the Our Father is addressed to God the Trinity rather than God the Father. This set of questions in Roman Catholic theology is vexed, as interpreters like Yves Congar have freely admitted.[45]

In contrast to this, classical Protestant theology has tended to hold to a direct and apparently naïve use of biblical language, taking some biblical statements about the three persons at face value without subjecting them to the sophisticated analysis of the medieval scholastic traditions. From the clear but unelaborated statements of Calvin ("the Holy Spirit is the bond by which Christ effectually unites us to himself")[46] to the more scholastic works of

---

44. See for instance A. N. Williams, *The Ground of Union: Deification in Aquinas and Palamas* (Oxford: Oxford University Press, 1999); Bruce D. Marshall, "'Ex Occidente Lux'? Aquinas and Eastern Orthodox Theology," in *Aquinas in Dialogue: Thomas for the Twenty-First Century*, ed. Jim Fodor and Frederick Christian Bauerschmidt (Oxford: Blackwell, 2004), 19-46.

45. Yves Congar, *I Believe in the Holy Spirit*, vol. 2 (New York: Crossroad Herder, 1997), 79-99.

46. Calvin, *Institutes* 3:1.1; McNeill/Battles, 538.

Owen and Turretin, the indwelling of the Holy Spirit in the believer is described, without nuance or qualification, as a direct personal office proper to the third person of the Trinity distinctly. On the Reformed side of Protestantism, this commitment is strengthened by two things: a notorious lack of squeamishness over the notion that direct divine action can move the human will without obliterating properly human freedom; and a preference for categories of interpersonal fellowship as opposed to categories of ontological participation. It is worth noting, however, that the Wesleyan and Pietist offshoots of Protestantism affirm the Spirit's direct personal presence, either not noticing or not caring that their commitment to libertarian human agency might equally lead them to install created grace as a buffer between God and human action.

The doctrine of the Trinity, as an ancient landmark of consensual Christian belief, has long been the site of great ecumenical convergence (the *filioque* notwithstanding). If the varied theological and confessional traditions have anything in common, it is the ancient doctrine of God, or theology proper. However, with the recent re-centering of the doctrine on the economy of salvation, certain latent tensions have come to the surface. Oddly, the more clearly the doctrine of God's triunity is integrated into soteriology (an integration demanded by exigencies internal to both doctrines), the more the Trinity will be elaborated in terms shaped by confessional concerns and disputes regarding soteriology. When Trinity and gospel are closely linked, contentions about the character of the gospel also show up in the doctrine of God. This is something of a paradox in recent developments. The ecumenical centrality of trinitarian confession, however, is no illusion. We should gamble on the possibility that the convergence of the various doctrinal traditions in the doctrine of God might have a greater depth of ingression in the Christian church's web of belief than do the details of the various soteriological elaborations. Greater attention to the connection of Trinity and gospel could then be expected to open new avenues of approach to some deadlocked problems. For example, in the thicket of questions surrounding the direct personal presences of Son and Spirit in the economy of grace, it may be possible to marshal economic-trinitarian resources before undertaking a re-description of the zone between God and man traditionally populated by accounts of appropriations, uncreated energies, and created grace. The economic Trinity itself may contain adequate resources for addressing the concerns that arise here: the enhypostatic Christology of post-Chalcedonian conciliar thought puts the eternal Logos personally into the economy in a way that deserves further exploration, and a proper mission of the Holy Spirit as the agent of divine indwelling is the pneumatological parallel. Between these two hypostatically distinct missions, there may be enough space for a satisfactory account of human freedom.[47] The way forward is a more determined commitment to these two real presences (and only downstream from them, the "real presences" spoken of in sacraments). In this way, Christian theology can confess the integral doctrine of the Trinity in a way that acknowledges, with all the saints and also with appropriate conceptual integrity and rigor, "what is the breadth and length and height and depth, and to know the love of Christ" (Eph 3:18).

The economy of salvation is the matrix of the doctrine of the Trinity. Trinitarian theology's task is always to speak rightly about God in himself on the basis of what God has made known to us in the history of his works and words for us and our salvation. It is tempting to say that this is the case even when what is made known in the economy is the immeasurable magnitude by which the triune God exceeds the economy of salvation. But why say "even"? If we have learned the lesson of God's economy, and met him there, we should say "especially." It is precisely this immeasurable transcendence of God over the economy that the economy itself, as a true revelation of the true God, confronts us with. In the following chapters, it is the same mystery that will be explored: most broadly in atonement and ecclesiology, but in more detail in the Christian life, in Christology, and in pneumatology.

47. Thomas A. Smail, *The Giving Gift: The Holy Spirit in Person* (London: Hodder and Stoughton, 1988), 66–73.

Trinity and Atonement

I T IS HARD TO DELINEATE the boundary between the doctrines of Trinity and atonement because each doctrine, taken at its most expansive, makes such heavy requisitions from the other. Unless material from each field is featured prominently in the other field, neither doctrine can be developed properly. Not even in the darkest ages of modernism did the situation ever quite degenerate into Trinity versus atonement; rather the two doctrines have tended to thrive or wilt in unison. These are not two hostile doctrines that stand in need of reconciliation to each other (to use language from atonement doctrine), nor are they simply the same subject matter subsisting distinctly in relation, nor do they indwell each other perichoretically (to use language from Trinitarian doctrine). Calibrating them to each other is a major task for any systematic theological vision, and expounding them in due proportion is a true test of any theologian's sagacity.

DOCTRINAL OBLIGATIONS OF TRINITY AND ATONEMENT

The obligation of the doctrine of the Trinity is to be a doctrine about God, which certainly ought to give Trinitarian theology more than enough work to keep it occupied. In fact, it is incumbent on Trinitarian theology to be a doctrine concerning God's eternal, essential being in a way that distinguishes itself from doctrines about God's outward actions: it concerns who God is rather than what God does. There must be something of a *sola* in Trinitarian doctrine, a protest that preserves this doctrine from being reduced and relativized. After we have said all we must say (and there is much) about the doctrine as a mystery of salvation, a map of our participation in the divine life, the structuring grammar of an ecclesial encounter with God, the pattern of

God's ways in the world, and so on, we must recall that the triune God has a self-sufficient life of its own, which is occupied with more than just being the transcendental referent of that mapping, structuring, and patterning. In the doctrine of the Trinity we are at all times speaking of a God who would already have been fully actualized even if he had never undertaken those actions that constitute him as the three-personed mystery of salvation.[1] To omit this note of distinction is to expose all the other content of Trinitarian doctrine to the risk of being merely a congeries of observations about what happens in the course of human events. A god entangled in world process by bands of necessity is a god dissolved and lost into world process.

Yet Trinitarian theology necessarily canvases a broader theological field, drawing at least from Christology and pneumatology if it is to have anything at all Trinitarian to say about God. It does not just add the doctrines of an eternal Son and an eternal Spirit to a doctrine of God, but fetches what it knows of their identities from the incarnate, crucified, risen Savior and his outpoured Spirit. That is, Trinitarian theology is an interpretation of the work of atonement. It takes up all the material of salvation history together as a whole and places it against the horizon of God's eternal being, in order to specify the Christian God by describing the connection between God and the economy of salvation. All the other work of the doctrine of the Trinity flows from this basis in the economy. It speaks about the eternal, triune being of God on the basis of that God's self-revealing works and words in the world.

The obligation of the doctrine of atonement is to be a doctrine about salvation, which certainly ought to give atonement theology more than enough to keep it occupied. Minimally, the doctrine of atonement must analyze a problem and explain its resolution: the problem of sin resolved by forgiveness, the problem of vice resolved by the power to be virtuous, the problem of mortality resolved by eternal life, the problem of oppression resolved by powerful deliverance, and so on. But the doctrine of atonement always outstrips this tidy problem-solution schema because it gathers its material from a wider range of truths. It cannot speak of a problem without describing the normative background situation, which the problem (conceptually if not chronologically) disturbs, and it cannot describe that background without describing its transcendent source. In this way the doctrine of atonement implicates and presupposes doctrines of creation and God, respectively.

---

1. Robert Sokolowski, *The God of Faith and Reason: Foundations of Christian Theology* (Washington, DC: Catholic University of America Press, 1995), 21–30.

Developed with appropriate amplitude, the doctrine of atonement can scarcely be contained or delimited to a single region within the terrain of Christian doctrine. As Adam Johnson argues, "We must keep firmly in mind the synthetic nature of the doctrine of the atonement, comprised as it is of the doctrines of the Trinity, divine attributes, Christology, hamartiology and eschatology (especially the doctrine of heaven/salvation)."[2] As a consummately comprehensive and synthetic doctrine (for what other message can Christian theology reflect on than the gospel message?), the doctrine of the atonement sometimes seems to be the unified field within which all the other doctrinal fields are comprehended. Johnson's list of the contents of atonement theology, for example, includes the doctrine of God: both the Trinity and the divine attributes. What he has in mind is not the possibility of atonement outflanking and surrounding Trinity, but atonement doctrine drawing its form and content from the form and content of the doctrine of God. Thus "it is the business of the doctrine of the atonement to unpack the reality of God's triune life as basis for God's saving activity in Christ."[3] As the doctrine of the atonement carries out that task, it too connects the economy of salvation to the eternal being of God.

Johnson's account of atonement is illuminating in this regard because, without distorting the doctrine of God, it presses the doctrine of God into service to the doctrine of atonement. The exposition of atonement theology has often suffered under the burden of arguments about its central idea or main point. Johnson argues that along with a certain kind of focus and unity, the doctrine of the atonement also has a "unique diversity proper to" the divine act of atoning. That diversity, he says, is

> The diversity proper to the triune God whose act this was, in the fullness of his divine attributes. 'God was in Christ,' accomplishing the work of reconciling 'all things' (1 Cor 5:19). God: Father, Son and Holy Spirit; the God of Abraham, Isaac and Jacob; the God who is merciful, gracious, patient, loving, good, kind, righteous, faithful, constant, wrathful, holy, omniscient.... This God, in the fullness of his character, was in Christ, reconciling all things to himself. And by means of this work 'all things' are taken up and reconciled to God by means of God himself, by means of the diversity and richness proper to God's own being and life.[4]

2. Adam J. Johnson, *Atonement: A Guide for the Perplexed* (London: Bloomsbury T&T Clark, 2015), 180.

3. Johnson, *Guide*, 67.

4. Johnson, *Guide*, 23.

Atonement, on this maximizing view, rises to the level of a mega-doctrine. In fact there seem to be only two such complex mega-doctrines at work in the Christian theological system: Trinity and atonement. These are thick descriptions of who God is on one hand, and what God does on the other. The being and act of God seem to practically exhaust the scope of Christian doctrine between them, without remainder and without any definite boundary between them.

This view of Trinity and atonement as the mega-doctrines of systematic theology is neither self-evident nor uncontroversial. Even when it is affirmed, it is not without its attendant dangers. We might describe two basic options available for relating the two complexes. First we will consider the schema of placing the Trinity within the atonement; and second the schema of placing the atonement within the Trinity. Gleaning the strengths from each schema while seeking to be instructed by the errors they have sometimes led to, we conclude with a constructive proposal designed to provide balance: the key to keeping the doctrines of Trinity and atonement rightly related is to coordinate them both within the doxological context that is their origin and goal.

TRINITY IN ATONEMENT

To place the Trinity in the atonement is generally an epistemological move. It begins with the premise, already noted, that anything we know about the triunity of God we know from what was revealed to us in the saving work of Christ. In classical idiom, this is because the temporal missions of the Son and the Holy Spirit are the gracious manifestations to us of the eternal processions of the Son and the Spirit within the divine being. By meeting the Son and the Spirit in the economy of salvation, we gain true knowledge of them as eternal Son and eternal Spirit, which they would have been without the economy of salvation. All of this is true, and the venerable doctrine of temporal missions as enactments, extensions, or prolongations of the eternal processions constitutes a classic theologoumenon with irreplaceable explanatory power. Yet care must be taken in its use. To speak of the Son's mission may unduly direct attention to the act of incarnation rather than to the passion, death, and resurrection of Christ. And it is the latter with which we have to do. An incarnation of the Son of God, which was not ordered to the passion, would be at best a speculative counterfactual possibility; the incarnation we actually know is one that is always "ordered to the passion."[5] So "the mission of the Son" refers to the

5. Hans Urs von Balthasar, *Mysterium Paschale: The Mystery of Easter* (Grand Rapids:

entire scope of the life, death, and resurrection of Jesus Christ, rather than just to the fact or the moment of his enfleshment.

The epistemological point is sometimes made more drastically, depending on how worried a theologian is about the dangers of abstraction. Fearing that incarnation and Trinity can function as mere conceptual principles rather than as the conclusions of exegetical insight and spiritual perception, John Behr rejects any formulation that would describe Christian theology as being constructed on the axes of Trinity and incarnation. He laments a modern situation in which the doctrines about God and Christ have already been received as established facts, and the story of the Bible is then fitted within those parameters:

> Trinitarian theology is made into a realm unto itself, requiring subsequent reflection on "the Incarnation" of one of the three divine persons: Triadology followed by Christology. In this perspective, the Trinity and the Incarnation are taken as being the linchpins of Christian theology—Christian faith is "Trinitarian" and "incarnational." This has become an unquestioned premise for most twentieth-century theology.[6]

It is an odd complaint, considering that a theologian like Behr affirms the triunity of God and the incarnation of the Son. What he objects to, however, is the tendency of these doctrines to float free of their origin and take on an unwarranted appearance of stability in the form of what he calls "familiar shorthand formulae." Trinity and incarnation, he insists, are not conceptual axes within which to understand the story of Jesus Christ's death and resurrection. The doctrines of the Trinity and incarnation were and are nothing but an exegetical interpretation of the death and resurrection of Christ.

Behr seems to be taking a step further than the epistemological claim that we only know about the Trinity through the passion, in that he is commending a more thorough revision of methodological assumptions. He argues for "the paschal foundation of Christian theology" in a stronger sense, in opposition to Christian theology "construed in terms of the gradual development of a dogmatic edifice," in which patristic thought can be divorced "from the given revelation of God in Christ, and . . . made to retell that revelation in a

---

Eerdmans, 1993), 12–13. An author who does justice to the speculative alternative case is Edwin Chr. van Driel, *Incarnation Anyway: Arguments for Supralapsarian Christology* (Oxford: Oxford University Press, 2008).

6. John Behr, "The Paschal Foundation of Christian Theology," *St. Vladimir's Theological Quarterly* 45, no. 2 (2001): 116.

different manner, so that the Word of God is no longer the locus of God's self-expression."[7] Christian doctrine as a whole, Behr argues,

> Quite simply is not based upon the supposed two axes of Trinity and Incarnation. . . . Rather, theological reflection, beginning with the original apostles and continuing with all those who follow in their tradition, develops as a response to the marvelous work of God in Jesus Christ, the crucified and exalted Lord.[8]

In our terms, Behr is contending for a doctrine of the Trinity that is configured interior to the doctrine of the atonement (or, as Behr would say, "the pascha") in such a way that the latter governs the former. "Christian theology is a response to the Passion of the Savior, and reflects on the work of God through this prism;" this reveals "the unity of all theology in the paschal faith."[9]

The argument has much to commend it, and certainly functions well as a corrective to the abstractness of some recent theology. But it is open to objections of at least a cautionary sort on two fronts. First, it risks being so cross-centered that it has to pretend that the character of God is not yet disclosed until the passion of Christ. But the character of the God of Jesus Christ is already established in the Old Testament before it opens up to display a wealth of inner riches in the passion of Christ. As Behr himself points out, even our narratives of the death and resurrection of Christ are already themselves exegetical and interpretive moves performed on key texts of the Old Testament: Psalm 110, Psalm 22, Isaiah 53. Unless we admit that God is already truly known through the history of his interactions with Israel, we cannot make sense, Trinitarian or otherwise, out of the paschal events. Pushed to extremes, Behr's "paschal foundation" reads as almost an Eastern Orthodox inflection of a Barthian protest, or at least an idea from the apocalyptic school of recent biblical studies.

In some theological proposals, the "Trinity in atonement" schema expands beyond its epistemological and methodological starting point and takes on ontological seriousness. Robert Jenson's drastic version of trinitarianism is a case in point. Committed to the proposition that "the primal systematic function of Trinitarian teaching is to *identify* the *theos* in 'theology,'"[10] Jenson offers a

7. Behr, "Paschal Foundation," 119.
8. Behr, "Paschal Foundation," 120.
9. Behr, "Paschal Foundation," 120.
10. Robert W. Jenson, *Systematic Theology*, vol. 1 (New York: Oxford University Press, 1997), 60. The italics are in the original.

revisionist metaphysic on its basis. Identity is a thing narrated in a history with meaningful coherence, and this applies to God above all: "Since the biblical God can truly be identified by narrative, his hypostatic being, his self-identity, is constituted in dramatic coherence."[11] Scott Swain has pointed out that in Jenson's work, God is not only identified by his historical actions in Israel and Christ, but is actually identified with them in a strong, ontological sense. Identifying God by the atonement is just good biblical theology.[12] Identifying God with the atonement requires, as Jenson consistently asserts, a complete rethinking of metaphysics, and a willingness to call God an event that takes place between Jesus and his Father. Here Trinity is inside of atonement because there simply is no outside of atonement.[13]

The most expansive critique of all these tendencies emerged in the late work of John Webster. Without deviating from a commitment to God's self-revelation in the saving economy, Webster began to be concerned that configuring the doctrine of the Trinity too nearly internal to the atonement inevitably distorted the shape of a systematic theology by failing to attend programmatically to the creator-creature distinction. As his attention increasingly shifted to the doctrine of creation, Webster began to valorize not the two mega-doctrines we have been discussing, but rather "two distributed doctrines" that make themselves felt pervasively throughout the entire theological system. The first distributed doctrine is the Trinity, "of which all other articles of Christian teaching are an amplification or application, and which therefore permeates theological affirmations about every matter." But instead of naming atonement (or salvation, or the economy) as the second such doctrine, Webster displaces it with creation. "The doctrine of creation," he says, "is ubiquitous. . . . It is not restricted to one particular point in the sequence of Christian doctrine, but provides orientation and a measure of governance to all that theology has to say about all things in relation to God."[14] The doctrine of creation "brackets and qualifies everything that is said about the nature and course of all that

11. Jenson, *Systematic Theology*, 1:64.

12. Scott R. Swain, *The God of the Gospel: Robert Jenson's Trinitarian Theology* (Downers Grove, IL: IVP Academic, 2013), 86.

13. The conclusion is pervasive in Jenson, in some of his most arresting formulations. See, for instance, his claim "that the Spirit rests upon the Son is not a phenomenon merely of the economic Trinity—there are in any case no such phenomena." Jenson, *Systematic Theology*, 1:143.

14. John Webster, "*Non ex aequo*: God's Relation to Creatures," in *God without Measure: Working Papers in Christian Theology*, vol. 1, *God and the Works of God* (London: Bloomsbury T&T Clark, 2016), 117.

is not God," and therefore must already be in place before statements about soteriology can be deployed fittingly.[15]

Without an operative doctrine of creation in place to govern statements about God's saving action, "the existence and history of created things may be assumed as a given, quasi-necessary, reality, rather than a wholly surprising effect of divine goodness, astonishment at which pervades all Christian teaching."

> Exposition of the history of grace as the final cause of creation . . . results in . . . presenting the relation of God and creatures as one between divine and human persons and agents who, for all their differences, are strangely commensurable, engaging one another in the same space, deciding, acting, and interacting in the world as a commonly inhabited field of reality.[16]

What beguiles theologians into this disordered exposition is often "the sheer prominence and human intensity of the central subject and episode of redemption history." In short, the attention given to Jesus Christ the Savior leaves theology so enraptured with the story and the drama of the economy of salvation that it becomes very difficult to get the necessary perspective, "the setting of the work of grace in the work of nature."[17] The result is disastrous:

> Such an arrangement of Christian doctrine raises an expectation that what needs to be said about the natures of God and the creatures of God, and therefore of their relation, may be determined almost exhaustively by attending to the economy of salvation—the history of election and reconciliation in the missions of the Son and the Holy Spirit. Accordingly, if God and creatures are chiefly conceived as dramatis personae in an enacted sequence of lost and regained fellowship, talk of the non-reciprocity of their relation seems theologically and religiously unbecoming.[18]

At the end of his career, Webster was just beginning to deploy the doctrine of creation as one of the tools that could keep the doctrine of the Trinity from being distorted by absorption into the doctrine of atonement. Perhaps there are other theological tools that could serve equally well, and other ways of approaching this set of issues without making Webster's move of promoting the

---

15. Webster, "*Non ex aequo*," in *God without Measure*, 1:117.
16. Webster, "*Non ex aequo*," in *God without Measure*, 1:118.
17. Webster, "*Non ex aequo*," in *God without Measure*, 1:118.
18. Webster, "*Non ex aequo*," in *God without Measure*, 1:118–19.

doctrine of creation to the status of the second distributed doctrine alongside the doctrine of the Trinity. In his earlier work, Webster himself was more tentative about letting the doctrine of creation relativize the doctrine of salvation, directing attention to "the scope of the *opera Dei exeuntia*," which is "wider than that of the single theme of salvation, however widely ramified that theme may be."[19] Webster's Trinity-creation duo fits well with the Reformed Thomist grammar he developed, in which the task of Christian theology was to confess God, and then all things in relation to God. Even for those who cannot accept Webster's prescription, it stands as an instructive warning about the dangers of the controlling power of the Trinity-atonement duo, and a helpful vantage point on entire Trinity-in-atonement schema.

ATONEMENT IN TRINITY

Alongside the schema of locating Trinity in atonement, a number of recent theological projects can be described as locating atonement in the Trinity. That is, they confess the eternal being of God as Father, Son, and Holy Spirit, and then confess the greatness of what this God has accomplished in the economy of salvation, and then ask about the transcendental ground of what they have seen in salvation history. Generally these theologies are characterized by wonder and astonishment at the greatness of what God has done in the atonement. It is this high view of redemption accomplished that leads them to turn back to God and ask, what is there in God that forms the basis of this great salvation? Or, to put the question in more modern Trinitarian idiom, what is the immanent Trinitarian analogate of economic atonement?

Certain answers suggest themselves immediately and must be immediately rejected. Since the atonement requires the Son to suffer in his human nature on our behalf, an influential tradition of modern theology has affirmed that there must be something like suffering in the divine essence. And since the atonement requires the Father to give his Son over, some theologians conclude that there must be the transcendental possibility of divine self-abandonment in eternity, perhaps as a breach or gap between the Father and the Son. Jürgen Moltmann has been the most significant advocate of rejecting the classical doctrine of divine impassibility in favor of a radically cross-centered, radi-

---

19. Webster, "*Rector et iudex super omnia genera doctrinarum?* The Place of the Doctrine of Justification," in *God without Measure*, 1:163. This essay was originally published in 2009; "*Non ex Aequo*" (cited in notes 14–18 above) in 2014.

cally Trinitarian doctrine of divine suffering, "the pathos of God." Moltmann asserted that "the theology of the cross must be the doctrine of the Trinity and the doctrine of the Trinity must be the theology of the cross."[20] He even described the cross as the event of God's self-abandonment in history. If this is not an entirely Hegelian doctrine of God, it is at least a fairly thoroughly historicized one, and Moltmann was intentional about this: "The doctrine of the Trinity is the conceptual framework that is necessary if we are to understand this history of Christ as being the history of God."[21] Moltmann puts the atonement into the heart of the Trinity, eternally and essentially. "If a person once feels the infinite passion of God's love," he argues, "then he understands the mystery of the triune God. God suffers with us—God suffers from us— God suffers for us."[22] For Moltmann, the doctrine of the Trinity itself is not a statement about the being of God in itself, but always already a doctrine of the redemptive suffering of God for us.

The fortunes of full-blown theopaschism have risen and fallen over the past forty years. While the affirmation that God suffers seems to arise spontaneously from considering the depth of God's commitment to redeeming fallen sinners, very few theologians are willing to follow through with a complete rejection of the venerable tradition that teaches divine impassibility. Impassibility is just too tightly integrated with a number of other divine perfections to be excised without doing permanent damage to the doctrine of God. The suffering of Jesus Christ is an essential element of our redemption, but there must be something else present in the Trinity that forms the ground and possibility for the Son to appropriate the suffering of our nature and take it to himself.

Some more cautious answers have included Nicholas Wolterstorff's discussion of justice in the Trinity.[23] He nimbly considers whether the justice that God brings about on earth has a transcendental ground in the being of the Trinity, and makes some crucial distinctions on his way to answering. "If the whole of justice involves the rendering of judgment, then there is no justice within the Trinity." However, justice as judgment is derivative from what Wolterstorff calls primary justice, which "consists of treating persons

---

20. Jürgen Moltmann, *The Crucified God* (New York: Harper & Row, 1974), 241.

21. Jürgen Moltmann, "The Trinitarian History of God," in *The Future of Creation* (Philadelphia: Fortress, 1979), 81.

22. Jürgen Moltmann, *The Trinity and the Kingdom* (New York: Harper & Row, 1981), 4.

23. Nicholas Wolterstorff, "Is There Justice in the Trinity?," in *God's Life in Trinity*, ed. Miroslav Volf and Michael Welker (Minneapolis: Fortress, 2006), 177-87.

with due respect for their worth."[24] This sounds like something that does obtain between Father and Son in the Spirit; in fact, it sounds like something that is merely a redescription of interpersonal love. Wolterstorff's approach to the question of what there is in the Trinity that manifests itself as justice or atonement among us is exemplary in several ways. Edward T. Oakes has attempted something similar when handling the question of whether there is distance in the Trinity, or an interval or gap between the persons.[25] As an interpreter of Balthasar, Oakes is concerned to provide some necessary groundwork for some of Balthasar's more daring speculative moves. Confronted with instances of diastasis and distance in the theology of redemption, Balthasar famously attempted to find room for those distances within the distinction between the Father and the Son. Creation seems to require a metaphysical distance from God. While the Son is certainly not metaphysically distant from, even different from, the Father, Balthasar argued that the principle of uncreated personal distinction in the Trinity is what makes possible the principle of creation's distinction from the creator. Even the interval of alienation in hell is not a distance that outflanks the distinction between Father and Son. If Balthasar's more venturesome formulations are hard to affirm, Oakes carefully navigates what is and is not acceptable here: "distinction (*diakrisis*) yes, distance (*diastasis*) no."[26] Similar caution should be urged on any number of contemporary projects that seek to find in the Trinity the primal origin of what is manifest in the economy. Hospitality, for instance, may be a form of grace in salvation history, and may be unpacked as a kind of generosity that makes room and lets others be. But any attempt to locate hospitality in the being of God will shipwreck on the etymology of philoxenia: love for aliens. Whatever we can say about the Father, Son, and Spirit making room for each other, we can never describe them as overcoming estrangement, pacifying hostility, compensating for unworthiness, breaking down barriers, bridging a gap, transversing a distance to come to each other, or solving interpersonal problems. It simply won't do. Atonement is not in the Trinity in that way.

24. Wolterstorff, "Justice in the Trinity," 185.

25. Edward T. Oakes, SJ, "Diastasis in the Trinity," in *A Man of the Church: Honoring the Theology, Life, and Witness of Ralph Del Colle*, ed. Michel René Barnes (Eugene, OR: Pickwick, 2012), 125–47.

26. Oakes, "Diastasis," 125.

ATONEMENT AND THE PRAISE OF TRIUNE GLORY

For systematic theology, there is a perennial question of how to handle the doctrine of the Trinity and the doctrine of the atonement together in a way that adequately displays their overlap and differentiation. None of the approaches that we have considered above are without their merits, and each of them provides something that should not be omitted from a satisfactory treatment of this complex theme. In particular, the question of correlating the eternal Trinity with the historical atonement is a vexed one. The waves of historicism are always threatening to capsize the theological boats, yet history must have its proper place in this doctrine. How shall we keep our wits about us, surrounded by such outsized themes and exposed to such dangers of error? When all the options have been considered, the best way to coordinate these two mega-doctrines is to look back to the origin of both doctrines, and forward to their goals. Fortunately, the origin and goal is identical. Trinitarian theology and atonement theology arise from, and terminate in, the same response to God: praise. Doxology summons us to say what God has done, and who he is. Any elaboration of the doctrines of Trinity and atonement must move within this doxological sphere, and any attempt to coordinate their obligations with each other must take its bearings from its orienting task: to praise God in both conceptual profusion and reverent restraint.

A relatively minor and certainly neglected theologian from the Methodist tradition may offer the clearest example of a well-digested solution to using praise to solve the problem of relating Trinity and atonement as major loci in a system. William Burt Pope's three-volume *Compendium of Systematic Theology*[27] faces the problem squarely. The doctrine of God must come very early in a theological system; almost first, depending on how much methodological groundwork is necessary. But for a theologian committed to a maximal development of the atonement, the content of the doctrine of God must be derived from its most conspicuous display in the course of salvation history. Indeed, Pope is committed to the proposition that "the gradual unfolding of the mystery of redemption is also the gradual unfolding of the mystery of the Triune God."[28] This being the case, an early doctrine of God will have to smuggle in material from a

---

27. William Burt Pope, *A Compendium of Christian Theology: Being Analytical Outlines of a Course of Theological Study, Biblical, Dogmatic, Historical*, 3 vols. (London: Wesleyan Conference Office, 1879).
28. Pope, *Compendium*, 2:101.

later doctrine of atonement. Alternatively, a theologian could provide a sketchy initial doctrine of God and then wait until after the discussion of the atonement to describe more fully what has been learned about the divine Trinity and perfections from "the gradual unfolding of the mystery of the Triune God."

What Pope does is split the difference and double the doctrine of God. In the early chapters of his *Compendium*, he provides a solid treatment of God's triunity, perfections, and glory. The discussion is solid, orderly, and well proportioned. After these sections, he moves on to the doctrines of creation, humanity, then sin, Christology, and salvation. He wraps up an excellent and lengthy discussion of salvation with a section on "The Finished Atonement." It's at the end of this section that Pope makes his crucial move. Though he already discussed the Name of God, the Attributes of God, and the Trinity, Pope now sets aside several pages to take these doctrines up again. Why? Because

> In the finished work of Christ, the Name, Attributes and Government of God are most fully exhibited and glorified. The triune Name is made known; the Love and Righteousness of God have their highest and best manifestation, as the expression of the Divine will, and the Moral Government of the Supreme is supremely vindicated.[29]

In his characteristic style, Pope summarizes vast stretches of biblical teaching with a suggestive quotation from Scripture: "The Son, addressing the Father a prayer which regards the Atonement as accomplished, declares: I have manifested Thy name unto the men which Thou gavest me out of the world" (John 17:6).[30] Pope unpacks this "manifestation of God's name" as the revelation of the name "Father" that was brought to us by the Son and completed in the Spirit. He goes on to explain the principle of revelation behind this:

> The name of the Triune God is especially made known and therefore glorified in the meditation of the Incarnate Redeemer. The revelation of the Trinity is bound up with the revelation of redemption; the development of one was the development of the other, and both were perfected together.[31]

The doctrine of the Trinity, in Pope's presentation of it, is not a bit of esoteric information about God, but a fact made known when God put salvation

29. Pope, *Compendium*, 2:276.
30. Pope, *Compendium*, 2:276.
31. Pope, *Compendium*, 2:276.

into effect: when the Son and Spirit entered human history decisively, the Trinity was revealed. "Our Lord pronounced The Name of the Father, and of the Son, and of the Holy Ghost only after His resurrection. The mystery of His perfect love unfolded the mystery of His perfect essence."[32]

Although the glorification of the eternal Trinity is the main point Pope wants to make, he goes on to ponder the way the finished atonement glorifies God's name in other ways: "that Name is not only the Triune Name, but the assemblage of the Divine perfections." Again Pope is torn in two directions: On the one hand, he has already discussed the Divine perfections in the doctrine of God in volume 1, but on the other hand he cannot bypass their revelation in the finished work of the atonement:

> In the New Testament it is obvious that with scarcely an exception every reference to the combined or individual perfections of God refers to their exhibition in the work of Christ. At least, all other allusions lead up to this. Not to repeat what has already been made prominent under the Divine Attributes, it may suffice to mention the new and perfect revelation of the holiness and love of God as disclosed in the Atonement.[33]

What Pope is up to here is undercutting the inadequate notion that Christian theology can start by defining the characters of its story ("in this corner, God; in that corner, man") and then go on to describe the actions they undertake. In the case of God, the only way Christian theology can get started is to admit that God has most definitively revealed himself in Christ the redeemer, so we have to describe the saving work of Christ as the beginning of our theology. If the doctrine of God started on page one, the doctrine of redemption had to have been on page zero, or perhaps in a long and all-determining preface. In other words, by treating the name, triunity, and attributes of God in the middle of volume two, Pope underlines the fact that Christian thought has been presupposing the finished atonement all along. Volume one, page one of Pope's *Compendium* was already normed and formed by the work of Christ:

> There is nothing that belongs to our conception of the Divine nature which is not manifested in His Son, Who both in His active and in His passive righteousness reveals all that is in the Father. Man, in fact, knows God only as a God of redemption; nor will He ever by man be otherwise known.

32. Pope, *Compendium*, 2:277.
33. Pope, *Compendium*, 2:278.

Throughout the Scriptures of truth we have a gradual revelation of the Divine Being which is not finished until it is finished in Christ; God also, as well as man, is *en Autō peplērōmenos*, COMPLETE IN HIM. It is not enough to say that the Trinity Whom Christians adore is made known in Jesus, and that this or the other attribute which theology ascribes to Him is illustrated in His work. God Himself, with every idea we form of His nature, is given to us by the revelation of Christ. The gracious and awful Being Who is presented in the Christian Scriptures is not in all respects such a Deity as human reason would devise or tolerate when presented. But to us there is but ONE GOD; and we must receive Him as He is made known to us through the mystery of the Atoning Mediation of His Son. His Name is proclaimed only in the Cross; there we have His Divine and only Benediction; and every Doxology in Revelation derives its strength and fervour from the Atonement.[34]

Doxology is no excuse for imprecise thinking or careless expressions. The rigor of systematic theology ought to be kept in place even as we acknowledge that praise is the medium in which the problem of balancing Trinity and atonement can be resolved graciously. Theology is in fact best offered as praise to the God of salvation when it comes forth in the form of appropriately measured description of the being and act of the atoning Trinity.

One of the central idioms of late twentieth-century Trinitarian theologizing was the terminology of economic and immanent Trinity, largely in response to Karl Rahner's celebrated *Grundaxiom*, "the economic Trinity is the immanent Trinity, and vice versa."[35] Translated into these terms, the two schemas we have considered in this chapter would run as follows: Locating the Trinity inside the doctrine of the atonement would mean that the economic or atoning Trinity is the immanent Trinity, or that the three-personed God we meet in salvation history simply is the three-personed God of his own eternal identity. This is an attempt to recognize the earnestness and intimacy of the divine self-giving that constitutes Christian salvation. That first half of Rahner's Rule is, to that extent, true and necessary to affirm, within certain limitations that ought to be obvious. What must be simultaneously maintained is that the conditions

---

34. Pope, *Compendium*, 2:279.

35. I surveyed its origin and influence in Fred Sanders, *The Image of the Immanent Trinity: Rahner's Rule and the Theological Interpretation of Scripture* (New York: Lang, 2004). More recently I have argued that the terminology itself has a distorting bias and ought to be used much more circumspectly, in Sanders, *The Triune God* (Grand Rapids: Zondervan, 2016), 147–56.

of the economy of salvation, or of the work of atonement, bring with them a host of considerations. To say that in the atonement we are dealing with the immanent Trinity is to say "the economic Trinity is the immanent Trinity under the conditions of the economy." But to the extent that God is giving himself to us under the conditions of the economy, God is not alienated from his aseity or failing to be free in the very act of intervening.

Locating the atonement inside the Trinity would bring us into alignment with the more controversial second half of Rahner's Rule, "the immanent Trinity is the economic Trinity." Rahner's vice versa has always run the risk of collapsing God's identity into the process of redemption, and translation into our present terms would make that danger even more evident. What would it mean to take that further step of saying that the eternal God simply is the atoning God? Such a locution could easily mean that God is nothing but what he is for us and our salvation. That must not be affirmed or implied. Karl Barth's great question is again relevant here: "What would 'God for us' mean if it were not said against the background of 'God in Himself?'"[36] But if we said such a thing with an intent to praise the God of our salvation, we might mean, with William Burt Pope, that "the revelation of the Trinity is bound up with the revelation of redemption; the development of one was the development of the other, and both were perfected together."[37] In this way, the doxological setting of these two mega-doctrines helps keep their claims within the proper bounds, keeps the two doctrines rightly related to each other, and ensures that the obligations of each are faithfully carried out.

36. Karl Barth, *CD* 1/1, 171. See also Hans Joachim Iwand, "Wider den Mißbrauch des 'pro me' als methodisches Prinzip in der Theologie," *Evangelische Theologie* 14 (1954): 120–24.
37. Pope, *Compendium*, 2:276.

Trinity and Ecclesiology

F ORMALLY SPEAKING, the three most influential approaches to explicating the relation between ecclesiology and the doctrine of the Trinity can
be identified as communion, mission, and structural analogy. The communion approach emphasizes the overlap between trinitarian perichoresis and
churchly koinonia; it locates the church in eucharist-centered ecumenicity, and
thrives in the context of *communio* ecclesiologies. The mission approach connects the Father's sending of the Son and Spirit with the church's sending to the
world; it locates the church's being in the work of mission, and thrives in the
context of *missio Dei* ecclesiologies. The structural analogy approach identifies
patterns of correspondence between the immanent order of the trinitarian
persons and the ordered polity of church leadership; it tends to accompany
or illustrate the other two approaches and rarely stands on its own. But while
these three approaches serve to articulate a connection between the doctrines
of church and Trinity, attention should be given first of all to the underlying
impulse to make that connection at all. There is a trinitarian itch that these
diverse ecclesiological impulses all seek to scratch. That itch or impulse runs
deep, and has much to do with the way the doctrine of the triune God is related
to the history of salvation.

When Robert W. Jenson published his *Systematic Theology* in two volumes, he structured it according to a distinction between "God himself on
the one hand and on the other hand everything else."[1] The distinction is a time-
honored, scholastic one, and in its classic form in theologians like Thomas
Aquinas, it dictates a strict limitation of the doctrine of God followed by a wide
expanse for the works of God *ad extra*. But Jenson modified the distinction
considerably to make it serviceable for his own project: in his systematics,

1. Robert W. Jenson, *Systematic Theology*, vol. 1 (New York: Oxford University Press,
1997), x.

"Christology and pneumatology, together with discussions of the historical Jesus, of the doctrine of atonement, and of the resurrection, are drawn back into the doctrine of God, swelling that doctrine to make half the total work."[2] Jenson's distinctive theological commitments, including his revisionist metaphysic based on a narrative construal of divine identity, dictated that the work of the Son and the Spirit, especially in their incarnation and outpouring, were part of the subject matter constituting the doctrine of the Trinity even *ad intra*. Moving the historical Jesus and the atonement into the doctrine of God proper is a drastic way to make a point about God's involvement with history. It raises the question of whether anything at all counts as a work *ad extra*. In the preface of volume 2, Jenson famously conceded that "organizing the work on the plausible principle that finally all Christian teaching in one way or another tells God's own story would of course have obliterated the point."[3] And so Jenson moved creation, the church, and eschatology to a spacious second volume. But in doing so, he worried aloud that perhaps the doctrine of the church in particular actually belonged in the first volume after all. There is something about ecclesiology that aligns it more with the identity of the triune God than is the case with creation and eschatology. "The church," after all, "is not in the same way an *opus ad extra* as is the creation, even when it is perfected in God."[4] Some of the connections are obvious: the church can scarcely remain a straightforward *opus ad extra* after the incarnation and Pentecost have come to be in some way *opera ad intra*.

For all the idiosyncrasies of his theological project, there is something in Jenson's treatment of ecclesiology and the Trinity that is not just peculiar to him, or to the decisions he made in structuring his *Systematic Theology*'s table of contents. His deliberations make especially clear one aspect of the relation between these two doctrines. So intimate is the link between God and church that the impulse to articulate their connection is perennial in Christian theology. And when the trinitarian dynamic of the Christian doctrine of God is made explicit, numerous links to ecclesiology emerge: As the people of God, the body of Christ, and the temple of the Holy Spirit, the church is the point at which the triune God touches creation. There seems to be specifically trinitarian warrant for giving ecclesiology a greater depth of ingression into the divine life than any other created reality. The locus on the church, in Jenson's

2. Jenson, *Systematic Theology*, 1:x.

3. Robert W. Jenson, *Systematic Theology*, vol. 2 (New York: Oxford University Press, 1999), v.

4. Jenson, *Systematic Theology*, 2:167.

terms, seems readily drawn back into the doctrine of God under the pressure of a consummated trinitarian soteriology.

Though the tendency is perennial, including the church within the Trinity has been particularly attractive to modern theologians. In theological regimes that prefer to leave the creator-creature boundary unpoliced, the church is in danger of being simply deified. But even theologians who articulately confess the boundary between creator and creature when attending to the doctrine of creation sometimes find it difficult to maintain the distinction with equal clarity when they turn to the doctrine of the church. Something about ecclesiology seems to invite, if not actual transgression of that boundary, at least bold approaches to it. The scriptural rhetoric of intimacy and fulfillment gathers special intensity in what the Bible says about the church, God's particular treasure and "peculiar people" (1 Pet 2:9). Francis Turretin confessed as much in beginning his locus on the church by calling the church "the primary work of the Holy Trinity (*primarium S. S. Trinitatis opus*), the object of Christ's mediation and the subject of the application of his benefits."[5] Turretin's brief expression encapsulates a crucial tension in rightly relating the doctrine of the Trinity to the doctrine of the church: confessing it as on the one hand to be truly *primarium* and on the other hand as still just an *opus*; as the recipient of Christ's mediation and the Spirit's application, but after all a work and a creature. Before we turn our attention to the three influential modern approaches to relating ecclesiology and Trinity (that is, by way of communion, mission, and structural analogy), we should secure good order on this frontier between the creator and the redeemed creature that is the church.

TRINITARIAN DEDUCTION OF ECCLESIOLOGY

For an especially clear set of guidelines on how to navigate these issues, we can turn to the theology of John Webster, who cultivated a special methodological awareness of what was at stake in relating theology proper and ecclesiology. Webster certainly wanted to recognize the close link between them. He recommended that ecclesiology should be developed by way of a kind of "trinitarian deduction" in which the reality of the church was traced back into the prior reality of the Trinity. "A doctrine of the church," he said,

---

5. Francis Turretin, *Institutes of Elenctic Theology*, vol. 3 (Phillipsburg, NJ: P&R Publishing, 1997), 1.

"is a function of the doctrine of the Trinity."[6] Broadly, the trinitarian deduction of ecclesiology requires an account of divine action that begins with the divine life itself and then moves outward to God's free actions by way of a processions-missions structure:

> Intellectual apprehension of the being of the church requires us to explicate it as an element in the covenantal economy of God's goodness towards creatures; this, in turn, requires a theology of the divine missions, which is itself rooted in a theology of the inner-divine processions. Like all Christian doctrines, the doctrine of the church is to be traced back to the immanent perfections of God's life and his free self-communication in the *opera Dei exeuntia*. (177)

The relevant line can be traced in either direction: In the order of being, it runs from the inner life of God out into creation via the divine missions; in the order of knowing it begins with the reality of the church and runs back through the missions into the processions. The result is that the doctrine of the church is "an extension of the Christian doctrine of God" (178). To put it this way is to make a high claim for the nature of the church, but it is even more obviously to cede decisive priority to the doctrine of God. The church is, in this account, the manifestly derivative reality, receiving its dignity from its relation to its source. To claim that "dogmatics arrives at the doctrine of the church by trinitarian deduction'" is to identify ecclesiology as a "derivative doctrine" in which the absolutely prior "doctrine of God is directly at work" (181).

One benefit of setting ecclesiology in this relation to the doctrine of God is that it enables Webster to do justice to the social and historical particularity of the church, without relegating the church to the status of merely a human society with no divine background or basis. The church is certainly a social-historical entity, and Webster even speaks of this in a metaphysical register by saying that the being of the church is "a form of human society characterized by a certain estrangement from other such forms." But this is only one side of the church's being. "Ecclesiology has a proximate and a principal *res*," and its principal *res* is not the empirically observable social-historical phenomenon; that is only the proximate *res*. The church's principal *res* is "the temporal processions

---

6. John Webster, "In the Society of God: Some Principles of Ecclesiology," in *God without Measure: Working Papers in Christian Theology*, vol. 1, *God and the Works of God* (London: Bloomsbury T&T Clark, 2016), 177. Hereafter, page references from this work will be given in parentheses in the text.

of God and the eternal processions from which they are suspended" (177–78). To state the relation this way is obviously not to promote the church to divine status, but to recognize that the being of the church cannot be accounted for without reference to something decidedly beyond and above it. That something beyond is the triune God in his free actions of salvation and in the infinite divine life from which those actions arise. "The temporal economy, including the social reality of the church in time, has its being not in se but by virtue of God who alone is *in se*" (179). In this way, Webster recognizes "the human assembly as what it is," precisely by referring it to "certain antecedent divine works" that are "the exemplary cause of the church's temporal assembly" (190).

The wisdom of including within the definition of the church such an entirely transcendent reference is that it anchors ecclesiology in an order of being that is higher than a merely historicized ontology allows for. Webster identified one of the most troublesome and besetting problems of modern theology to be this philosophical bias in favor of historicism in ontology; he characterized it as "a conviction, part metaphysical and part theological, and often only half-articulated, that the real is the social-historical." It is a conviction with far-reaching doctrinal consequences. In ecclesiology, Webster noted that one consequence of this conviction is that it "commonly promotes the metamorphosis of what I have called the proximate *res* of ecclesiology into principal *res*" (178). That is, if what is fundamentally, metaphysically real is that which is social-historical, then the observable, social-historical reality of the church is all that makes it what it is. With the eclipse of the reference to any reality that transcends the church, ecclesiology becomes nothing but a series of indicators pointing to the social and the historical in itself. Thereon follow consequences for any of the standard approaches to relating ecclesiology and trinitarianism. Social reality taken in isolation is a poor imitation of the *communio* at the heart of *communio* ecclesiology, but it is easy to see how the thinner notion could be substituted nearly undetectably for the richer notion. Likewise, historical process taken in isolation is a poor imitation of the missional movement at the heart of *missio Dei* ecclesiology, but with the alteration of background metaphysical assumptions about God's reality above and beyond historical process, *missio Dei* ecclesiology could easily be transformed into a mere affirmation of historical development or church expansion. As for the strategy of identifying structural analogies between the immanent Trinity and ecclesial polity, Webster cautions that "the relation of theology proper and ecclesiology is best explicated not by setting out two terms of an analogy but by describing a sequence of divine acts both in terms of their ground in the immanent divine being and in terms of their creaturely fruit" (182). Webster's trinitarian deduction of ecclesiology shows the way to safeguard the reality of both *communio* and *missio Dei* ecclesiology, and, to a much lesser extent, even the appeal to putative structural analogies. "To speak of the church's being, dogmatics is required to speak of God who alone has being *in se*; to speak of the church's acts, dogmatics is required to speak of the *opera Dei interna et externa*" (180). It secures an anchoring of ecclesiology in the doctrine of the Trinity without which these other two strategies would be exposed to the risk of losing their own best insights. "Because Christian dogmatics does not concede the self-evidence and primacy of the social-historical . . . its account of the church is an extension of the doctrine of God, and so of teaching about God's immanent perfection and goodness" (180). The trinitarian deduction of ecclesiology is, in other words, Webster's characteristic "theological theology" extended to the task of keeping ecclesiology properly theological.

So far we have appealed to Webster mainly for his insights into the formal dynamics of how to relate Trinity and ecclesiology. But we have not yet stated the actual content of his trinitarian deduction of ecclesiology. That content is bracingly traditional and can be stated in terms drawn largely from the Bible itself and from some Reformed confessional expansions of scriptural motifs. Webster's trinitarian deduction of ecclesiology is a matter of "tracing how particular external works of God with respect to the church may be appropriated to particular persons of the godhead" while bearing in mind that the external works of the Trinity are undivided (183). The Father's appropriation in ecclesiology is centered in "the primal reality of the inner-divine life" in which "the Father is properly and personally *autotheos*" (183). Because of this primacy, election is appropriated to the Father as the one who chooses, and adoption as the paternal ground responsible for "the bestowing of status, a status which fulfils natural sociality but only by way of redemptive grace" (183).

There is more to say about the Son's relation to ecclesiology, but Webster limits himself mostly to the task of "ensuring that the full compass of Christology is brought to bear on the matter" (184). Vigilant to keep Christology from being misconstrued as an endorsement of historicist ontology, Webster warns that attention must be given not only to the incarnation but also to the eternity of the divine Logos as well as to his ascension and enthronement. "When too narrow a selection of Christological material is deemed pertinent, ecclesiology suffers disfigurement" in this regard: "The person and work of the Son can be so identified with his incarnate presence that his eternal pre-existent deity recedes from view; or the post-existence of the Son in his state of exaltation can come to be retracted" (184). When the Son's pre-existence and post-existence are eclipsed by his incarnate presence and "temporal career" narrated in the gospels, the result for ecclesiology is a loss of interest in any question but "what kind of continuity" obtains "between the incarnate and the ecclesial body" (184). The result is a reduction of the full scope of biblical category of the church as the body of Christ, and the danger of relativizing Christology to ecclesiology rather than vice versa. Webster calls this "the ecclesiological functionalization of Christological doctrine" (184). It is to be resisted by identifying Christ as the lord of the church in the full scope of his eternal deity, his work as reconciler, and his rule as the ascended one.

Webster completes the material content of his trinitarian deduction of ecclesiology by indicating the Holy Spirit's appropriation in the church: "There is a stream of life which flows from heaven towards creatures, whose source is God the Father and whose power is God the Son; this is the Holy Spirit, by whom God's covenant with his rational creatures takes social-historical shape" (188). Thus the work of God is traced from the "primal reality of the inner-divine life" in the Father all the way through the actual "social-historical shape" of the reconciled community taking its creaturely place among other social-historical communities. By doing this descriptive work of showing ecclesiology to be deduced from the doctrine of the Trinity, Webster establishes a doctrinal context in which ecclesiologies of communion and mission can succeed in rising above the social-historical and making contact with the doctrine of the Trinity. To these we now turn.

Communion and Mission

The ecclesiological motifs of *communio* and *missio Dei* can easily claim ancient roots and biblical warrant, but both received their classic formulations in the twentieth century. In fact, they emerged from official twentieth-century ecumenical discussions and are in their own ways marked by these ecumenical origins. Both *communio* and *missio Dei* ecclesiologies have a certain breadth and inclusiveness that evince how they were designed not only to be congenial to a diversity of confessional traditions, but also to serve as explanations of this diversity. In both cases, this ecumenical origin has advantages. It lends itself to large and comprehensive patterns of thought, to schemas that take in a maximum amount of claims and information, and thus are more easily connected to a doctrine as comprehensive as the doctrine of the Trinity. Not just any ecclesiology is expansive enough to be convincing in its appeal to trinitarian theology; *communio* and *missio Dei* ecclesiologies both are, mainly because they arise from ecumenical ambitions.

The communio ecclesiology, as classically stated by J.-M. R. Tillard on the basis of an analysis of the documents of Vatican II, had dialogue with the Eastern Orthodox churches especially in mind. The title of his book, *Church of Churches*, captured the intention to include multiple ecclesial fellowships within the one overall ecclesial reality of a church already constituted by fellowship. "We have recognized in communion the profound being of the Church of God. Church of Churches, it is a communion of communions, linked to God who is revealed as the eternal communion of three Persons."[7] Already here in Tillard's formulation, it is evident that the view of overlapping ecclesial communions has a certain priority. The appeal to the Trinity is, if not quite an afterthought and not merely a rhetorical ploy, at least a kind of final extension of the ecclesial motif. The center of gravity for *communio* ecclesiology is the church's *koinonia*, especially as it is constituted by eucharistic fellowship. How much weight to give the underlying sacramental theology is a major decision in evaluating *communio* ecclesiology. The eucharistic fellowship can be understood as a participation in the death and resurrection of Jesus Christ, a mediatorial encounter through which believers have fellowship with God. Or it can be understood in a less traditional way, as a more direct sacramental participation in the fellowship of the Trinity. In this way of construing sacrament, what is being participated in is divine perichoretic unity. Communion in the sense of eucharist comes to be viewed as a participation in communion in the sense of perichoresis. When this more expansive use of the communion motif takes hold, it risks over-determining the kind of things that can be said about the Trinity. That is, as Webster warned, it can functionalize the doctrine of the Trinity by pressing it into the shape demanded by the notion of communion already worked out at the churchly level.

What kind of construal of the Trinity is required to underwrite *communio* ecclesiology? All things being equal, a certain type of strong social trinitarianism seems most congenial to serve as the transcendent ground of ecclesial fellowship. In some influential authors like Jürgen Moltmann and Leonardo Boff, this becomes fairly explicit. But *communio* ecclesiology and social trinitarianism are not linked by necessity; they do not logically entail each other. And a certain late twentieth-century enthusiasm for *communio* ecclesiology has perhaps given way to a more critical phase of cautious appeal to the motif, especially at those places where it is most in danger of introducing distortion into trinitarian theology. Brian Doyle points out that after all "the vocabulary

---

7. J.-M. R. Tillard, O. P., *Church of Churches: The Ecclesiology of Communion* (Collegeville, MN: Liturgical Press, 1992), 169. The French original was published in 1987.

of *communio* is not sufficiently represented in the tradition of Christian reflection on the Trinity to be the primary analogy employed in contemporary
trinitarian theology." He admits that "no one denies that *communio* plays a
role within historical trinitarian theology. However, its relatively minor role
and its absence from the ecumenical creeds have caused some to ask whether
this concept can carry the weight of an orthodox Christian theology of God."[8]
Doyle also makes the biblical case that "although *koinonia/communio* is a biblical concept, it is rarely used in the Scriptures in reference to God."[9] *Communio*
ecclesiology, it seems, provides a rich source of resonances and connections
between the doctrine of the church and the doctrine of the Trinity. But in the
final analysis, it requires tremendous discipline to make proper use of it, and
that discipline comes from sources rather far afield from merely ecclesiological
concerns. A fully-formed doctrine of the Trinity, worked out according to its
own proper sources and norms, must already be in place if *communio* ecclesiology is to make limited but meaningful connections to it.

 Missio Dei ecclesiology likewise arose in the setting of twentieth-century
ecumenical discussions, although those discussions were first of all about the
nature of Christian witness and mission rather than about the nature of the
church. Where *communio* ecclesiology coalesced in Vatican II's intentional
discussions of ecclesiology, the conversation about *missio Dei* started almost
as an alternative to, or attempted relativization of, the church. That is, in world
missionary conferences where it was widely perceived that Christian mission was being in some ways held captive to the constraints of the established
churches and their programs, the note of God's own mission was introduced
as an expansion of the Christian message beyond the sphere of the church.
As David Bosch traces the spread of the *missio Dei* motif, it entered the discussion through the influence of Karl Barth, and made its first major impact
on a mission conference at Willigen in 1952: "it was here that the idea (not
the exact term) *missio Dei* first surfaced clearly. Mission was understood as
being derived from the very nature of God. It was thus put in the context
of the doctrine of the Trinity."[10] While it would be too much to say that the
emphasis on God's own mission started as an anti-ecclesiology, the idea was
definitely used to relativize the church by bringing in something larger, more
theocentric, more theological: "In the new image mission is not primarily an

---

8. Brian M. Doyle, "Social Doctrine of the Trinity and Communion Ecclesiology in
Leonardo Boff and Gisbert Greshake," *Horizons* 33, no. 2 (2006): 247.

 9. Doyle, "Social Doctrine," 247.

 10. David Bosch, *Transforming Mission: Paradigm Shifts in Theology of Mission* (Maryknoll, NY: Orbis Books, 2011), 399.

activity of the church, but an attribute of God. God is a missionary God."[11] The idea has nevertheless made its way into the self-understanding of the churches, and has in the process become a key element in actual ecclesiologies. Ecclesiologies of this kind tend to be actualistic, and to locate the being of the church in the very witness of the church toward the outer world. As a movement, the missional movement of the twentieth century insisted that rather than simply explaining how churches could add an emphasis on mission to their current ecclesiologies, the goal should be to think of church as altogether mission. An ecclesiology that locates the church within the *missio Dei* has the advantage of tracing the trajectory from God's action through to the church's own actions. We might say that such an ecclesiology is closely engaged with the economic Trinity, because it confesses itself to be brought into existence by the sending of the Son and Spirit. Bosch explains the advantages thus:

> [I]t cannot be denied that the *missio Dei* notion has helped to articulate the conviction that neither the church nor any other human agenda can ever be considered the author or bearer of mission. Mission is, primarily and ultimately, the work of the Triune God, Creator, Redeemer, and Sanctifier, for the sake of the world, a ministry in which the church is privileged to participate. Mission has its origin in the heart of God. God is a fountain of sending love. This is the deepest source of mission.[12]

At its best, *missio Dei* ecclesiology can carry out something like Webster's trinitarian deduction of ecclesiology, and it can certainly make good on the confession that the church is a creature. At its worst, *missio Dei* ecclesiology can be ontologically thin, simply refusing to make statements about the being of the church, preferring verbs to nouns. But in most cases the refusal to engage in metaphysical reflection simply leaves one at the mercy of an age's background metaphysical assumptions, and if Webster is right, these are likely to be biased toward historicized ontologies and a metaphysical privileging of the social-historical. This outcome would be ironic in several ways. Colin Gunton once argued that the main advantage of bringing Trinity and ecclesiology into conversation is that ecclesiology can then benefit from the highest-level metaphysical reflection in Christian doctrine, which is contained in the trinitarian dogma. "The development of the doctrine of the Trinity was the creation, true to the gospel, of a distinctively Christian ontology; but . . .

---

11. Bosch, *Transforming Mission*, 400.
12. Bosch, *Transforming Mission*, 402.

its insights were for the most part not extended into ecclesiology. What happened was that the vacuum was readily filled by rival ontologies."[13] John Flett has argued that a proper understanding of God's mission would not treat it as something subsequent to, or incidental to, his being. Flett interprets Karl Barth's trinitarian theology as requiring that God's mission belongs properly within his own eternal self-determination.[14] That is certainly a metaphysical claim, though it runs close to what we have called a historicized ontology. At any rate, *missio Dei* ecclesiology must be vigilant on the ontological front, and must invoke theologically informed metaphysical commitments if it is to be true to its own interests.

These two broad approaches to relating ecclesiology and the doctrine of the Trinity stand in an interesting tension with each other. We might say that *communio* is more Catholic and *missio Dei* more Protestant; that is certainly true to their origin stories and to the bulk of the literature devoted to them. *Communio* tends to be ontically thick, trading on notions of participation and assuming profound continuity between what it means to say that both God and the church are constituted by communion. *Missio Dei* tends to be ontologically thin or underdeveloped, and stands in danger of inheriting an unexamined set of metaphysical commitments. *Communio* tends to focus on the immanent Trinity; *missio Dei* on the economic. In face of the danger of treating ecclesiology sub-theologically as an indicator of a merely social-historical entity, *communio* is at risk of reduction to the social, *missio Dei* in danger of reduction to the historical. In terms of the desired deduction of ecclesiology from the doctrine of the Trinity, *communio* ecclesiology clearly intends to strike home in the heart of God's eternal being, while *missio Dei* clearly intends to trace God's actions out into history. Both approaches are broad in scope and capable of accommodating many different elements and emphases, and this is an advantage. Large ecclesiological categories have the best chance of aligning with large claims like the doctrine of the Trinity. All of this is to be expected, as one observer noted of the benefits of linking Trinity and ecclesiology:

> If the ecumenical movement is looking for a basis for a common understanding of church and of mission, an obvious choice is the trinitarian understanding of God. Both the new trinitarian-based *koinonia* concept in

13. Colin Gunton, *The Promise of Trinitarian Theology* (Edinburgh: T&T Clark, 1991), 62.
14. John Flett, *The Witness of God: The Trinity, Missio Dei, Karl Barth, and the Nature of Christian Community* (Grand Rapids: Eerdmans, 2010), 214–15.

World Council of Churches (WCC) Faith and Order's thinking on church unity, and the increasingly trinitarian understanding of *missio Dei* in recent church thinking on the theology of mission, are based on a return to the common trinitarian understanding of God.[15]

STRUCTURAL ANALOGIES

Compared to the previous two approaches for relating Trinity and ecclesiology, our third approach, the quest for structural analogies, has a peculiar status. On the one hand, it is a recurring favorite on the popular level with considerable influence. For some people, it simply seems axiomatic that church structures ought to correspond to the structure of the Trinity. On the other hand, unlike *communio* and *missio Dei*, the structural analogy approach has not attracted many scholarly advocates, and has rarely been given extensive conceptual articulation. We will take up one case study in order to clarify what is and is not at stake in this approach, but we should bear in mind that none of the theologians involved in this case study treated the production of structural analogies to be some kind of sufficient basis for their entire ecclesiologies. They operated with other ecclesiological models for most of their work, but supplemented them with structural analogies in certain limited areas.

The case study is a three-way conversation enacted by Miroslav Volf in his book *After Our Likeness: The Church as the Image of the Trinity*. Volf engages, from a Free Church perspective, with Roman Catholic and Eastern Orthodox ecclesiologies respectively in the works of Joseph Ratzinger and John Zizioulas. As the title of his book signals, Volf proceeds as if "the thesis that ecclesial communion should correspond to trinitarian communion enjoys the status of an almost self-evident proposition."[16] The interesting thing is that in this discussion, three different ecclesiologies correspond to three different accounts of the Trinity.

In Volf's presentation, Ratzinger's ecclesiology represents an overriding interest in catholicity, which grounds all the internal relations in a constant reference to the whole: "The one Christ acting as subject in the church is rep-

15. Matthias Haudel, "The Relation between Trinity and Ecclesiology as an Ecumenical Challenge and Its Consequences for the Understanding of Mission," *International Review of Mission* 90 (2001): 401.

16. Miroslav Volf, *After Our Likeness: The Church as the Image of the Trinity* (Grand Rapids: Eerdmans, 1997), 191. Hereafter, page references from this work will be given in parentheses in the text.

resented by the one visible head of the church, namely, by the pope as head of the universal church, and by the bishop as head of the local church. Thus only the one pope and the one bishop, and not the college of bishops, can be grounded as structural elements through the doctrine of God" (71–72). As a result, Volf argues, for Ratzinger,

> relations between Pope and bishops as well as between the individual bishops and congregation members (or priests) must necessarily be structured *hierarchically*. Just as the one substance of God (or the Father) is over Christ, so also must the one who is to vouch for the totality of the church, namely the Pope as *vicarius Christi*, be over the bishops, and the bishops over congregation members (or priests). (72)

Volf's critique of Ratzinger centers on the way he conceives the relation of person to community: persons, divine and human, appear as pure relations who never stand on their own. "Whereas it initially seemed as if pure relationality would relativize the hierarchical structure of relationships, in reality it merely gives free hand to the power of the hierarchs" (72). Everything must be related to the whole, and what that concretely means in ecclesial structures is necessary subordination of each person to the one bearing the office of catholic unity. Just as Ratzinger's trinitarianism prioritizes the one substance of God, his ecclesiology prioritizes the office of pope.

In Volf's account of John Zizioulas, the Orthodox voice in the conversation, it is the monarchy of the Father as the source of the Son and Spirit that comes to the fore. "Just as in the Trinity the one (the Father) constitutes the many (the Son and the Spirit) and at the same time is conditioned by them, so also does the one (Christ and bishop as *alter Christus*) constitute the many (the church) and at the same time is conditioned by them" (123). Volf summarizes: "Whereas in Zizioulas we encounter a mutual (albeit asymmetrical) relation between the one and the many, in Ratzinger we encounter an (almost completely) one-sided relation of the whole and the one to its concrete realizations" (123). Volf is careful and evenhanded in his reporting, but his treatments of his interlocutors is necessarily compressed, and the final point of comparison emerges clearly: in his own way, each of these two authors ground a necessary hierarchy and subordination of the laity in the analogate communion of the Trinity.

For his part, Volf appeals to a more thoroughly social model of the Trinity, in which the relations among the trinitarian persons are complementary and the persons themselves are perichoretic subjects. Perhaps the most difficult aspect of the book is that Volf's main constructive moves in the doctrine of the Trinity itself occur in the span of a few pages that rely on a series of footnotes invoking Jürgen Moltmann's trinitarian theology. Central to his account is a refusal to conflate divine processions with trinitarian relations as such. As a result, Volf argues that "one must distinguish between the constitution of the persons and their relations" (216). Son and Spirit receive their divinity as persons from the hypostasis of the Father by way of the relations of origin, but for Volf this is not all there is to say about the trinitarian relations. In addition to these person-constituting unilateral relations of origin (which would put Volf in very close agreement with Zizioulas), there are also mutual relations among the three that are more complex, diverse, multilateral, and polycentric. Volf, following Moltmann, insists on a distinction between constitutional and relational levels of the triune life, which "are, of course, not to be conceived as two temporally sequential steps, but rather as two dimensions of the eternal life of the triune God" (217). These pluriform, perichoretic relations have equal ontological status with the relations of origin.

Much of Volf's own proposal relies on this distinction being valid. It is a distinction that Moltmann first drew in the course of ecumenical dialogue about the *filioque*, and in that context it enabled Moltmann to recognize the elements of truth in both Eastern and Western views. At the level of procession, Moltmann rejects the *filioque* completely: the Father is the sole source of divinity, and to obscure this fact is to subordinate the Spirit to the Son one-sidedly. But at the level of relational form, Moltmann admits that "the *filioque* has its proper place." He goes on to offer a paraphrase of the creed: We believe in "the Holy Spirit, who proceeds from the Father of the Son, and who receives his form from the Father and from the Son."[17] If the constitutional/relational distinction is correct, it not only resolves the *filioque* problem (as Moltmann argues), it opens up a whole sphere of immanent Trinitarian activities where polycentric and reciprocal relations among the three persons can be recognized. It is in this new territory that Volf finds warrant for his ecclesiological vision.

> If this distinction . . . is persuasive, then the unilinear hierarchical relations can disappear from the trinitarian communion, since maintaining that the Father constitutes the Son and Spirit says nothing yet about how the relations between them are structured. In any case, within salvation history

---

17. Jürgen Moltmann, *The Trinity and the Kingdom*, trans. Margaret Kohl (Minneapolis: Fortress, 1980), 171.

they do appear as persons standing in reciprocal relationships to one another. With regard to the immanent Trinity, salvation history thus allows us to infer the fundamental equality of the divine persons in their mutual determination and their mutual interpenetration; even if the Father is the source of the deity and accordingly sends the Son and the Spirit, he also gives everything to the Son and glorifies him, just as the Son also glorifies the Father. Moreover, within a community of perfect love between persons who share all the divine attributes, a notion of hierarchy and subordination is inconceivable. Within relations between the divine persons, the Father is for that reason not the one over against the others, nor "the First," but rather the *one among the others.*[18]

Having established this distinction, Volf summarizes his position over against the Catholic and Orthodox interlocutors: "The structure of trinitarian relations is characterized neither by a pyramidal dominance of the one (so Ratzinger) nor by a hierarchical bipolarity between the one and the many (so Zizioulas), but rather by a polycentric and symmetrical reciprocity of the many" (217). Stated prescriptively, "The more a church is characterized by symmetrical and decentralized distribution of power and freely affirmed interaction, the more it will correspond to the trinitarian communion" (236).

In arguing that the church is or should be the image of the Trinity, Volf is not insensitive to the dangers of unwarranted assimilation of divine and human realities. In fact, one of the first tasks he undertakes in the constructive part of his book is to put in place definite limits to the correspondences and analogies that are permissible. Without these limits of correspondence in place, Volf admits that "reconstructions of these correspondences often say nothing more than the platitude that unity cannot exist without multiplicity nor multiplicity without unity" (191), or, on the other hand, they seem to be exhortations for us to act like God. These options are too little and too much, respectively. Volf therefore takes pains to clarify the limits. Because "the mystery of the triunity can be found only in the deity itself, not in the creature," every attempt to conceive correspondences to the Trinity is chastened. Mediations are necessary, and Volf provides three. On the one hand, he clarifies that at the conceptual level we are dealing at all times with constructed models and not with God himself, "who always remains hidden in the light of his own being" (198). Secondly, Volf argues for a wide gap between the use of terms

---

18. Volf, *After Our Likeness*, 217. Italics in original. Hereafter, page references from this work will be given in parentheses in the text.

like "person" and "communion" in the two contexts of Trinity and ecclesiology. Thirdly and most substantively, Volf employs a far-reaching eschatological proviso, reminding us that there is a wide difference between "the historical and the eschatological being of Christians," and that "for a sojourning church, only a dynamic understanding of its correspondence to the Trinity is meaningful" (199).

Volf's proposal repays study because it is as good as the structural analogy approach gets. But after he has been fair to Ratzinger and Zizioulas, and after he has put his careful limitations and methodological provisos in place, he still has to make a case that his Free Church ecclesiology corresponds in some meaningful way to the structure of the immanent Trinity. And in order to do this, he introduces new levels of conceptual complexity into his account of the Trinity. It is a lot of work for a limited payoff, especially when we consider the awkward spectacle of a Roman Catholic theologian finding in the Trinity structures corresponding to the papacy, an Eastern Orthodox theologian finding structures corresponding to world Orthodoxy, and a Free Church theologian finding structures that correspond to free association. In less capable hands, the structural analogy approach fares even worse. There is little to be said in its favor.

CONCLUSION

The goal of articulating the connection between ecclesiology and the doctrine of the Trinity is to let the doctrines mutually illuminate each other, but with a decided priority given to letting the doctrine of the triune God illuminate the doctrine of the church. Confessing the connection properly will probably entail, as we saw with Jenson, running right up to the boundary of what can be said about God's intimacy with his redeemed creatures. But we do not want to transgress the boundary between creator and creature; we want to be able to confess, as in Turretin's formula, the church as "the primary work of the Holy Trinity" (*primarium S. S. Trinitatis opus*); both primary and a work; both exalted to fellowship with God and yet a creature. In order to maintain good dogmatic order that lets the doctrine of God retain its commanding role within the structure of theology, something like Webster's trinitarian deduction of ecclesiology is necessary. With these guidelines in place, ecclesiology can make limited use of *communio* and *missio Dei* motifs, and at most a strictly chastened use of structural analogies. Webster's decisions and warnings were guided not just by the architectonics of how the doctrines in a dogmatic system hung together, but also by a commitment to approach the task of theology in a way that gave definite priority to Scripture. He described theology as a work that is at the service of the word of God when it modestly indicates "the worlds of meaning in Scripture." Theological texts succeed "when they attain a certain transparency to the Bible, when concepts and patterns of argument are sufficiently light that they can be seen not as an improvement upon Scripture, but as a means whereby it can, as it were, be repeated."[19] These words stand as an apt warning in the territory of trinitarian ecclesiology. At their worst, some attempts to articulate the connection between church and Trinity run afoul of this charge to stay transparent to Scripture's own terms and indications. It is very easy for trinitarian ecclesiology to take on a kind of baroque hyper-development that leaves the main lines of Scripture far behind. A more appropriate goal would be not to turn heads with clever new ways of arguing, but to repeat, in the context of describing the church and the triune God, what Scripture says.

---

19. John Webster, "Reading Theology," *Toronto Journal of Theology* 13, no. 1 (1997): 57.

Trinity and the Christian Life

E VERY ACCOUNT OF THE CHRISTIAN LIFE is suspended from a particular doctrine of God. Any soteriology is dependent on its presupposed
doctrine of God for its terms, its structure, and its scope. The doctrine of the
Christian life is always aligned in some way with the doctrine of God, but it
can be well aligned or poorly aligned. In this chapter I would like to sketch a
way of aligning the doctrine of the Christian life with a well-formed doctrine
of the Trinity. "Well-formed" means, in this instance, a classical doctrine of
the Trinity, complete with an explicit affirmation of the eternal processions
of the Son and the Holy Spirit from the Father, together with an account of how
these processions are presupposed by the sending of the same Son and Holy
Spirit into the economy of salvation. The goal of this exercise is to ground the
gospel of God in the character of the God of the gospel.

GLORIOUS IRRELEVANCE

There are two errors to be avoided in undertaking this task, and it may be
worthwhile to point them out before proceeding with the exposition of how
the Christian life presupposes the triune God. First, a description of the difference the Trinity makes for the Christian life, if it is to be a helpfully dogmatic description, must not merely be a rehearsal of the work of God in the
economy of salvation. Because the Christian life is immediately grounded
in God's saving actions, there is certainly much to say about the work of the
Father, Son, and Spirit in constituting the reality that is the Christian life.
There is even much to say about how all the work of God is grounded in the
character and being of God, such that he acts toward us as the one he is, and
the graces of the Christian life take on the character of the Gracious One who
is the electing God, the creating and providential God, the saving God, and

the perfecting God. Further, none of this can be elaborated concretely without making specific reference to its trinitarian character, because the one God who gives the Christian life its reality and identity is, to the uttermost depths of being, Father, Son, and Holy Spirit. All the external works of the triune God are indivisibly and identifiably the concerted work of these three, and every aspect of the Christian life is most fruitfully described in terms of the Son and the Holy Spirit carrying out the Father's will.

Second, a description of the triune God that intends to highlight how it is aligned with the doctrine of the Christian life must resist the distorting influence of rushing toward relevance. It must devote its attention to the revelation of God's identity first, without asking in advance which elements of that description might later prove relevant for the doctrine of the Christian life. Many recent theological projects have erred at this point, describing the immanent Trinity in a way that underwrites practical concerns and goals, attending selectively to only those elements of trinitarianism that are judged to be relevant for soteriology or spirituality. Many such efforts to apply the Trinity to the Christian life, as Daniel Keating observes, have "become unmoored from the very reality they so ardently labour to apply. Caught up in the enthusiasm to make the Trinity applicable and relevant to any and every aspect of Christian life, they sometimes too readily select and appropriate one aspect of Trinitarian doctrine to the detriment of others, thus diminishing or deforming the doctrine of the Trinity itself."[1] In much modern theology, the doctrine of the Trinity has suffered from being too relevant, or too immediately relevant.

It seems that there is something gloriously irrelevant about the doctrine of the eternal processions, in that if the doctrine is true, it is something true of God's own identity, true before and apart from the salvation of fallen creatures, indeed apart from the very existence of any creatures. The Father always begat the Son, and there was never a time when the Son had not been begotten. It is this Christological and pneumatological aspect of the doctrine of God that we now place in alignment with the doctrine of the Christian life.

The task, then, is to describe the coherence or alignment of the doctrine of the Trinity with the doctrine of the Christian life. To set out the task in this way is to highlight the fact that it is not enough to link Christology and pneumatology to the doctrine of the Christian life, a task always necessarily undertaken by any account of the person and work of Christ and the Spirit. But to turn to the eternal generation of the Son and the eternal procession of the

---

1. Daniel Keating, "Trinity and Salvation," in *The Oxford Handbook of the Trinity*, ed. Gilles Emery, OP, and Matthew Levering (Oxford: Oxford University Press, 2012), 442–43.

Spirit is to turn resolutely to theology proper, that is, to the doctrine of God, and not merely to the mediatorial work of the persons sent into the economy. Consideration of the mediatorial office of Christ always necessarily includes a consideration of soteriology, and consideration of the work of the Spirit necessarily" includes consideration of the Christian life. Not so the doctrine of God. There is more to God's life than the saving of creatures. Hypothetically, and counterfactually, God would be God without having freely taken on the administration of redemption; though thanks be to the God of salvation, we have never known a God who prescinded from saving, who withheld his sovereign covenant faithfulness to his uncompelled and unexacted promise. The God whose story is told in the Bible is the God who is caught in the act of rescue. Still, as John Webster insists, "The salvation of creatures is a great affair, but not the greatest, which is God's majesty and its promulgation."[2]

A Particular God and a Determinate Sort of Salvation

Now, because God comes absolutely first in any possible order of being, the doctrine of God determines the doctrine of the Christian life—theology norms and forms soteriology and everything downstream from it. A particular God will accomplish a determinate sort of salvation. A God having a certain character, or specified attributes, will bring about a salvation commensurate with that divine character. There are two proofs of this: the first is a proof from comparative religion, in which a wide variety of God concepts are found to be correlated with a wide variety of quite diverse soteriologies. Nirvana, Valhalla, and Paradise are not just different words for referring to the same thing, but are names for competing alternative visions of human fulfillment. The second proof is from the history of Christian doctrine. The major clarifying moments in the development of the Christian doctrine of God were yoked to moments of greater clarity about the character of Christian salvation. Nicaea, as defended by Athanasius, is the signal instance. The decisive step forward taken in that theological moment was the proof that Jesus Christ had to be confessed as fully divine, consubstantial with the Father, if salvation were to be sufficiently anchored. But notice that the Nicene proof only works if a particular notion of soteriology has been specified or at least presupposed. The Arian Christ—a mighty creature, called into being

2. John Webster, "'It was the Will of the Lord to Bruise Him': Soteriology and the Doctrine of God," in *God without Measure: Working Papers in Christian Theology*, vol. 1, *God and the Works of God* (London: Bloomsbury T&T Clark, 2016), 148.

ex nihilo by the high God before the ages themselves were set in motion—could be counted as competent to save only if the content of salvation were decisively downgraded. Whatever salvation the Arian Christ could deliver could only be a salvation made available by a third party, not so much a mediator as an intermediary, and one who, while towering imposingly above his worshipers (could such a being truly have human brothers?) must nevertheless be recognized as remaining infinitely lower than God. The Athanasian insight, in other words, is that soteriology is our best orientation to the truths of theology. In the order of discovery, and of tracing out a path of understanding, we often begin with the character of salvation and then reason our way to the confession of the character of the God who has thus saved.

What, then, is the significance of the doctrine of the Trinity for the doctrine of the Christian life? Beginning from the doctrine of the Christian life, we can say that the God who adopts sinners into a filial relationship in which they cry Abba! Father! must be a God in whom the relationship of Father and Son already exists. Or beginning from the doctrine of God we can say: It is the eternal Son who becomes the incarnate Son to propitiate the Father and bring into being adopted sons. Or, to trace again the trajectory from here to there, we are born again through the work of the one who was born of the virgin because he was of the Father's love begotten before the world began to be. Or again from above to below, the eternal, internal streaming of the life of God streams forth into the human nature of Christ, whose death and resurrection cause the streaming forth of new life in redeemed sinners. Or again, from below to above, we are given life by the death and resurrection of the indestructible human life of the one to whom the Father (who has life in himself) gave also to have life in himself. Or again, from above to below, the one who shared the glory of the Father before the world existed came among us full of grace and truth so that we who beheld his glory are among those many sons whom he leads to glory.

All the long lines of the life in Christ reach up toward the life of God in himself. All the trajectories of soteriology are launched toward something greater than soteriology. Indeed, without the doctrine of eternal generation, soteriology stops short of saying what it wants to be able to say. The task of soteriology is only half done when it describes what we are saved from, and even when it specifies the agent of salvation. Soteriology finds its real footing when it announces what end we are saved to; and that goal or direction of salvation has never been better stated than in the doctrine of trinitarian adoption. The character or the relationship that grace brings us into, at great cost to God the Father, is the filial character, the dependent relationship of a sonship that is not simply a created relationship but is our created participation in his uncreated filiality. As Ivor Davidson says, "At the heart of the *beneficia Christi* of which the gospel speaks lies a specific blessing: the opening up of the eternal Son's native sphere to others, the drawing of contingent beings into the realm of his intimate, eternally secure relation to his Father."[3]

Let us look first to the way the classical dogmatic tradition has described "the eternal Son's native sphere," then to its opening up for our inclusion, and finally to the benefits of the doctrine of the eternal processions for the doctrine of the Christian life.

From Eternal Processions to Temporal Missions

Classic trinitarianism has taught that the Son and the Spirit proceed eternally from the Father by way of two distinct, eternal, internal processions. The leading edge of this doctrine was the confession of the eternal generation of the Son; the elaboration of the Spirit's own personal mode of origination came later. That a "son" should come from a "father" is evident from the metaphors themselves (just as a "logos" should come from a speaker), and so speaking of the Son as "begotten" was natural for the early Christian tradition. The rise of Arianism, however, called for a conceptual defense of this simpler biblical language: Arians argued on the one hand that if the Son was begotten of the Father, there must have been a time before he was begotten, and on the other hand that all things come from the Father, so the Son is not qualitatively different from creation for his being generated. In response, the formulators and defenders of Nicaea argued that the begetting of the Son was not temporal, but eternal: He was always begotten of the Father, and there was never a time when the Father was the Father without the Son. Further, they distinguished between the Son's being begotten by the Father and the world's being created by the Father through the Son. Just as "a man by craft builds a house, but by nature begets a son," reasoned Athanasius, God brings forth eternally a Son who has his own nature: the Son is proper offspring to the Father's essence, and is not external to him."[4]

When this argument is extended include the Holy Spirit, the Christian doctrine of God is completed in its trinitarian form. When we meet the Son

3. Ivor J. Davidson, "Salvation's Destiny: Heirs of God," in *God of Salvation: Soteriology in Theological Perspective*, ed. Ivor J. Davidson and Murray A. Rae (Burlington, VT: Ashgate, 2011), 161.

4. Athanasius, *Contra Arianos* 2.62.

and the Holy Spirit in salvation history, we meet divine persons. They are eternal, and there was never a time when they did not already exist as persons of the Trinity, as God. Their coming into our history is not their coming into existence. But their coming into our history is an extension of who they have always been, in a very specific, trinitarian way. When the Father sends the Son into salvation history, he is doing something astonishing: he is extending the relationship of divine sonship from its home in the life of God, down into human history. The relationship of divine sonship has always existed, as part of the very definition of God, but it has existed only within the being of the Trinity. In sending of the Son to us, the Father chose for that line of filial relation to extend out into created reality and human history. The same is true for the Holy Spirit: when he is sent to be the Spirit of Pentecost who applies the finished work of redemption and live in the hearts of believers, his eternal relationship with the Father and the Son begins to take place among us. Having always proceeded from the Father in eternity, he now is poured out by the Father on the church.

There are helpful terms available for all of this, in the traditional theological categories of trinitarianism. At the level of the eternal being of God, the Son and the Spirit are related to the Father by eternal processions. The Son's procession is "sonly," or filial, so it is called generation. The Spirit's procession is "spiritly," so it is called spiration, or, in a more familiar word, breathing. Those two eternal processions belong to God's divine essence, and define who he is. The living God is the Trinity: God the Father standing in these two eternal relationships to the Son and the Spirit. These processions would have belonged to the nature of God even if there had never been any creation or any redemption. But turning our attention from God's eternal being to the temporal salvation he works out in the economy of salvation, we see that by God's unfathomable grace and sovereign power, the eternal trinitarian processions reach beyond the limits of the divine life and extend to fallen man.

Behind the missions of the Son and the Holy Spirit stand their eternal processions, and when they enter the history of salvation, they are here as the ones who, by virtue of who they eternally are, have these specific relations to the Father. For this reason, the Trinity is not just what God is in himself, but that same Trinity is also what God is among us for our salvation. This is an account of how eternal processions give rise to temporal missions, or how the immanent life of God is freely extended to form the economy of salvation. Without entering into a full description of the Christian life, we can describe how the trinitarian processions give the Christian life its distinctive character.

BREADTH AND LENGTH OF THE CHRISTIAN LIFE

God has sent the Spirit of his Son into our hearts crying Abba! Father! In the words of Gilles Emery, "the filiation of the Son is the foundation of all human sonship and of filial adoption by the Father . . . salvation consists in the reception of adoptive sonship by which humans become children of God. This sonship by grace is a participation in his personal relationship to the Father, an assimilation to his mode of existence that is completely referred to the Father."[5] So we have characterized "the native sphere of the Son" and indicated that salvation is adoptive affiliation. Much more ought to be said about the cost of that affiliation. Attending to the goal and purpose of salvation is a vital task, but doctrines of the Christian life that focus on that task are notorious for eliding, or simply not making conspicuous enough, the fact that none of it works without the atonement. Even Irenaeus and Athanasius found it difficult to write at length on the incarnation with its trinitarian background, without distracting attention from the cross and resurrection, and their commentators are in constant danger of the theological error of exalting Christmas over Easter. These things ought to be tighly integrated, not simply taped together or added as elements on a list. J. I. Packer once remarked that the best three-word summary of New Testament soteriology is "adoption through propitiation,"[6] an admirable formula that succeeds in giving equal weight to both halves while ordering the latter (propitiation) to the former (adoption). The theological challenge is how to maintain those proportions when saying more than three words. I bring it up here because I am recommending that we invest heavily in the conceptual schema of eternal processions and salvific adoption, but I do not want to give the impression that taking on this venerable trinitarian-incarnational schema will remove our theological need for constant vigilance to ensure we are not leaving anything out of the full counsel of the word of God. The doctrine of eternal generation does not automatically solve every soteriological problem. It only solves most of them.

In particular, a doctrine of the Christian life properly joined up with a fully elaborated doctrine of eternal processions pushes us to comprehend, with all the saints, the breadth and length and height and depth, and to know the love of Christ that surpasses knowledge. Breadth, length, height, and depth: the doctrine of eternal processions underwrites an expansiveness and comprehen-

---

5. Gilles Emery, *The Trinity: An Introduction to Catholic Doctrine on the Triune God* (Washington, DC: Catholic University of America Press, 2011), 126–27.

6. J. I. Packer, *Knowing God* (Downers Grove, IL: InterVarsity Press, 1993), 214.

siveness that the doctrine of the Christian life fares poorly without. I have assigned these four directions, more by way of convenience and fittingness than by way of necessity, to four directions that Christian soteriology is directed by an alignment with eternal generation. Breadth points to the expanse of the whole economy of salvation. Length indicates the span between the two eternal persons sent into that economy, the Son and the Holy Spirit. Height gestures toward the fact that what takes place between the Son and Spirit here among us in the economy of salvation corresponds to the reality of God in himself, and depth shows how far down into the details of soteriology the doctrine of eternal generation descends.

The breadth: Modern exegetes are stumped by the confidence with which the classical dogmatic tradition affirmed eternal generation. With microscopic accuracy we examine the individual scenes of salvation history and can barely find eternal sonship there, never mind a relation of origin or begetting behind it. What we need to grasp is that the judgment about eternal processions is a holistic judgment, a conviction that the entire scope of God's economy is communicating the sonship of the Lord. It is a judgment about the total economy, the one unified work of God that arises with creation and moves on prophetically to consummation. Such a judgment is not unthinkable: a parallel situation in the modern period is the development and expansion of biblical theology. Sober exegetes debate the prospects of a biblical theology that encompasses the entire Bible and, without suppressing individual voices, nevertheless treats Holy Scripture as a single book brought about by a single divine author and having one identifiable central message. That is a vast thought. But greater still is the classic Christian commitment to the whole economy of salvation as a single purposeful work of God that displays his wisdom and delivers his word. That wisdom and that word are the Spirit of God and the Son of God, which brings us to the category of length.

The length is about confessing the unity of the Son and the Spirit as an economy-spanning unity grounded in an immanent trinitarian commonality—both Son and Spirit have their eternal origins from the Father and so both are sent to us from the Father. The theology of the eternal Son provides a stronger than average rationale for the unity of the work of the Son and Holy Spirit on their coordinated mission from the Father. That the work of the Son and the work of the Holy Spirit go together is clear from the basic facts of the Scriptural witness. Even a unitarian reading of the New Testament would admit as much, while insisting that there is a monopersonal God behind that threefold pattern. It is the glory of the trinitarian reading of the New Testament, on the other hand, that it perceives in the coordinated work of the Son and the Holy Spirit an eternal background of consubstantiality that accounts for the coherence of their work. It is not just that Christ and the Holy Spirit are often seen to be in open collaboration with each other. The reason for this collaboration is that they are, together with the Father who sent them, the one God of Israel, carrying out the one plan of Redemption. The classical Christian view grounds the coherence of the economy in the coinherence of the Trinity.

Now, the procession-mission model adds no greater depth or scope to the trinitarian anchoring of salvation history in the being of God. Even a minimal trinitarianism affirms the deity of the three and their eternal unity. No theology offers a vision deeper or wider than this grounding in God, even if it is the kind of trinitarianism that refuses to acknowledge eternal processions. But a well-ordered trinitarianism replete with the conceptual specifications of the procession-mission model has the great advantage of displaying the distinctiveness of the Son and the Holy Spirit (their *idiotētes*, their distinguishing marks, the ways they are not each other) in a way that is equally illuminating whether these two are contemplated at the bottom of the economic-immanent axis, or at the top. The same momentum of fromness helps us recognize and confess (on the one hand) the eternal Son and the eternal Holy Spirit who came from the Father in different ways, and (on the other hand) the same eternal-now-incarnate Son and the same eternal-now-outpoured Holy Spirit here among us in the economy.

Under the rubric of length, we have at last overcome a besetting tendency to give more attention to the Son than to the Holy Spirit; or at least to eternal generation than to eternal spiration. We have extended our consideration to include the entire scope of both processions. With what warrant? Assumed here is the same warrant that led us to talk about grasping the entire economy of salvation as a single whole. The patristic mindset that first accomplished that task was a mindset gifted in holistic thinking, graced with a sense of totality even when the details were sketchy, certain of the gestalt emerging from all the dots and lines. Our own modern intellectual cultures have the opposite strengths, a gift for details even at the cost of having lost the big picture. As a result, we tend to approach the doctrine of eternal generation as an isolated thing, with a desire to keep it strictly and chemically separated from other doctrines. But it did not arise in such a piecemeal fashion, and it is no wonder that it has seemed less persuasive and compelling to moderns when approached in such a way. If we are to rehabilitate the doctrine, it should not be an isolated doctrine of eternal generation that is described or defended, but the whole thing, along with the generative matrix that produced it in the first place. Let us not be conceptually stingy with this doctrine. God loves a cheerful giver.

Eternal generation demands a link with pneumatology because it is one part of the doctrine of processions within God, of which there are two. And the whole doctrine of eternal generation and spiration, understood as internal processions, is a doctrine of remarkable fecundity. The classical dogmatic tradition does not just barely manage to confess eternal generation—it situates that confession within a recognition that these processions, these "comings-from," are the highest and most generalized way of saying what Scripture says in a rich variety of ways: the trinitarian relations are an interconnected and overlapping nexus of richly structured exchanges that make up the life of the living God. There are glorifyings, illuminatings, restings upon, motivatings, givings and receivings, shinings forth, mutual insidedness and in-beings, postures toward, and intimations of a blessed exchange for which we have no adequate concepts or terms. These are not reduced to, but are summarized as, relations of origin. When the classic tradition says "eternal generation," it is not excluding all this. The relations of origin are capacious. In fact, in a neglected but important turn at the end of his treatise on the Trinity in the *Summa Theologiae*, Thomas Aquinas subjects the notion of internal procession to a surprising analysis: he points out that procession of a divine person from another entails procession into or toward something.[7] In the case of the Son, he proceeds from the Father and into the divine nature; that is, the more completely he goes out, the more completely he arrives in. The more perfectly he is distinct from the Father, the more perfectly he is God the Son. His eternal generation has an eternal terminus in God. His emergence is immersion. It is not only ineffable but also undiagrammable. Aquinas makes much of this from-to structure of the processions in God; moderns have made little. In fact, what moderns have rejected is the minimized doctrine of eternal generation when they should have given the fully elaborated version a closer look.

Height and Depth of the Christian Life

About the height of eternal processions, there is little to say beyond what has already been said. Eternal sonship is the transcendent ground of incarnational sonship; eternal generation is the transcendent ground of the sending of the Son and Spirit. The economy is a revelation of God's character. This is what elevates our talk of salvation into something truly deserving the name *theology*: it is about God.

7. Thomas Aquinas, *Summa Theologiae* 1:43, question 2.

Regarding the depth: How far down into the details of the doctrine of the Christian life does the doctrine of eternal processions go? It imparts to the doctrine of the Christian life a fundamental character that allows the doctrine of salvation to maintain a poise between two opposite errors. On the one hand, all the language about salvation in the New Testament can be misunderstood as a host of metaphors without deeper referent. Kinship and adoption can be a way of talking, and other apostolic language drawn from contexts like temple, courtroom, or politics can also be construed as poetic ways of saying that God chooses to do some saving act. But there is a too-blunt appeal here to the divine will, and a nominalistic and voluntaristic current that deflates what Scripture has to say. On this account we are said to be sons metaphorically, and the Christian life is flatly and straightforwardly one of obedience to a supreme power. Christian soteriology runs the risk of being the kind of salvation that could be traceable to a Unitarian supreme being. He is lord, we receive his salvation and then imitate his character. Whenever the Christian life is presented as merely taking in a new set of ideas, taking on a new set of activities, and perhaps feeling certain new emotions, the minimizing error is in effect.

At the opposite extreme is a maximizing error. Some of the promises and announcements of the New Testament can be misinterpreted as breaking down all distinctions, and chiefly that between creator and creature, and promising total immersion in the being of God, with a depth of ingression into God's essence that is quite startling to contemplate. One is reminded of the Rhineland mystics and their tendency to make statements so extreme in their piety that they resulted in impiety. Spiritual teachers have spread a way of talking about salvation as being "Godded with God" and "Christed with Christ." Angelus Silesius routinely wrote things like, "the blessedness of God, His life without desire, He doth as much from me, as I from Him acquire."[8] Whenever the Christian life is described as theosis, and careful distinctions between God and creation are not observed and policed, this maximizing error is in effect.

If these two tendencies represent minimalist and maximalist doctrines of the Christian life, enacting errors of deficiency and excess respectively, then dogmatic soteriology following the classical guidelines can leave them to fight it out between themselves. A doctrine of the Christian life grounded in the eternal generation of the Son can keep to its course, confident that it is not speculative in affirming participation in sonship. Gilles Emery again: "Sonship by grace conforms believers to the Son; it 'makes them similar' to the Son; it

---

8. Lines like these seem calculated to drive Karl Barth to distraction; indeed, I quote this one from a chain of "pious blasphemies" reported by Barth in *CD* 2/1, 282.

enables them to be associated with the very sonship of the Son in relation to the Father."[9] This is a high claim, but not too high. As John Calvin says, "God, to keep us sober, speaks sparingly of his essence."[10] Instead, he speaks lavishly of his only Son and our adoption into sonship. And when we imitate the sonship of Christ, we are doing it from the inside, so to speak, having been placed in the relationship of created sonship opened up and extended to us by the mission of the only begotten Son. The soteriology of trinitarian adoption, well-connected to the doctrine of eternal generation and spiration, finds the balancing point and enables us to affirm our distinction from, and our intimacy with, God. This is what Kevin Vanhoozer means when he asserts that "the Gospel is ultimately unintelligible apart from Trinitarian theology." He is articulating what a number of contemporary theologians have converged on confessing: "Only the doctrine of the Trinity adequately accounts for how those who are not God come to share in the fellowship of Father and Son through the Spirit."[11]

Emery indicates how such a soteriology avoids the minimalist extreme as well:

> This conformation to the Son, by the Holy Spirit, renews human beings who thereby become 'new creatures.' . . . The Son is the 'ontological' model of the new being of believers. This new being blossoms in the imitation of the holy life of Christ, lived wholly for his Father. The Christian vocation is thus filial by essence.[12]

Formed and normed by the doctrine of the immanent Trinity, that is, the eternal processions that are the life of the living God, the doctrine of the Christian life is also filial by essence.

9. Emery, *The Trinity*, 127.

10. Calvin, *Institutes* 1:13.

11. Kevin Vanhoozer, *The Drama of Doctrine: A Canonical-Linguistic Approach to Christian Doctrine* (Louisville: Westminster John Knox, 2005), 43–44.

12. Emery, *The Trinity*, 127.

Salvation and the Eternal Generation of the Son

THE GOAL OF THIS CHAPTER is to draw a very close connection between the doctrine of eternal generation and the doctrine of salvation, so that the two theological loci may mutually illuminate each other. Although it is almost always valuable to juxtapose any two doctrines within the Christian theological system, the motivation in this case is deeper than mere curiosity about what sparks may fly when any two doctrines collide. Eternal generation and soteriology are not just any two doctrines selected at random. What we need to see is that these two doctrines presuppose each other in a special way. In other words, the mutual illumination of eternal generation and soteriology is not so much a matter of two distinct light sources held close to each other, but two topics both suffused with the radiance of the one light source of all proper theological reasoning: the God of our salvation.

This claim, that soteriology and some element of trinitarian theology have a uniquely close relationship, would not be sustainable if the soteriology in question were a relatively low one, or if the Trinitarian theology in question were a relatively thin one. But the claim's warrant applies to a high soteriology and an elaborate Trinitarianism. What this chapter commends is a correlation between a high view of salvation and an elaborate doctrine of the Trinity. By "a high view of salvation" we mean one that is explicit about salvation's origin in God's self, stemming from the divine self-determination, self-revelation, self-communication, self-donation, and self-impartation. Soteriology is often presented in a highly abbreviated form that investigates its results and articulates its processes, but pays scant attention to its abiding and constantly present source in God. Such treatments of soteriology can be all foreground and no background, to the doctrine's diminishment. The appropriate background for the gospel message is an elaborate, or conceptually rich, doctrine of the Trinity. By "conceptually rich" we mean a doctrine of the Trinity that, in line with the great, central tradition of Christian thought, has made explicit the biblical dynamic of how the one God reveals himself in a way that corresponds to the manner of his existence in eternity: as the begetting Father, the begotten Son, and the proceeding Spirit. A contemporary articulation of the doctrine of the Trinity, if it is indeed to be articulate, ought to make extensive use of the traditional categories of eternal relations of origin within the divine essence. The doctrine of eternal relations of origin teaches that there are two processions in God that have been revealed in temporal missions of the Son and the Holy Spirit among us (the incarnation and Pentecost). This revelation happened at the level of the economy of salvation, resulting in adoption, reconciliation, and indwelling at the level of personal experience in the church. Eternal processions ground temporal missions which ground full salvation. To trace the same logic backward: believers are fully saved because in the fullness of time the Father sent the Son, from whose fullness we have received. This Son is he who was sent because he had eternally proceeded from God the Father in the life of the blessed Trinity.

A Supporting Witness

The fact that the doctrine of the eternal generation of the Son enjoys a good fit or close correlation with soteriology may rank highest among the reasons why it is a theologically and spiritually satisfying doctrine. It shows that the doctrine of eternal generation has systematic and existential advantages. Most of these can be traced in the way it provides a norm and a form for trinitarian soteriology. This belongs on the credit side of the ledger for eternal generation. However, the doctrine of eternal generation must not be based on its benefits for, or its alignment with, the doctrine of salvation. The only argument capable of establishing the doctrine of eternal generation is a biblical argument, and real warrant for believing eternal generation must be the warrant of a right interpretation of Scripture.

The demand for recourse to scriptural revelation of eternal generation has been widely shared in the Christian tradition. The reason for this is that eternal generation is an integral part of the doctrine of the Trinity, and all things trinitarian are made known by God alone. They do not belong among the invisible things understood by what is seen, nor to the truth that can be demonstrated by arguing back from creaturely effects. The same Thomas Aquinas who had at least five ways to prove God's existence resolutely denied that God's triunity could be proven demonstratively by argument. Rather, if we are to become aware of the truth that God has an eternal Son, God will have to tell us. John of Damascus begins his doctrine of God with a florilegium of three New Testament quotations: first from John, then from Jesus (according to Matthew), and finally from Paul:

> No one hath seen God at any time; the Only-begotten Son, which is in the bosom of the Father, He hath declared Him (John 1:18). The Deity, therefore, is ineffable and incomprehensible. For no one knoweth the Father, save the Son, nor the Son, save the Father (Matt 11:27). And the Holy Spirit, too, so knows the things of God as the spirit of the man knows the things that are in him (1 Cor 2:11).[1]

The harmonious witness of the apostles, then, testifies that knowledge of the Father, Son, and Holy Spirit is something only brought about by those three persons who have the requisite, insider knowledge. Hilary of Poitiers similarly said that he taught the divine sonship of Jesus because "the Father bears testimony to Him, He Himself makes such a profession about Himself, the Apostles preach it," and "devout people believe it."[2] Knowledge of the Trinity is a secret locked up in the Trinity until the Trinity crosses over to spread it abroad among us. "Why," asks question 25 of the Heidelberg Catechism, do you speak of three, Father, Son, and Holy Spirit . . . since there is only one divine being?" Answer: "Because that is how God is revealed in God's own word . . . these three distinct persons are one true eternal God."[3] The seventeenth-century Lutheran theologian Johann Gerhard put it more combatively in one of his theses on the revelation of the Trinity: "The mystery of the Trinity should and also can be proved not from the streams of the fathers, nor from the murky pools of the scholastics, but from the utterly clear springs of the Holy Scriptures."[4]

For these reasons we must give decisive priority to clear biblical revelation of the identity of God the Son and his relation to God the Father, and avoid the temptation of reverse-engineering a savior to fit a salvation. The theological task cannot be reduced to seeking after whatever doctrine of God satisfies the demands of soteriology. The doctrine of God takes normative theological

---

1. *An Exact Exposition of the Orthodox Faith* 1:1, in *Saint John of Damascus: Writings*, trans. Frederic H. Chase Jr. (New York: Fathers of the Church, 1958), 165.

2. Hilary of Poitiers, *On the Trinity* 1:25, in *The Trinity*, trans Stephen McKenna (Washington, DC: Catholic University of America Press, 1954), 21.

3. *Heidelberg Catechism*, question 25.

4. Johann Gerhard, *Theological Commonplaces: On the Nature of God and On the Trinity* (St. Louis: Concordia, 2008), 274.

precedence over the doctrine of salvation that hangs from it, and any warrants drawn from soteriology are retroductive at best.[5]

JUSTIFICATIONS FOR AN APPEAL TO SOTERIOLOGY

There are nevertheless three justifications for an appeal to soteriology as an important supporting witness in the case for eternal generation: first, as we have said, a relation of fittingness obtains between them; second, the two doctrines are already entangled as revealed doctrines; and third, contact with soteriology has motivational force.

The first justification for an appeal to soteriology is that although the eternal generation of the Son could not for the first time be established on the basis of our adoptive sonship—which would be a case of the soteriological tail wagging the Christological dog—it is valid to reason a posteriori about the fittingness that links the triune God of salvation and the trinitarian work of salvation. Speaking of the role of rational argument, Aquinas puts it this way: we do not use it "to prove a root [of doctrine] sufficiently . . . [but to] show that consequent situations are in harmony with the root already posited."[6] There is thus some persuasive force to the insight that our salvation is a blessedly "consequent situation" that is "in harmony with" the Son's eternal generation "already posited." Salvation by adoption is the salvation than which nothing more fitting can be imagined by a triune God.

The second justification is that a truly biblical doctrine of salvation is itself a matter of revelation, so appeal to it is not an appeal to any other source than God's own self-witness. In fact, we might even say that soteriology is the native biblical soil of trinitarian theology, because it is conspicuously true that God did not make these things known as merely verbal announcements ("I have a Son") but as explanations accompanying the accomplishment of salvation ("This is my Son"). It is not the case that we had an intact doctrine of the Trinity and then waited expectantly to see how that triune God would save us. It is the case that the one God of Abraham, Isaac, and Jacob fulfilled his promises by sending forth his Son, a Son he apparently already had, so that the New Testament retroactively adjusted the Old Testament doctrine of God

---

5. For "retroductive warrants" in theological method, see Francis Schüssler Fiorenza, "Systematic Theology: Task and Methods," in *Systematic Theology: Roman Catholic Perspectives*, vol. 1, ed. Francis Schüssler Fiorenza and John Galvin (Minneapolis: Fortress, 1991), 77.

6. Thomas Aquinas, *Summa Theologiae* 1:32, article 1.

to accommodate what must always have been true if Jesus is Lord and God is unchanging. Thus to appeal to the doctrine of salvation is to take recourse to the same subject matter that funds our canonical doctrine of God. It is of course a matter of decorum and accountability, with a decent respect to the opinions of other theologians, that when we argue from soteriology we should strive to keep our chain of reasoning as short as possible, our scaffolding of presuppositions as evident as possible, and our network of inferences as modest as possible.

The third justification for making an appeal to soteriology is that if the doctrine of eternal generation is to thrive within the intellectual culture of systematic theology today, it requires more than just demonstration. Retrieving it will also be a motivational and persuasive undertaking. Rhetoric, in the tradition of Aristotle, is the art of finding the available means of persuasion. "Available" refers to those elements that are at hand for, or are able to avail with, a particular audience. Considered in itself, the truth has a superabundant panoply of persuasiveness. But persuasion is the art of matchmaking between certain elements of the truth and the receptivity of a particular audience. We are living through a fraught and awkward era for trinitarian biblical interpretation. For good reasons and for ill, the passages our forebears taught us to consult on this doctrine do not function for us as they did in previous centuries. The Johannine Comma, which launched a thousand trinitarian sermons with its "three that bear witness in heaven," has gone missing. Fair enough; the text-critical case for it is far too weak to support its evidential use. The interpretation of the word *monogenēs* bristles with footnotes and hesitations, and is rarely rendered "only-begotten." This is peculiar but not in itself a matter of great doctrinal weight. Proverbs 8, whatever it means, is not a key player in trinitarian theology now as it manifestly was in the fourth or sixteenth centuries. These are just a few examples at the text-critical, lexical, and allegorical levels. Battalions of trinitarian verses have gone down under heavy fire from the steady Socinianizing forces of historical criticism. Scholarly reinforcements for traditional doctrines like eternal generation, such as those gathered in this volume, are beginning to make themselves known. It seems that after all the besieged fortress of biblical trinitarianism may in fact give proof through the night that the creed is still there. In the interim, many defenses of eternal generation have been based on temporizing tactics, such as letting church tradition carry the weight that the Bible has seemed unable to bear. This is sometimes propped up with a robust account of doctrinal development, wherein the Bible provides some raw materials, but the early church makes something actually trinitarian out of them. This is a short-sighted and inadvisable strategy. If we are to believe in the Trinity, we ought to do so on the same grounds as the church fathers did: because it is a biblical doctrine, not because it is a patristic doctrine. It would not have become the latter if it had not been the former, at least if we believe the testimony of the fathers. To help motivate the present generation to gather its wits for a more robust biblical doctrine of eternal generation, a galvanizing strategy is to show eternal generation's deep resonance with the gospel. About eternal generation the apostles have much to say, but if we are too sluggish to hear it, it has become, in a literal rendering of Hebrews 5:11, *dys*-hermeneutical: hard to speak in interpretation. During this dark age of dyshermeneutical trinitarianism, we will gather strength to go forward into Scripture from a vivid apprehension of salvation.

THREE CONNECTING THEMES FOR TRINITARIAN SOTERIOLOGY

With these motivations clarified, we turn now to three themes that illuminate the close connection between eternal generation and the gospel: first, metaphysical sonship; second, being from the Father; and third, considering God relatively.

"See what kind of love the Father has given to us, that we should be called children of God; and so we are."[7] The Christian experience of adoption to be children of God is founded on a reality, rather than ventured from a figure of speech. Speaking in terms of literary craftsmanship, the concept of sonship may be thought of as a powerful metaphor, one that serves especially well to integrate and focus the entire semantic domain of biblical language about family, household, and inheritance. But sonship is also more than a metaphor, because naming the Christian experience of salvation by the name *adoption* (whether as "son-making" or as "placing in the position of a son") is not an exercise in evocative metaphorical description. It instead descends from that Father [*patēr*] from whom every fatherhood [*patria*] in heaven and on earth has its name.[8] The relation of Father to Son is a relation in God, which is brought down to or given over to us; or, to say the same thing, into which we are exalted and incorporated. "Multitudes of us," says Hilary of Poitiers, "are sons of God; He is Son in another sense. For he is God's true and own Son, by origin and not by adoption; not in name only but in truth; born and not created."[9] Or as the *Heidelberg Catechism* asks and answers: "Why is He

7. 1 John 3:1.
8. Eph 3:14–15.
9. Hilary, *De Trinitate* 3:11.

called God's only begotten Son, since we also are the children of God? Because Christ alone is the eternal, natural, Son of God; but we are children of God by adoption, through grace, for his sake."[10] The relation of sonship is his by definition and ours by some kind of extension of the term's meaning, on the basis of a gracious and costly exchange. If we are to call soteriological sonship metaphorical in any sense, it would be in a sense that demands metaphysical grounding in trinitarian sonship. The doctrine of eternal generation is what specifies the metaphysical foundation behind the metaphorical extension of sonship to us.

At some times in the history of trinitarianism, theologians have considered whether it might be adequate to stop at the assertion of mere sonship—coeternal, coequal, metaphysical sonship—instead of going on to the language of begetting or eternal generation. The proper response is that much would be lost, obscured, and rendered inarticulate by stopping short of generation. William Burt Pope put it this way:

> Those who would efface the interior distinctions of generation and procession in the Godhead surrender much for which the earliest champions of orthodoxy fought. They take away from the intercommunion of the divine persons its most impressive and affecting character; and they go far toward robbing us of the sacred mystery which unites the Son's exinanition in heaven with his humiliation as incarnate on earth.[11]

Pope is speaking circumspectly, but his point is that the Son stands eternally in a relation of origin to the Father that explains his sending. The Father sends the Son and not vice versa. This is not because the Father has more authority than the Son, but because the Father eternally Fathers the Son. To call the Son a Son without going on to confess the "interior distinctions of generation" is to truncate the filial relation in a way that immediately entails a less potent account of soteriology.

Confronting a similar reticence to pursue eternal sonship all the way up into eternal generation, W. G. T. Shedd took another line of argumentation. Shedd was concerned about theologians who were so cautious to stay within the bounds of scriptural terminology that they embraced the word "Son" but

10. *Heidelberg Catechism*, Question 33.

11. William Burt Pope, "Methodist Doctrine," in *The Wesley Memorial Volume*, ed. J. O. A. Clark (New York: Phillips and Hunt, 1881), 176. "Exinanition" is an obscure English word for emptying; it seems to be Pope's way of using Latin word roots to avoid the connotations that had built up around the Greek word *kenōsis* in nineteenth-century theology.

refused to extend it to some antecedent process of the production of the Son. Shedd pointed out that this truncation was an inconsistent one, because the eternal relations of origin are analytically contained in the biblical names, properly understood.

> These trinal names, Father, Son, and Holy Spirit, given to God in Scripture, force upon the theologian the ideas of paternity, filiation, spiration, and procession. He cannot reflect upon the implications of these names without forming these ideas and finding himself necessitated to concede their literal validity and objective reality.[12]

Shedd draws from the proper names their corresponding verbs: the theologian "cannot say with Scripture that the first person is the Father and then deny or doubt that he 'fathers.' He cannot say that the second person is Son and then deny that he is 'begotten.'"[13] In fact, he goes one further grammatical step while insisting that it is not really a further step at all: "Whoever accepts the nouns Father, Son, and Spirit as conveying absolute truth must accept also the corresponding adjectives and predicates—beget, begotten, spirate, and proceed—as conveying absolute truth."[14]

Confessing eternal generation is the consequence of grounding adoptive sonship in a higher sonship that belongs to the essence of the living God. It is especially when considered in relation to salvation that we see why that relation must be solidly grounded in a conceptually rich confession of what makes sonship sonship: as Ivor Davidson says, "At the heart of the *beneficia Christi* of which the gospel speaks lies a specific blessing: the opening up of the eternal Son's native sphere to others, the drawing of contingent beings into the realm of his intimate, eternally secure relation to his Father."[15]

The second theme that connects eternal generation to soteriology is the notion of being from the Father. "Every good and perfect gift is from above, coming down from the Father of lights."[16] Not only do all created gifts come from the Father, but creation itself as a whole comes from the Father. The Son, too, comes from the Father. But the Son comes from the Father in a

12. William G. T. Shedd, *Dogmatic Theology*, 3rd ed., ed. Alan W. Gomes (Phillipsburg, NJ: P&R Publishing, 2003), 245.
13. Shedd, *Dogmatic Theology*, 246.
14. Shedd, *Dogmatic Theology*, 246.
15. Ivor Davidson, "Salvation's Destiny: Heirs of God," in *God of Salvation: Soteriology in Theological Perspective*, ed. Ivor Davidson and Murray Rae (Routledge, 2010), 161.
16. James 1:17.

wholly other way than the way the world comes from the Father. Clearing up the desperate confusions over these two ways of being from the Father was the urgent business of the pro-Nicene theology of the early church. There are at least four ways of being from the Father, or of coming from God, and it is crucial to distinguish them.

The first way: The Son comes from the Father by filiation, or by eternal generation. "Begetting is not an event of time, however remote, but a fact irrespective of time."[17] This is a relation of from-ness or of-ness that is part of the definition of God, as the Son is God of God, light of light.

The second way: The world comes from God by creation, and the difference is marked in the Nicene Creed's phrase that the Son is "begotten, not made," because, as Athanasius says, "a man by craft creates a house, but by nature begets a son." Here Christology and cosmology are distinguished and creation *ex nihilo* begins to be more clearly articulated because of trinitarian theology. The creator-creature distinction must be recognized even though our concern is not primarily with the doctrine of creation, but with soteriology.

The third way: When the Son is sent into the world, he comes from God in yet another way, a new way. The eternally generated one (first way) takes to himself a created nature (second way) and is the subject of an economic sending, a temporal mission that reveals his eternal generation as he brings metaphysical sonship into the realm of creatures (third way). When he comes from God in this new and unique way, he is not two sons, as if he added a created sonship to the uncreated Sonship. There is one Son, who always came from the Father in the first way, and took up a nature created in the second way to be the instrument of his coming in the third way.

The fourth way: When he who comes from God the first way is sent among those who come from God the second way in this unparalleled third way, is the creator-creature distinction transgressed? May it never be! But it is infiltrated, spanned, and surprisingly fulfilled as the eternal generation of the Son reaches its "strangely logical final conclusion"[18] in the way the Son of God enters into the far country. And this establishes a fourth way of being from the Father, or of coming from God. When creatures, fallen and atoned for, are joined to the eternally begotten one, these who come from God as creatures are given their share in the trinitarian way of coming from God as sons. Eternal generation grounds regeneration.

17. H. C. G. Moule, *Outlines of Christian Doctrine* (London: Hodder and Stoughton, 1902), 59.

18. Karl Barth, *CD* 4/1, 203.

The final theme that connects soteriology and eternal generation is the notion of God considered absolutely and relatively. Systematic theology has traditionally distinguished the doctrine of God into two treatises: the doctrine of God's unity of being, and the doctrine of God's trinity of persons, or *de deo uno* and *de deo trino*. There is plenty of material content to discuss under each heading, and so long as the treatises adequately inform and presuppose each other, it is a fine distinction. Another title for that distinction is "God considered absolutely" and "God considered relatively." This was a common way of handling the distinction in the period of Protestant scholasticism. For example, in Johannes Quenstedt's theological system, he begins chapter 9 with the title "On God Relatively Considered; that is, on the Most Holy Trinity." He elaborates on the distinction:

> The consideration of God is twofold, one absolute, another relative. The former is occupied with God considered essentially, without respect to the three persons of the Godhead; the latter, with God considered personally. The former explains both the essence and the essential attributes of God; the latter describes the persons of the Holy Trinity, and the personal attributes of each one.[19]

The distinction could be paraphrased less precisely as "God from the inside, God from the outside." In more current theology, Scott Swain says, "the truth of the Trinity does not concern relations external to God's most excellent being; for example, the relation of creator to creature or of divine king to creaturely subject. The truth of the Trinity concerns relations internal to God's being . . . the truth of the Trinity is internal to the hidden depths of God's being."[20] The point is that knowledge of the Trinity is knowledge of God from within. Gerald Bray says that "Christians have been admitted to the inner life of God. . . . The God who appears as One to those who view him on the outside, reveals himself as a Trinity of persons, once his inner life is opened up to our experience."[21] It

19. Johannes Quenstedt, cited in Heinrich Schmid, *The Doctrinal Theology of the Evangelical Lutheran Church* (Minneapolis: Augsburg, 1889), 134.
20. Scott Swain, "Divine Trinity," in *Christian Dogmatics: Reformed Theology for the Church Catholic*, ed. Michael Allen and Scott R. Swain (Grand Rapids: Baker Academic, 2016), 82.
21. Gerald Bray, "Out of the Box: The Christian Experience of God in Trinity," in *God the Holy Trinity: Reflections on Christian Faith and Practice*, ed. Timothy George (Grand Rapids: Baker Academic, 2006), 45–46.

is a striking claim, but it is the one we have been moving toward in our entire argument that a high soteriology and an elaborate trinitarianism cohere.

Trinitarian theology arises from the biblical conviction that Jesus Christ must be described as internal to God, as something to be considered under the heading "God, relatively or relationally considered." That is why confessing the deity of Christ has never been considered quite good enough: the Nicene formula is not that Jesus Christ is God, but that he is "God of God, light of light," and is of one substance with the Father, which is a relational statement. In his life among us, we have not just beheld God, but the glory of the only begotten. To omit the begottenness is to omit the internal relation that is the secret of salvation, the deep link between God and the gospel. Trinitarian soteriology, then, stands on eternal generation. Eternal generation is implicit as the background of salvation as the Bible presents it. It only needs attention, unfolding, or paraphrasing. For the sake of salvation, then, let us attend, let us unfold, and let us paraphrase. Confessing processions and missions, let us proceed with our mission.

Salvation and the Eternal Procession of the Spirit

T HIS CHAPTER IS AN ESSAY in triangulation, locating the doctrine of the Holy Spirit by inference from other doctrines, and with reference to those other doctrinal loci. Such an indirect strategy is necessary because of some peculiarities of pneumatology. While the doctrine of the Spirit is not obscure in itself, its exposition is beset with certain ambiguities that resist a more straightforward method. These pneumatological ambiguities become theologically troublesome especially in relation to the doctrines that border it: the Trinity, Christology, and the relation of God to creation. These contiguous doctrines generally have clearer boundaries, and histories in which they have been more elaborately formulated; as a result, they can draw attention away from pneumatology. Instead, this chapter attempts to borrow clarity from these surrounding doctrines for the consolidation of pneumatology. It takes three steps toward placing pneumatology within a comprehensive doctrine of God. First, it analyzes the pattern of biblical naming of the Holy Spirit; second, it relates pneumatology to the doctrine of divine processions and missions that is fundamental for classical trinitarian theology; and third, it explores the fruitfulness of using the less biblically obvious category of *gift* as a description of the third person of the Trinity. The Holy Spirit is God, and is from God: by triangulation this chapter undertakes to specify the meaning of both sides of this statement.

NAMING THE THIRD PERSON OF THE TRINITY

To speak about the third person of the Trinity is not yet to invoke any name, because the phrase "third person of the Trinity" is not so much a name, nor even an identifying description, as it is a kind of doctrinal map locating this one by triangulation from other plottable doctrinal points: it directs us to find the Spirit in the trinitarian taxis at location three. It says something like,

"Go to the Father, follow the way of procession, and when you get to the Son you are not quite there yet; make a left turn and proceed to the terminus of pneumatology lane." The phrase "third person of the Trinity" is also fairly obviously an invocation of a set of theologoumena honored by long usage but not found in the words of Scripture. The key words *Trinity, person,* and even *third* are not given to us in the very words of scriptural revelation. These words are offered as conceptual paraphrases that give an account of the overall meaning of what Scripture says on these topics. One disadvantage of using this elaborate theological terminology of "third person of the Trinity" is that it could lead to abstraction and distraction. In order to avoid these pitfalls, we need to make careful use of it and handle it intentionally as a schematic way of saying what Scripture says, while regularly taking recourse to the way Scripture actually speaks. But there are also distinct advantages of using this elaborate terminology. One advantage is that it conjures for our minds the overall doctrinal matrix within which we are speaking of this person, while also picking out precisely the Spirit in distinction from the Father and the Son. This is one of the constant duties of pneumatology: to pick out the Holy Spirit within the Trinity, without lifting the Holy Spirit out of that trinitarian matrix. We want to be able to ponder this one in particular, but not this one in isolation. The phrase "third person of the Trinity" does this rather abstractly and schematically, but it does locate the Spirit. Let us now follow Scripture in actually naming the third person of the Trinity.

Scripture names the third person of the Trinity in many ways, and Christian theology has the task of responding appropriately to this biblical pattern of naming in a way that is both responsive to God's word, confessing the identity of the Spirit, and responsible to its own office of teaching, following "the pattern of the sound words"[1] that we have heard from the apostles and prophets. Serving the Lord and serving the church in this way, the theological work of pneumatology is a particular mode of conceptually "guarding the good deposit entrusted to" us, which Paul tells Timothy is something that must itself be done "by the Holy Spirit who dwells within us."[2] There is something reflexive or self-involving here, if we apply this phrase "by the Holy Spirit" to pneumatological study. All theology, as a catechetical guarding of the good deposit by a disciplined following of the pattern of sound teaching, must take place "by the Holy Spirit who dwells in us," but the doctrinal locus of pneumatology is uniquely a field of doctrinal work simultaneously *by* the Spirit and *about* the Spirit. At its most instructive, Christian pneumatology serves as a foreground-

1. 2 Tim 1:13.
2. 2 Tim 1:14.

ing of what has always already been going on as the pervasive background of all theology, and can catalyze the deepest moments of insight and awareness. But great care is required here, because at their least instructive, exercises in pneumatology can become doctrinally diffuse, saying nothing much in particular; or vacuous, holding open a place to be assigned some content at a later time; or distracting, inviting the mind to pursue any number of other subjects in quest of the long-awaited definitive treatment. This is the danger theologians confront when directing attention to the Holy Spirit: to come away with a lot of good ideas, each of which is interesting, promising, and in itself perfectly correct, but moving in so many directions that it no longer feels like one doctrine. In other words, one of the desiderata for responsible pneumatology is that once done, it should stay done. A well-ordered and well-functioning doctrine of the Holy Spirit should secure a solid and permanent basis for all the things we need to say in the full scope of the doctrine. The Spirit blows where it wills, but pneumatology ought to stay put.

The biblical pattern of naming, I suggest, provides a foundation for a stable pneumatology. That pattern establishes a relation between God and God's Spirit that is precisely what was selected for further development by the central traditions of Christian theology. Viewed thus as an expansion of a biblical pattern of naming, the ancient patristic notion of the procession of the Spirit serves as a safeguard against pneumatological chaos. The pneumatology of the early church developed and articulated these concepts in part with this goal of stability in mind; especially the line of Alexandrian thinkers from Origen through Didymus the Blind, Athanasius, and Cyril were especially attentive to the way the doctrine of eternal procession served as a grounding or integrating concept for the vast and disparate array of ways the Scripture speaks of the Holy Spirit. This first phase of the argument will not be carried out in the mode of commentary on patristic arguments, though: instead it will be a brief demonstration on the grounds of the matter itself, which is the pattern of words used by Holy Scripture in naming the Spirit.

In one sense, the difficulty we encounter in expressing pneumatology could be called the Bible's fault. The Holy Spirit's own self-revelation and self-naming in inspired Scripture is diverse. In the Old Testament we meet references to the Spirit of God, but already there is diversity and plurality in the multiple divine names used: we hear of the Spirit of Elohim and the Spirit of Yahweh; even the Spirit of Adonai and of the Most High. This Spirit is by Isaiah 11 the Spirit of wisdom and understanding, the Spirit of counsel and might, the Spirit of knowledge and the fear of the Lord. Elsewhere, the pattern of naming splits off even more, so that no sooner do we learn that the Spirit indwells the temple than we have to learn that the glory also indwells, and that spirit and glory are, if not synonyms, at least acceptable parallelisms. And so begins the proliferation of new nouns that can serve as ciphers of the Spirit: holiness, glory, power, cloud, presence. In poetic parallelisms, all of these can point to the Spirit without invoking the expected name. In the thicket of these many Old Testament names, the most constant element sometimes seems to be "of." And in fact, there lies the real biblical root of the doctrine of procession. The fundamental pattern in the Spirit's self-naming is ofness. The ofness itself is also complex, of course: sometimes it signifies identity (the Spirit of God is God); sometimes it signifies distinction (not just God, but the Spirit of God). Other divine self-descriptions also follow this logic, including a range of self-descriptions that we have no reason to think of as especially pneumatological: both the face of God and the name of God are used with the same tension, signifying God yet also signifying something from God. We might almost say, in these instances, that God is on both sides of the "of:" God of God, to use the Nicene idiom. In a phrase like "Spirit of God," the word *Spirit* sometimes functions adjectivally, meaning "divine Spirit." "Spirit of holiness," on this construal, signifies "Holy Spirit," a name not prominent in the Old Testament, and not especially hypostatized when it does occur.[3] "Of" can function generatively (what comes from God) or genitively (belonging to God, characterizing God). However we interpret "of," the ofness we interpret is a primal element of the biblical revelation.

What the New Testament adds is a certain consolidation, but not a straightforward linguistic one. It is true that the New Testament writings promote the term "Holy Spirit" to the dignity and function of a proper name, above all in the baptismal formula "in the name of the Father and of the Son and of the Holy Spirit."[4] Here is an apostolic, or even a dominical, way of thinking and speaking of what goes by so many names in the Old Testament. But while there is a definite consolidation of pneumatological reference, it is not exactly a consolidation of names. In fact, the New Testament actually expands our catalog of names, and does so more or less predictably, on the threefold lines suggested by the baptismal formula: Spirit of the Father, Spirit of the Son, Spirit of Jesus, Spirit of Christ, Spirit of adoption, and so on. The New Testament consolidation, in other words, is not a consolidation of names but of sending, because central to New Testament pneumatology is the fact that the Spirit is sent.

---

3. In the Old Testament, the adjective *holy* and the noun *spirit* are only combined in Ps 51:11 and Isa 63:10.

4. Matt 28:19.

We are about to turn our attention from revealed names to the revelation of the Spirit's sending. Before we do so, let us clarify why our way forward through a theology of names is, if not exactly blocked, at least not a clear enough road to proceed on straightforwardly. As we have seen, "Father, Son, and Holy Spirit" is in every way imaginable a venerable formula, and the way it assigns a name to the third person of the Trinity is, to say no more, eminently useful for clear theological discourse. Nevertheless, this form of words does not provide everything we might wish for as we take up the project of pneumatology. Consider these three observations about what the name "Holy Spirit" in the baptismal triad does and does not provide. First, Holy Spirit as the name of the third person in a doctrinal formula is not distinct: holy is common to the divine being, and so is spirit. But combined, somehow they become the name that picks out the third person. Second, Holy Spirit is not a relational name. Father implies Son and vice versa, but Holy Spirit does not imply any correlative terms. Father and Son are relational realities with relational names; Holy Spirit is a relational reality without a relational name. Father and Son are family words, but Holy Spirit is not. Greek and Latin traditions, as we will see, have offered two different ways of making the Spirit's name serve these relational ends: in Greek, speaking of Spirit as breath, and in Latin speaking of Spirit as gift. Third, Holy Spirit is not a necessarily personal name; it is not obviously about somebody rather than something. The whole matrix of New Testament language about the Spirit seems to pick up on this aspect of the name, and speaks of the Spirit as poured out, or as given.

None of the difficulties listed here are insurmountable; they merely require a careful handling of the Bible's manifold ways of speaking, and a willingness for theologians to take on the task of specifying what is meant by the variety of occurrences of the name Holy Spirit. One good example of a theologian who gladly takes on this task is Herman Witsius, whose exposition of the Apostles' Creed alerted readers to the variety of ways to construe the word *Spirit* as it occurs in Scripture:

> The term *Spirit*, when used with respect to God, is taken either essentially, or personally, or metonymically. It is taken essentially when it is ascribed to God, in reference to the essence common to all the persons, personally, when it is attributed to some one person, whether the second or the third, metonymically, when it denotes certain effects or gifts.[5]

5. Herman Witsius, *Sacred Dissertations on What Is Commonly Called the Apostles' Creed*, vol. 2 (Edinburgh: Fullarton & Co., 1823), 304. An even more detailed account can be found

The guidance Witsius provides does not come from digging deeper into the historical or grammatical context of each appearance of the word *Spirit*. It comes rather from his commitment to bring the overall context of Scripture, read cumulatively and canonically, to bear on any individual occurrence of the word. He moves from whole to part, considering the full witness of Scripture to the revelation of the triune God, and then offering a rough taxonomy of possible meanings of any occurrence of the word under investigation. In doing so, he considers more than just the analysis of revealed names. He also considers the salvation-historical matrix of divine actions within which these names are given. That is to say, the main reason he is unconfused by the ambiguity of the word *Spirit* is that he has already taken his bearings from the economy of salvation, and in particular from the epochal event of the Father and Son sending the Spirit.

A theology of revealed names must arise from, or ride along on the momentum of, economic-soteriological analysis. The central tradition of pneumatology has widely recognized this, but has rarely made it explicit, partly because it has always pursued pneumatology comprehensively and organically in a way that does not bifurcate names and sending. Especially if we attend to patristic exegetical writings, we find extensive development of the recognition that the Spirit is sent from God, and a confident tracing of this sending back into the eternal being of God by recognition of an eternal procession. In short confessional formulas, the theology of names often comes to the fore, and especially in pneumatology the narrative about the Spirit's sending is somewhat backgrounded and left implicit. But read sympathetically, the Nicene fathers and those in their tradition work out their name theology and even their precise terminology on the basis of a mission-and-procession theology. This explains why, in his *Fifth Theological Oration* (Oration 31, On the Holy Spirit), Gregory of Nazianzus was able to rest the whole doctrinal and hermeneutical complex of pneumatology on a single statement of Jesus containing a single key word: John 15:26, which says "the Holy Spirit who proceeds from the Father."[6] In conflict with opponents who deny the deity of the Spirit, Gregory elevates the word "who proceeds" (Greek *ekporeuetai*) to the status of a technical term for the eternal relation of origin by which the Spirit

---

earlier in this Protestant Scholastic tradition, in Petrus van Mastricht's *Theoretical-Practical Theology*, vol. 2, *Faith in the Triune God* (Grand Rapids: Reformation Heritage Books, 2019), 571–72.

6. Gregory of Nazianzus, Oration 31, in *On God and Christ: The Five Theological Orations and Two Letters to Cledonius*, trans. Lionel Wickham (Crestwood, NY: St. Vladimir's Seminary Press, 2002), 122.

eternally is from God. Nazianzus recognizes that this saying of Jesus includes two elements: Jesus refers to the time "when the Helper comes, whom I will send to you from the Father, the Spirit of truth, who proceeds from the Father." Nazianzus installs the distinction between missions and processions at the comma between "I will send to you from the Father" and "the Spirit of truth who proceeds from the Father." He offers this as an interpretation of Scripture, in a hermeneutical synthesis of the full biblical witness to the Spirit. This is how classical trinitarian theology wove together the theology of revealed names and the theology of divine missions.

MISSION AND PROCESSION

With consideration of the mission of the Spirit, pneumatology falls most definitely into line with Christology, because Christ and the Spirit are co-sent in the New Testament. The two sendings are significantly brought into relation to each other in the argument of Galatians 4:4–6: "When the fullness of time had come, God sent forth his Son" and "sent the Spirit of his Son into our hearts, crying, 'Abba! Father!'" The logic that establishes eternal generation applies in parallel fashion to the eternal procession of the Spirit. The God who sent a Son must have always had a Son, and the God who sent a Spirit must have always had a Spirit. These two temporal missions reveal eternal processions, indicating an eternal fromness in the life and being of God. These processions in the divine life can be called the internal works of God that simply are God. They are goings-forth that are first of all internally realized, and as such fully realized, fully perfect, and satisfied in all their dynamics. By grace they open up to temporal sendings. This is the classic doctrine of the trinitarian processions and missions, and it is the most important conceptual tool for confessing the identity of the Spirit as God. But before pursuing its pneumatological implications further, we should attend to the way it demarcates the eternal, always-already-perfectly-accomplished life of God proper, and the free, gracious actions into which God enters. Very loosely, the distinction being recognized here is between the inner life and the outer actions of God. We can expound it more fully by refusing for a moment to expound the dynamic in terms of the missions-processions terminology, and instead speaking initially in a slightly more abstract way. We can speak of the actions of God, internal and external. Employing the concept of "action" to talk about what God does, we will say that God is the source of all sorts of things in the world. But then if we turn around and ask about what God is doing when considered apart from these doings in the world, we have a choice to make. One option is to say that in the divine life there is no action, only being. We could then describe be-ing as something very alive, and as something greater than action, while carefully avoiding the word "action" because we want to save it for what God does with the world. You can go pretty far with this option. Question: What's God doing when he's not doing anything? Answer: Be-ing, but in a divine way. Apophatic silence descends, perhaps a bit prematurely, before the flash of insight that is supposed to give us a glimpse of what we are talking about by choosing this language.

But another, less standoffish option is to apply the category of action to the divine life in itself, and then to specify what those actions in the life of God are. And this is the path that the main stream of trinitarian theology in fact pursued. Building on what Augustine called *opera* and the Cappadocians called *energeia*, Latin-language theology developed a distinction between the inward acts of the Trinity and the outward acts. What are the inward acts of the Trinity? They are generation and procession, concepts that had long been fundamental to trinitarianism, but which now came under the general conceptual framework of "actions" in God. Theologians in the classic tradition of trinitarian doctrine have found it easy to confess that the external actions of the Trinity are undivided. One reason is that they started from a clear confession that the internal actions of the Trinity were not undivided. Or, to put it less double-negatively, the internal actions of the Trinity are distinct and distinguishable as real relations that stand in relative opposition to each other. This relative opposition is crucial, because the key thing about these actions is that each of them has a person of the Trinity at each end. The Father begets or generates the Son, which puts Father and Son at opposite ends of the relation. The Spirit proceeds from the Father ("at least from the Father," we can ecumenically agree, prescinding for now from *filioque* questions), putting Spirit and Father over against each other within the divine life. This polarity or opposing-relation is why the inward works are not called undivided: they mark the distinctions among the persons. The formula used by the Council of Florence in 1439 is what has become the classic statement of the principle: *In Deo omnia sunt unum, ubi non obviat relationis oppositio*: "In God all things are one except where there is opposition of relation."[7]

In the second volume of his *Systematic Theology*, Wolfhart Pannenberg advocates making use of the category of action, and of distinguishing between

---

7. Eastern Orthodox readers may understandably be suspicious of the declarations of the filioquist Council of Florence, but the principle of relations of opposition can also be traced in older, Greek sources like Gregory of Nazianzus and John of Damascus.

internal and external actions of God. One advantage he points out is that it helps conceptualize divine aseity: the notion of internal actions is "a great gain for the actual understanding of God that God should be thought of as active." Pannenberg asks,

> Does there not have to be a world of creatures, or a relation to it, if God is to be thought of as active? Christian doctrine denies this by describing the trinitarian relations between Father, Son, and Spirit as themselves actions. To these divine actions in the creation of the world are added as actions of a different kind, as outward actions.[8]

Pannenberg calls for a high wall of distinction between internal and external actions:

> The acts of the trinitarian persons in their mutual relations must be sharply differentiated from their common outward actions. This differentiation finds support in the rule that posits an antithesis between the inseparable unity of the trinitarian persons in their outward action relative to the world and the distinctiveness of their inner activities relative to one another, which is the basis of the personal distinctions of Father, Son, and Spirit.[9]

In other words, external acts of the Trinity are undivided because the internal acts of the Trinity are distinct relative to one another. Because this is true, we can recognize that "God does not need the world in order to be active. He is in himself the living God in the mutual relations of Father, Son, and Spirit. He is, of course, active in a new way in the creation of the world."[10] The internal actions of the Trinity thus help us conceive of God in himself as the living and active God, not a God waiting for a created, historical stage on which to be living and active. They enable a confession of dynamism as part of the divine life, as a form that aseity takes. And they do this in an orderly way, without illegitimately manufacturing any new content for trinitarian theology. The content provided by the category of action continues to be what it has always been: the generation of the Son and the procession of the Spirit. Anchoring the livingness and activity of God in eternal generation and eternal spiration, the older theology had the conceptual space to declare the external works of the Trinity undivided.

8. Wolfhart Pannenberg, *Systematic Theology*, vol. 2 (Grand Rapids: Eerdmans, 1994), 1.
9. Pannenberg, *Systematic Theology*, 2:3.
10. Pannenberg, *Systematic Theology*, 2:5.

By contrast, any theology that denies or downplays the eternal generation of the Son is likely to need the historical manifestation of the incarnate Son to carry all the meaning and significance; and any theology that downplays the eternal procession of the Spirit is likely to require the historical manifestation of the Spirit to function as an exhaustive and fully satisfying pneumatology. A theologian with a weak grasp of the internal actions of the Trinity is a theologian who will need to make too much of the separateness of the external actions. Such a theology is bound to exploit the external actions for more than they can contain, and is under considerable pressure to read them as the actions of three different agents doing three distinct things. In extreme cases, for example Moltmann at his most drastic,[11] the events in the history of salvation may turn out to be the actual ground of the distinctions among the persons of the Trinity. There is an understandable desire to recognize the cross of Christ as the place where all the action is. But to fail to recognize that the action was in the being of God before it was among us is to give away too much. As Karl Barth asked Moltmann in a 1964 letter, "Would it not be wise to accept the doctrine of the immanent trinity of God?"[12]

For pneumatology in particular, exclusive preoccupation with external actions at the expense of internal actions has a disfiguring effect. The underlying reason for this has to do once again with the biblical revelation itself, which does not identify a single, central way the Spirit works, but instead offers a baffling diversity of works of the Spirit. Theologians and exegetes have long recognized this. Consider this telling sentence from Basil of Caesarea's fourth-century treatise *On the Holy Spirit*:

> Through the Holy Spirit comes our restoration to Paradise, our ascension to the Kingdom of heaven, our adoption as God's sons, our freedom to call God our Father, our becoming partakers of the grace of Christ, being called children of light, sharing in eternal glory, and in a word, our inheritance of the fullness of blessing, both in this world and the world to come.[13]

It is a magnificent collocation of what the Holy Spirit does for believers and is redolent of the whole sweep of the biblical witness. Some of Basil's phrases

11. "The economic Trinity not only reveals the immanent Trinity; it also has a retroactive effect on it." Jürgen Moltmann, *The Trinity and the Kingdom: The Doctrine of God* (Minneapolis: Fortress, 1993), 160.

12. Karl Barth, *Letters 1961–1968*, ed. Jürgen Fangmeier and Hinrich Stoevesandt, trans. and ed. Geoffrey W. Bromiley (Grand Rapids: Eerdmans, 1981), 175.

13. Basil of Caesarea, *On the Holy Spirit* (Crestwood, NY: St. Vladimir's Seminary Press, 1980), 59.

are obviously from a single passage of Scripture, while others evoke a journey of biblical theology from Genesis ("Paradise") to Revelation ("the world to come"). In context, the sentence is part of Basil's book-length argument for the deity of the Holy Spirit, and it is a key passage for that argument. These great benefits of receiving the Spirit are of such a character that they could not be given to us by any person who was not God. That is implicit in the fact that Basil links the Spirit's work to the trinitarian work of salvation. "Through the Holy Spirit comes our . . . adoption as God's sons, our freedom to call God our Father, our becoming partakers of the grace of Christ." The Spirit makes good to us the work of the Father and the Son; therefore he too is God.

But formally, the main thing to notice about this list is that it is a list. There is something about the work of the Holy Spirit that makes theologians start making lists. There is a manifoldness, an overflowing fullness, a profusion of specificities, and a diffusion of bounties that makes pneumatology take the form of lists. At the systematic level, often the real constructive challenge for pneumatology is not so much filling out the list of the many works of the Spirit, but finding a way to comprehend them all under one organizational, summarizing category or notion. Many of the most edifying discussions of pneumatology are strong on the listing and weak on the gathering.[14] Think of what a contrast that is with the work of Christ: though there are infinite facets to the work of Christ and it can be contemplated under various illuminating headings (office, status, moment, object, etc.), it is always obvious that these are various ways of getting at the one work of Christ. Not so with the Spirit: accounts of his work tend more toward sprawl and diffuseness. This phenomenon probably accounts for some of the unsettledness we experience in pneumatology, and the way every book on the Holy Spirit seems in some ways to be starting the project all over from the beginning again. The character of the revelation tends toward wonderful, glorious, listhood.

When we speak of missions revealing processions, we are not speaking of any sending. Not all sendings reveal eternal processions. God sends prophets, apostles, servants, angels, and all manner of other emissaries. But when God the Father sends the Son and the Spirit, we meet God in sendings that have an infinite depth behind them: self-sendings in which God sends God; sendings in which God is God with us. This is the economic Trinity, in which we see that the "of" in the locution "Spirit of God" goes all the way back into the depths of God. For a doctrine of God to be in earnest, it must take this step,

14. This applies, I think, even to Abraham Kuyper's great treatise *The Work of the Holy Spirit* (New York: Funk and Wagnalls, 1900).

seeing the processions behind the missions, or, in modern idiom, confessing in the economic Trinity the revelation and presence of the immanent Trinity.

GIVING OF THE GIFT

We have observed the fact that much of the biblical revelation of the Spirit tends toward a diffuseness, but needs to be understood against a more unified background, the background of its eternal depth in the one procession of the Spirit within the eternal life of God. The history of theology is a history of trying to find faithful ways of foregrounding this deep scriptural background, and making it functional or operational for confessing the theology of the Holy Spirit. In the history of the doctrine, a few proposals have been especially influential. Chief among these is Augustine's strategy of pressing the biblical notion of gift into service as a usable name for the third person of the Trinity. Augustine is keenly aware of precisely the terminological ambiguity we have been examining: Spirit is a word for God, but somehow also the word for the third person of the triune God. He puzzles over this repeatedly, including in the fifth book of his *De Trinitate*. When Jesus affirms to the Samaritan woman in John 4:24 that "God is Spirit," Augustine notes that it seems to be a reference to the Father (who seeks worshipers), to the Holy Spirit (symbolized by the water Jesus will provide), and to God as a whole, that is, to the divine nature or the Holy Trinity.[15] By what standard can the theological reader make these distinctions? Augustine's solution moves on two lines simultaneously. First, he employs an argument from the nature of the Holy Spirit's place in the economy of salvation, broadly considered: the Spirit is given by the Father and the Son. And secondly, on the basis of this giving, Augustine lifts up the word *gift* and presses it into service as a name, a name that is inherently relational.

In an essay on pneumatology, Robert Louis Wilken expounded the logic of this Augustinian move by noting how pneumatological naming is shaped by the unique role of the Holy Spirit in the economy of salvation. The distinctiveness of the doctrine of the Holy Spirit depends on the way it arises from recognition of the Spirit's work in salvation history. Wilken's orienting question is whether Pentecost can be considered a peer of Easter, noting that "in some ways the history of the feast of Pentecost can serve as a metaphor for the development of the Christian doctrine of the Holy Spirit."[16] That development,

---

15. Augustine, *On the Trinity* 5.11.12.
16. Robert Louis Wilken, "Is Pentecost a Peer of Easter? Scripture, Liturgy, and the Pro-

as we have already mentioned, is different from Christology. The doctrines about Christ practically jumped off the pages of Scripture and into orthodox theological confession, as compared with the way the biblical witness about the Holy Spirit gradually emerged and without often being the focus of conciliar attention. Comparatively speaking, the history of Christology is the striking appearance of the solar disc of sunrise pushing back the darkness, while pneumatology is the slow dawning of an overcast day that imperceptibly turns the night into morning. Putting the contrast differently, Christological progress always turned on confronting a heretical teaching in order to refute it and to defend the truth, a truth that became clearer in the course of conflict. Progress in pneumatology, on the other hand, was always marked by a process of culling Scriptures and exploring relationships among passages. In pneumatology, Wilken says, "the Fathers are less engaged in defending something than in searching for something. Only gradually and after they peered intently at the murkiness before them, does the goal of their quest come clear."[17]

Within this gradual process, one of the key clarifying moments was when a particular Latin theological tradition pressed the word *gift* into pneumatological usage. Wilken points to Hilary of Poitiers as the first theologian to speak confidently about the Holy Spirit in terms of the many biblical passages in which it is "the distinctive characteristic of the Spirit, that he is given, received, and possessed." Drawing on this pattern, Hilary calls him the *donum fidelium*, the "gift to the faithful."[18] Gift, in other words, is a shorthand way of referring to being given, received, and possessed. Hilary has noticed something distinctive about the biblical language for the Holy Spirit, namely, that there is a field of terms in the Bible associated with the Spirit that variously depict being given and poured out, on the one hand, and being received or indwelling, on the other. That is, the gift is seen not only from the perspective of the giver, but also from that of the recipient. What is given enters into the life of the recipient and becomes his own, which in turn relates the recipient to the giver. Gift, as presented in the Scriptures, has built into it overtones of reciprocity and mutuality.[19]

Though there is more gradual progress, the next leap forward seems to be Augustine's decision to trace the characteristic gift-ness of the Spirit back

prium of the Holy Spirit," in *Trinity, Time, and Church: A Response to the Theology of Robert W. Jenson*, ed. Colin E. Gunton (Grand Rapids: Eerdmans, 2000), 159–60. Wilken's chapter title draws on the clever phrasing, as well as the theological proposals, of Robert Jenson.

17. Wilken, "Pentecost," 163.
18. Wilken, "Pentecost," 165.
19. Wilken, "Pentecost," 166.

from the church's experience into the immanent being of God. It is Augustine who, agreeing that the Spirit is the gift to mankind in the history of salvation, thinks to ask the question, "Was he already gift before there was anyone to give him to?" (*De Trinitate* 5.15.6). As Wilken paraphrases the question, "does the term 'gift' as a designation of the Holy Spirit only apply to the economy?"[20] The pneumatological move here is parallel to the Christological. If Christ is the Son of God for us, he must have been the eternal Son of God; and if the Spirit is gift to us, he must have always had the character of gift. But whose gift to whom? In the absence of creatures, the exchange would have to be between the Father and the Son. Yet it is just here, at the move to the eternal inner life of the Trinity, that gift seems too impersonal a term to serve well.

At this point, it begins to matter that Hilary did not simply use proof texts to identify Spirit with gift, but rather worked with the thrust and logic of a wide range of texts to derive a fuller account of the Spirit's characteristic role as marked by reciprocity and mutuality. Augustine took this approach one step further by annexing to this gift-reciprocity-mutuality cluster the word *love*. In order to distinguish the proprium, the distinctive character of the third person as manifested in the economy, we must think in terms of a gift of self-involving love that creates communion. "Augustine wants to say not only that the gift of the Holy Spirit creates a communion between God and the believer but also that the Spirit is the 'communion' between Father and Son."[21] And that, finally, is why the third person is specially called Holy Spirit, even though the other two persons are holy and spirits, and God in general (the one triune God) is holy and spirit. As Augustine says, "He is properly called the Holy Spirit . . . with good reason. Because he is common to them both, he is called properly what they are called in common."[22]

This particular Latin pneumatological tradition that reached its ripe formulation in Augustine is a powerful integrative proposal. It is perceptive in its recognition of the giving, mutuality, and reciprocity effected by the third person of the Trinity in the economy of salvation. It is also perceptive in taking the next step of asking what divine reality lies behind the history of salvation: A "who" question about a person of the Trinity cannot be fully answered without taking recourse to the eternal Trinity, to God in himself without any necessary reference to us and our salvation. As for the decisive step of transposing this insight about the gift into the eternal being of God, it functions

20. Wilken, "Pentecost," 167, citing Augustine, *De Trinitate* 5.15.6.
21. Wilken, "Pentecost," 172.
22. Augustine, *De Trinitate* 15.19.37, cited in Wilken, "Pentecost," 172.

properly for pneumatology as long as we keep in mind that it is intended as a heuristic help to making sense of what Scripture actually says, and that it is carefully designed to solve certain problems we would encounter if we tried to do pneumatology by working exclusively with the data of the revealed names. It leverages the Spirit's mission to make the most of the insights delivered by the names. We can pause here to note that other developments, from other theological trajectories, are also possible. In fact, there is a prominent development in the tradition of Greek-language theology, which addresses many of the same problems and finds strikingly parallel solutions. The tradition that stretches from Irenaeus to John of Damascus plays on the Greek word *pneuma* and emphasizes its underlying breath imagery. Just as word and breath both come out from the one who speaks, the Son and Spirit have their eternal origin in the Father, and both carry out among us a kind of characteristic extension of their way of being in the eternal life of God. This Greek tradition has different opportunities and shortcomings than we might trace in the Latin tradition. But both traditions take up biblical material and invest it with deeper significance than is evident in Scripture itself; both press key biblical terms into use for purposes that they do not serve in any explicit biblical argument. Above all, they are alternative strategies for doing exactly the same thing: anchoring the theology of the revealed names to a mission-procession theology, and making explicit the inherent relationality of the Spirit who is God, who is in God, and who is God. In both cases, and perhaps in other, less influential threads of Christian tradition, the presupposition is that the biblical revelation is perfect, but that we need to develop it carefully if we are to speak responsibly in the doctrine of the Spirit. A broadly Nicene pneumatology that understands itself to be not improving on the form of words given in Scripture but rather to be offering conceptual paraphrases that equip us to grasp what we are reading is a pneumatology that establishes the big picture and keeps the most important things in the foreground.

Thirdness and the Spirit Who Was Always Already There

In concluding this discussion of the third person of the Trinity, we can offer a brief justification for treating the third person third; a defense, really, and in that sense an apology, of getting around to the Spirit last. It seems to me that speaking third of the Spirit is not a problem, but is in fact a long and healthy tradition in Christian theology. It is a tradition in which the main lines of the Christian confession are established first without a focus on the Holy Spirit. But when, in a later move, reflection on the Spirit is added to those main lines, a world of greater depth opens up, and the full glory of trinitarian soteriology shines forth. Nothing changes, but everything is better when pneumatology is explicated at last. A few key examples demonstrate this.

Consider the Creed of Nicaea, which in 325 labored to say the right thing about the relation of the Son to the Father. At the end of the creed, having elaborately affirmed that they believe in the Son, the fathers of Nicaea added the unimpressive phrase, "and in the Holy Spirit." Fifty-six turbulent years later when this creed was retrieved and expanded at Constantinople (381), this paltry third article blossomed forth into the confession we recite in the Nicene Creed today: I believe in the Holy Spirit, the Lord and giver of life, who proceeds from the Father, who is worshiped and glorified together with the Father and the Son, who spoke through the prophets. What shall we say happened when the Creed of Nicaea, with minimal explicit pneumatology, added the rich pneumatology of 381? Trinitarianism itself came into its own. The whole statement of faith became richer, fuller, and deeper. It is worth noting that the creed of 325 did not omit all mention of the Spirit. It said little rather than much, but it did say something. The tradition we are considering is one that initially says little about the Spirit, but then later says much.

Second, a parallel development can be seen in one of the greatest pro-Nicene fathers, Athanasius of Alexandria. Most of his theology is a relentless hammering home of the Nicene recognition of the full deity of the Son, consubstantial with the Father. He only occasionally mentions the Holy Spirit, and never as a focus of attention in his own right. Athanasius had message discipline, and the message was, Arianism is false. But then, at the request of Serapion of Thmuis, Athanasius wrote a series of letters explaining the person and work of the Holy Spirit, which amount to a brief treatise so powerful and integrated that it is hard to believe Athanasius had held all that understanding about the Spirit subliminally in his mind throughout the Arian crisis. What happens when the Christological Athanasius extends his attention to explicit discussion of the Holy Spirit? His work achieves a rounded trinitarian contour that is a wonder to behold. Perhaps contour is the wrong metaphor; the shape and form of Athanasian theology do not change, but drawing out the pneumatological depths transfigures everything he says.

Third, the structure of Calvin's *Institutes* shows a similar dynamic. For various reasons, Calvin postpones much discussion of the Spirit until book 3, when he asks how the salvation that the Father has worked out in Christ can become ours. His answer is faith, but then he climbs high into the mysterious workings of the Spirit, and expounds a practical pneumatology of magisterial power.

Rather than tracing out this tradition in later examples, I want to reach back to the sources and suggest, reverently, that Holy Scripture itself follows a similar pattern in several places. The gospel of Matthew reaches a first climax in chapter 11 when Jesus says that nobody knows the Father except the Son, and vice versa, but reaches a rounded conclusion in 28 when the risen Christ extends that formula to include the third person, the Holy Spirit, whose work he left implicit in chapter 11. John's gospel likewise expends considerable energy on the dyadic relation of the Word to God, and then of the Father to the Son, before turning sustained attention to the Holy Spirit around chapter 14 and especially 16. In Romans, Paul works out the righteousness of God and the propitiation in Christ before turning his attention fully to the Spirit in chapter 8, in which Romans reaches a doxological and kerygmatic highpoint. To end with the broadest possible gesture at the structure of the entire economy of salvation, the Spirit, never absent but often anonymous in the early phases of God's work, is conspicuous precisely at the New Testament fulfillment of God's promises, when his name and character and distinctive work come into their own and become a matter of proclamation and teaching.

The point is that while it is wrong to neglect the Holy Spirit, it is also wrong to belabor pneumatology in a distracting way, or to attempt to lay a pneumatological foundation in the first moves of systematic theology. There is a wise tradition of establishing the main lines of theology before drawing out the implicit pneumatological realities that have undeniably been at work all along. At least in the order of instruction, this seems to be a prudent way of working for pilgrim theologians instructing the church. Late in Thomas Goodwin's book *The Knowledge of God the Father and His Son Jesus Christ*, he admits that his whole project has a dyadic, not to say binitarian, ring. "There is a third person in the Godhead, the Spirit of God the Father, and of Christ; who in my handling the point will fall in, and appear to be that only true God, as well as these other two named."[23] As it turned out, the Spirit did in fact "fall in" to Goodwin's later handling, not only in that book but especially when, in a later book, he developed an extended pneumatology. If the Spirit had not fallen in, we would judge Goodwin's dyadic start differently in retrospect. But Goodwin was able to make his implicit pneumatology explicit. We should recognize that this sort of move, from an undeveloped pneumatology to a strong and elaborate one in a subsequent movement, happens all the time in Christian theology, and is commendable.

The only reason it works at all, however, is that the Spirit who we recognize third was also there from the beginning, as the very condition of the possibility

23. Thomas Goodwin, "The Knowledge of God the Father and His Son Jesus Christ," in *The Works of Thomas Goodwin*, vol. 4 (Edinburgh: James Nichol, 1862), 351.

of confessing truth about the Father and the Son. In 1 Corinthians 2:12 Paul says, "Now we have received not the spirit of the world, but the Spirit who is from God, that we might understand the things freely given us by God." Here Paul recognizes the constitutive role the Holy Spirit is always already playing in all theology, and pointing to the divine initiative in the Spirit playing that role: we have received the Spirit for the purpose of understanding what God has given. God has given something, and has also given the understanding of it. He has given that understanding as an abiding principle of our spiritual understanding.

In a beautiful passage, John Henry Newman appealed to this pneumatological emergence to account for the strange way that Christian theologians talk. They have before them a reality to which they are attempting to do justice, and their propositions, proofs, decisions, and arguments must be understood as attempts to account for that reality. Newman puts it this way:

> Though the Christian mind reasons out a series of dogmatic statements, one from another, this it has ever done, and always must do, not from those statements taken in themselves, as logical propositions, but as illustrated and (as I may say) inhabited by that sacred impression which is prior to them, which acts as a regulating principle, ever present, upon the reasoning, and without which no one has any warrant to reason at all. Such sentences as "the Word was God" or "the Only-begotten Son who is in the bosom of the Father," or "the Word was made flesh," or "the Holy Ghost which proceedeth from the Father," are not a mere letter which we may handle by the rules of art at our own will, but august tokens of most simple, ineffable, adorable facts, embraced, enshrined, according to its measure, in the believing mind.
>
> For though the development of an idea is a deduction of proposition from proposition, these propositions are ever formed in and round the idea itself (so to speak), and are in fact one and all only aspects of it. Moreover, this will account both for the mode of arguing from particular texts or single words of Scripture, practised by the early Fathers, and for their fearless decision in practising it; for the great Object of Faith on which they lived both enabled them to appropriate to itself particular passages of Scripture, and became a safeguard against heretical deductions from them. Also, it will account for the charge of weak reasoning, commonly brought against those Fathers; for never do we seem so illogical to others, as when we are arguing under the continual influence of impressions to which they are insensible.[24]

24. This long passage is quoted at the end of Andrew Louth's little book *Discerning the*

This is the Christian mind, the angle of approach from which pneumatology makes sense, and makes sense of Scripture. In pneumatology, the mind "inhabited by that sacred impression . . . which acts as a regulating principle, ever present" is both the presupposition of all statements and the object of them.

And this is why Paul prays, in Ephesians 1:17, that God would give to Christians "the Spirit of wisdom and of revelation," that is, that they would be subject to the work of the Spirit. Pneumatology is the doctrine in which the prayer for illumination becomes the subject.

We could call this gift of a spirit of wisdom and revelation an invisible mission of the Holy Spirit, a sending of the Spirit to illumine our understandings to know the deep things of God, which only the Spirit knows properly and by nature. John Webster calls this divine operation the work of illumination, and glosses the language of Ephesians 1:17 in his description of it: "What sets in motion creaturely apprehension of the gospel is God himself: the inner glory of God in its outward splendor, the inner wisdom of the Spirit who knows God's depths and is in himself infinitely wise, and who communicates this to creatures."[25] He describes the same pneumatological illumination also in these terms: "God so orders rational creatures that there is a creaturely coordinate to this omnipotent and omnipresent divine radiance. We are not simply bathed in light; it does not simply shine over us or upon us. Rather, it illuminates and so creates in creatures an active intelligent relation to itself."[26] That is the condition and goal of the doctrine about the third person of the Trinity: even today may our Christian minds receive this Spirit of wisdom and revelation in the knowledge of God.

Mystery (1983), and Louth's footnote places it in Newman's *Sermons, Chiefly on the Theory of Religious Belief, Preached Before the University of Oxford* (London, 1843), 335–36.

25. John Webster, "Illumination," in *The Domain of the Word: Scripture and Theological Reason* (London: T&T Clark, 2012), 61.

26. Webster, "Illumination," in *Domain of the Word*, 57.

Trinitarian Theology, Gospel Ministry, and Theological Education

THE TRINITY IS BIG. The doctrine of the Trinity is central to Christian theology and existence, and in turning our thoughts to it, we enter into an intellectual and academic act of worship, an act in which our rational souls magnify the triune Lord, because our spirits rejoice in God our savior (Luke 1:46). If the poor, bedraggled word *evangelical* still means anything—and it does—it picks out a Christian whose spirit knows to rejoice in God the savior. But how can a soul—a little part of God's creation—magnify, enlarge, expand on, or embiggen, its Lord? Following the guidance of the Magnificat, as we have begun to do here, we can answer: when the Lord does magnificent things, the lowly can magnify the Lord. In Mary's Magnificat, it is because the mighty one has done *megala*, great things, that the handmaid's soul responds with *megalynō*, making him great in the sense of declaring him great in her speech (Luke 1:46, 49).

Here is the secret of praise: the Lord moves mightily, the creature responds verbally, magnifying not just the deeds of the Lord, but the Lord of the deeds. This is the secret of praise, and praise is the secret of trinitarian theology. Helmut Thielicke said that the doctrine of the Trinity is a doxology using the means of thought.[1] In the incarnation of Christ and the outpouring of the Holy Spirit, God does the biggest thing he ever did outside the happy land of the Trinity, and the redeemed of the Lord say so. They say so by speaking of divinity; by speaking in orthodox doxology of trinitarian divinity. Trinitarianism is a response to God's self-revelation in the Father's sending of the Son and the Holy Spirit. So it is big. And so, let the praise of the triune God be continually in our mouths. "Oh, magnify the Lord with me, and let us exalt his name together" (Psalm 34:3).

---

1. Helmut Thielicke, *The Evangelical Faith*, vol. 2 (Grand Rapids: Eerdmans, 1977), 174.

CHAPTER 8

Persuasion for Deeper Commitment

In commending the ministry of evangelical trinitarian theology, I am commending something that evangelical Christian theologians already value. But I am undeterred. I want Christian theologians to take what they already possess, and already value, and be persuaded to hold it more dearly and to value it more highly. I hope it is possible to make theologians value an even greater trinitarianism, and to possess an even more evangelical trinitarianism.

The kind of rhetoric appropriate to this task is epideictic rhetoric. Epideictic rhetoric is a type of persuasion that intends "to bring about a deepening and reaffirmation of values already held in the present," as Colin Kruse says.[2] In the present: that is, it is not like judicial rhetoric, which looks back on an event and seeks to persuade the jury to make a determination about its justice, either prosecuting or defending. Nor is it like deliberative rhetoric, which looks forward to a course of action and urges an audience to undertake it or debates how to undertake it. Unlike these, epideictic or demonstrative rhetoric is about our current status. It is not engaged in judicially determining if the Trinity is right, nor deliberatively deciding how to perform or carry out something related to the Trinity. It is demonstratively deepening our commitment to, and appreciation of, the doctrine of the Trinity. If this kind of rhetoric seems familiar, it is because it is a kind of rhetoric found in the pages of the New Testament. As Colin Kruse says of the rhetoric of 1 John, "the author is not seeking to defend himself or persuade his hearers to take some course of action; rather, he is trying to increase their adherence to the traditional truths of the community."[3] And the main technique in the toolkit of epideictic rhetoric is amplification: the act of magnification. By techniques of repetition, augmentation, comparison, accumulation, itemization, and so on, amplification seeks to make the truth loom larger, and to let believers dwell deeper in it.

We do not seek to magnify the Trinity because it is measly and in need of magnification; rather we seek to magnify it because it is big. Precisely because it is big, the soul wants to magnify it. But trinitarian praise is an art, and there are many right ways and many wrong ways to do it. I have seen, and may have occasionally been guilty of, many of the wrong ways of seeking to make much of the Trinity. I would like to point out a few of the false moves that are sometimes made, if you will bear with these confessions of a Trinity salesman.

2. Colin G. Kruse, *The Letters of John* (Grand Rapids: Eerdmans, 2000), 29.
3. Kruse, *Letters*, 29.

One of the most pervasive, perennially alluring missteps in teaching on the Trinity is the one that pretends to make much of the Trinity while in fact making much of the trinitarian theologian. It is an error as insidious as it is subtle. Let me share a concrete example. A well-meaning interviewer once asked D. A. Carson the following question: "What elements of the doctrine of the Trinity are largely overlooked in substantial swaths of today's evangelicalism? And what are the practical implications of such neglect?" On the face of it, it's a fine question, a prompt for the professor to display his insight, to level a critique, and to point a way forward. But Carson seems to have heard the hiss of the serpent in the sibilant syllables of the interviewer, because his curt reply was, "the question is a bit cheeky." That is a great response. Carson is not just being pedantic or contrary. I don't picture him removing his glasses and rubbing his weary professorial eyes as he leans back in his chair and sighs, "Your question, young man, is so ill conceived and badly formulated that no possible answer could approximate verity. Class dismissed." No, in this case Carson hears an invitation to criticize the church from a superior position, and declines because the wrong answer might magnify the mighty theologian alongside the almighty God, and to give that answer would be to shirk his duty. Even the rebuke is mild: "the question is a bit cheeky." Well, it takes one to know one, because that answer is a bit cheeky. And so, cheek to cheek with his interlocutor, Carson gives a full answer:

> The question is a bit cheeky of course, since it assumes that much *is* wrong. All of us know fine evangelical churches that are carefully trying to teach the whole counsel of God. While majoring on biblical exposition, they are also enthusiastic about teaching sufficient historical and systematic theology to give their members a sense of the historical continuity and of the doctrinal heritage of the people of God.[4]

Here is a recognition that good churches are out there getting the work done. The people of God are gathering to worship the Father, the Son, and the Holy Spirit. They are hearing the word of God about Jesus Christ in the power of the Spirit. They are praying to the Father by the mediation of the Son and the intercession of the Spirit. Trinitarian things are happening; evangelical trinitarianism is thriving. Can these churches do better? Of course. Can a theologian help them? Yes. But not by crouching in a cave and joining in Eli-

---

4. "SBJT Forum: The Relevance of the Trinity," *Southern Baptist Journal of Theology* 10, no. 1 (Spring 2006): 92.

jah's lament: "I have been very jealous for the Lord, the God of hosts. For the people of Israel have forsaken your covenant, thrown down your altars, and killed your prophets with the sword, and I, even I only, am left, and they seek my life, to take it away" (1 Kgs 19:10). How did the Lord reply to this lament? By telling Elijah to go to Damascus and give his mantle to a younger prophet. He has seven thousand faithful followers in reserve who have not bowed the knee to the sub-trinitarian Baal. Prophets who complain too sweepingly about the faithlessness of the people are apparently, if not exactly disqualified thereby, at least showing that they are near the end of their tenure in the office. Theologians who imagine themselves to be the last, best hope of the church should consider the warning of this biblical story.

Could evangelical churches go on to a better understanding of what they are doing, and of what it has to do with God being the Trinity? They could and they should. And they may be summoned to that better understanding by the kind of preaching, teaching, and theologizing that has the character of filling in the gaps, strengthening the things that remain, and drawing out latent resources that are already familiar, connecting the dots that are already in place. Evangelical theologians ought to join the church in praising the Trinity. They say, "Magnify the Lord with me, and let us exalt his name together." Otherwise we theologians run the risk of compromising the health that is already in the members of the body. We ought to take a kind of theological equivalent of the old Hippocratic oath: first, do no harm. The fancy name for a disease you catch in the hospital, from the doctors and nurses, is iatrogenic. I fear there is a lot of theological iatrogenesis abroad these days. Too often when theologians think they can fix what ails the church, they do so not because they are impressed by the bigness of the Trinity, but impressed with themselves, or with the superiority of academic discourse to ecclesial discourse. Many theological critiques of the church seem to presuppose that what the church's culture needs is an infusion of health from academic culture. But academic culture, even among Christian academics, is not self-evidently healthy, nor are its ways routinely appropriate to God's church. Consider this danger of self-magnification. Have you ever reflected on the cultural implications of the fact that every academic, as a condition of entering the guild, has carried out an extensive review of literature with the goal of demonstrating to the gatekeepers that nobody else has ever said what they are going to say? Dissertations and journal articles ought to be rigorously original of course, or why bother writing them? A well-informed review of literature is a useful tool for identifying where meaningful work is to be done. But just picture the consequences of requiring everyone in the club to be a certified original. An outsider might have cause to be skeptical of their claims to be bringing a new and unheard-of word. Of course, academic life also provides ample invitations to humility: to admire the work of others, to confront your own limits and stupidity every time you sit down to write or stand up to speak. There is no need to be embarrassed of academic work, which can be good, honest labor and a chance to walk in the ways of the Lord. But profsplaining to the saints as if they were not immersed in trinitarian life is not the way forward. Of course, we ought to have even more reason for self-doubt if we have a book to sell, which has all the answers in it.[5]

ON THE SCOPE AND PLACE OF THE DOCTRINE OF THE TRINITY

So let us speak of divinity. The Trinity is so big that the size and significance of trinitarian doctrine is difficult to estimate. Where should such a doctrine even go in the table of contents of a systematic theology? Should it go right at the beginning, as the full statement of the identity of the God who theology is about? Yes. And yet, you can't say very much about the doctrine of the Trinity until you have met Christ and the Spirit, and have handled a great deal of material in the vast fields of Christology and pneumatology; at least their persons if not their work. And once you have brought up the incarnate Son and the outpoured Holy Spirit, you are doing soteriology. So you could insert the doctrine of the Trinity into the middle of a system, but that placement would be awkward. Yet the doctrine of the Trinity can't be put off until the denouement of salvation history, for fear that for the duration of the theological system there will be nothing but discussion of a divinity that has not yet been specified or identified until the end. But if you start the system with all the specifications of the divinity as the Father who sends the Son and Spirit, you have to presuppose on page one that the reader is already more or less in on the whole story. You would already have to be in on the story to get in on the story. So the beginning won't work, the middle won't work, and the end won't work. A theological system could handle the doctrine three different times, insisting that these three are one; or a system could simply resolve to elaborate the doctrine of the Trinity at each point along the way. This last option may sound enticing for readers who simply cannot get enough trinitarian theology, or cannot get theology to be trinitarian enough. But the virtue of conciseness

5. Fred Sanders, *The Triune God* (Grand Rapids: Zondervan, 2016).

would be utterly lost. Incessantly expounding trinitarianism in a system would make the point so elaborately that it would obscure the point.

And the point to be made is that the Trinity is big. The doctrine of the Trinity is the Christian doctrine of God developed on the basis of God's actions in salvation history. It is the Christian answer to the question, "Who is God?" developed by reference to God's mighty acts, and chiefly the Father's sending of the Son and the Holy Spirit. The doctrine of the Trinity takes up the entire unified, coherent economy of salvation, and considers it against the background of God's own eternal being. It correlates God's identity with his free and gracious self-giving in the history of salvation. It refuses to treat salvation history as a series of discrete episodes of intervention, instead insisting that it is a comprehensive economy, carried out by God in all wisdom and insight, to save us by being himself for us, by being among us and for our salvation what he is in himself (and would have been without us), and to make himself known in the Father's sending of the Son and the Holy Spirit because the one God is, from eternity to eternity, the Father, the Son, and the Holy Spirit. It takes the whole Bible to make this point. In fact, you can picture the rise of the church's confession of trinitarian doctrine as the result of reading the full canon of Scripture left to right, Old Testament to New Testament, and then pursuing the question, "If these promises, and this gospel, go together and are true, what must we say about who the one God is?" If we say he is the God of the Bible's gospel, we have to say he is the One God who gave his Son because he has a Son—there is no Sonless God. He sent his Spirit because he has a Spirit—there is no Spiritless God. Commitment to the gospel of the Bible's God leads to praise of the God of the Bible's gospel.

We could go around that Bible-gospel-God circle many more times by way of amplification and magnification. Rehearsing the mutual entanglement of the canonical, the evangelical, and the theological is worthwhile work. But we have said enough to show that the doctrine of the Trinity is not just any doctrine. It is the doctrine of doctrines, a uniquely holistic and comprehensive confession. But to estimate the scope of the doctrine of the Trinity aright, and to locate it properly, we must find a way to describe it in a less external manner. Our musings about where to locate the doctrine in a systematic theology have a strangely extrinsic and formal sound to them, and the doctrine of the Trinity has a size and significance difficult to estimate from the outside. But there is a precise sense in which we are never quite speaking about the persons of the Trinity from outside. Discourse about the trinitarian persons is necessarily always discourse about God's internal self-relatedness. Here is what I mean. We are speaking of divinity, and can do so only because Scripture speaks of divinity. Augustine helpfully points out that in Scripture, "not everything that is said of [God] is said substance-wise. Some things are said [relation-wise], with reference to something else, like 'Father' with reference to 'Son' and 'Son' with reference to 'Father.'"[6] Note that by "relation-wise," Augustine is not pointing to God's relation to the world of creatures. That is because God's relation to things outside himself is never a symmetrical or equally reciprocal relation. It has to be what scholastics called a "mixed" relation, since the creature could not possibly exist without reference to that relation, but God, on the contrary, could exist and be fully himself without that relation. So the kind of relation Augustine is pointing out is an unmixed, eternal, internal relation. If we speak of those, we are truly speaking of divinity relation-wise, which is to say that we are speaking of the Trinity.

This is precisely how the doctrine of the Trinity was handled in systematic theology in the days of Protestant scholasticism. Recall seventeenth-century Lutheran theologian Johannes Quenstedt's instrucation that

> the consideration of God is twofold, one absolute, another relative. The former is occupied with God considered essentially, without respect to the three persons of the Godhead; the latter, with God considered personally. The former explains both the essence and the essential attributes of God; the latter describes the persons of the holy Trinity.[7]

Meanwhile, in the same century, Reformed theologian Francis Turretin said that "the absolute consideration of God (as to his nature and attributes) begets the relative (as to persons)."[8] For Turretin and company, the turn from absolute to relative simply is the turn from the doctrine of the one God to the doctrine of the triune God.

Those scholastics bring an appropriate coolness and abstraction to the difficult task of trinitarian theology. They specify rather surgically the sense in which our statements about the persons are statements about an insideness of God. But we could approach the insight from a more soteriological angle, and phrase it in a more evangelical idiom. In an essay entitled "Out of the Box: The Christian Experience of God in Trinity," Anglican theologian Gerald Bray says that knowledge of the Trinity is "inside knowledge." "Christians," he says,

---

6. Augustine, *De Trinitate* 5.6.

7. Quenstedt, cited in Heinrich Schmid, *The Doctrinal Theology of the Evangelical Lutheran Church* (Minneapolis: Augsburg, 1889), 134.

8. Turretin, *Institutes of Elenctic Theology*, vol. 1 (Phillipsburg, NJ: P&R Publishing, 1992), 254.

"have been admitted to the inner life of God . . . the God who appears as one to those who view him on the outside, reveals himself as a Trinity of persons, once his inner life is opened up to our experience. The Christian doctrine that has resulted from this is nothing more nor less than a description of what that experience of God's inner life is like."[9] To follow Scripture in speaking of divinity substance-wise is to speak from the outside, "absolutely considered." To follow Scripture in speaking of divinity relation-wise is to bring personal distinctions into our view, to speak from the inside, "relatively considered."

Seventeenth-century theologians saw this distinction as one that was implicit in a wide range of Scripture's own expressions. To take one concise example, John Davenant reads Colossians 1:3, "we give thanks to God and the Father of our Lord Jesus Christ" in this way: "He is described as well by his absolute name, that is, God; as by his relative title, that, the Father of Christ. The apostle employs both with the best design."[10] The same distinction, which theologians learned from Scripture, is one of the things at work in John 1:3, where the Word was with God and was God: one way to parse the Word's simultaneous withness and wasness, his being-with and his being, his distinction and identity, is as a case of essential and relative predication. The Word in terms of relation was *with*; in terms of essence, or described absolutely, the word *was*.

I hope that in this project of trinitarian salesmanship, I have not made the doctrine seem cheap. It is no good to offer discounts on a doctrine so vast and comprehensive. On the contrary, I am commending it as the treasure buried in the field of salvation history, and passing along an insider tip that you would be wise to sell all your hermeneutical belongings in order to lay hold of this great treasure. It is not just another doctrine, but the one that sums up the economy of salvation, the whole counsel of God, and the identity of the God of the gospel. How could it be cheap if it runs through the whole economy? It truly is "too big to fail."

Two-Handed Theology

In the task of propagating and encouraging evangelical trinitarianism, it is wise to emphasize the close relationship of the Trinity to the gospel. Evangelicals are

9. Gerald Bray, "Out of the Box: The Christian Experience of God in Trinity," in *God the Holy Trinity: Reflections on Christian Faith and Practice*, ed. Timothy George (Grand Rapids: Baker Academic, 2006), 45–46.

10. John Davenant, *An Exposition of the Epistle of St. Paul to the Colossians* (London: Hamilton, Adams, and Co., 1832), 55.

gospel people (it's in the name), so that means evangelical trinitarianism will be characteristically gospel trinitarianism. First, a word of caution: we do not want evangelical trinitarianism to be so distinctive from "mere trinitarianism" that it is a different thing after all. I'm reminded of a Lutheran theologian who said, "There is, thank God, no specific Lutheran doctrine on the Trinity."[11] And I could concur: there is, thank God, no specific evangelical doctrine on the Trinity, one that would be distinguished as a different doctrine than the normal Christian doctrine. But we may speak that shared doctrine with a characteristic accent, or walk its path with a telling limp. Certainly we want it to be truly ours, cultivated in our churches rather than shipped in from across town; really appropriated, and if not homemade then at least own-made.

To that end, it is always worthwhile to trace some of the many links between the Trinity and the ministry of the gospel. Just as we have seen that the revelation of God's triunity comes to us from God's side, that is, the inside, and that our speech about the Trinity is a reference to internal relations, we want to speak of divinity by pursuing this theme: that the gospel is God the Trinity opening up his life of fellowship to share it with us. So we come to an internal approach to gospel ministry.

Authentic gospel ministry is never without the Trinity; it is always within the Trinity. Every element of gospel ministry can be fruitfully analyzed to show its trinitarian depth. The crucial analytical question to ask is never simply, "Where can I find the number three in this?" The crucial analytical question is always, "What are the Son and the Holy Spirit doing in this ministry?" Trinitarian analysis of gospel ministry is more a matter of counting to two than to three. Because the Son and the Spirit are the sent persons, whose sending constitutes the economy of salvation and revelation, they are the persons to watch. The sending Father is available to us, active toward us, and engaged with us, in the twofold mission of the Son and Spirit. We do not look to the sky to wait for the coming of the Father; he always sends and is never sent. Irenaeus of Lyons used a homey illustration of this twofold sending: he talked about the Father's two hands. When gnostics said God was too high to touch the world, delegating it rather to angelic intermediaries, Irenaeus replied, "God the Father is never without his two hands, the Son and the Spirit."[12] The image should of course not be taken literally. As Didymus the Blind said, "Be careful not to descend to lowly things, forget what we are discussing, and thereby depict in

11. Hermann Sasse, quoted in Carl L. Beckwith, *The Holy Trinity: Confessional Lutheran Dogmatics*, vol. 3 (Ft. Wayne, IN: The Luther Academy, 2016), xi.
12. Irenaeus, *Against Heresies* 4.20:1.

your mind a variety of bodily limbs and begin to imagine to yourselves their sizes, their inequalities, and other body parts."[13] By hand, Irenaeus means agency, personal presence, and effective power. By calling the Son and Holy Spirit the Father's two hands, Irenaeus draws our attention to the differentiated unity of God's work. In doctrinal terms, this Irenaean two-handedness can be described as the constant correlation of Christology and pneumatology. It is remarkable how much the New Testament vision of ministry opens up to our understanding when we direct careful attention to the distinguishable and coordinated work of the Son and the Holy Spirit. And it is equally remarkable how much the Father's presence and power are discernible in the work of his two emissaries, because to be in the grip of Christ and the Spirit is to belong to God the Father.

Many modern theologians have noted the wisdom of this "two-handed" approach to theology. The late Ralph Del Colle, for example, wrote that "Christ and the Spirit are God's way into the depths of the human condition, the divine grip, so to speak, upon our fragile and tenuous reality. To know this, to realize that one is in the grasp of divine knowing, is the beginning of all Christian theology."[14] Irenaeus's image is a helpful clue to indicate the essential unity (one God) and hypostatic diversity (three persons) of divine action, and the need of systematic theology to recognize that unity of trinitarian action by distinguishing Son and Spirit precisely in order to affirm their inseparability. The classic Augustinian rule holds that "the external acts of the Trinity are undivided,"[15] and the equally classic Cappadocian way of saying it is that every action of God is an action from the Father, through the Son, in the Holy Spirit.[16] The Irenaean image offers a different strategy for articulating

13. Didymus the Blind, *On the Holy Spirit* (Yonkers, NY: St. Vladimir's Seminary Press, 2011), 171.

14. Del Colle, *Christ and the Spirit: Spirit Christology in Trinitarian Perspective* (Oxford, 1994), vii.

15. "*Opera ad extra indivisa*," but see Henri Blocher's fuller quotation of the neglected context, "*servato discrimine et ordine personarum*," "the distinction of the persons being preserved." Blocher, "Immanence and Transcendence in Trinitarian Theology," in *The Trinity in a Pluralistic Age: Theological Essays on Culture and Religion*, ed. Kevin Vanhoozer (Grand Rapids: Eerdmans, 1997), 120.

16. Based on a loose reading of their more interpersonal idiom, the Cappadocians are sometimes wrongly interpreted as teaching that the three persons are distinct agents who cooperate, rather than three persons with inseparable power and operation. Lewis Ayres dismantles this misreading in "On Not Three People: The Fundamental Themes of Gregory of Nyssa's Trinitarian Theology as Seen in *To Ablabius: On Not Three Gods*," *Modern Theology* 18, no. 4 (October 2002): 445–74.

the same dynamic: God has two hands, and always uses both of them. If God the Father is ambidextrous, theologians ought to be similarly two-handed in describing his work.

One of the benefits of the modern revival of scholarly interest in the doctrine of the Trinity is that pneumatology and Christology have increasingly pressed themselves into the foreground of systematic theology as two doctrines that need to be treated together. But before they can be treated together, their distinctness must be recognized. The two doctrinal areas have their own distinctive conceptualities and vocabularies, and can even be described as following different, relatively independent grammars.

The scriptural witness presents the Son and the Spirit in distinctive ways, using different terms and different narrative patterns. Alert readers are rarely at risk of confusing the Son and the Spirit in the New Testament. Broadly speaking, the Son of God makes his personal, direct entrance into salvation history at the incarnation, while the Spirit makes his at Pentecost, and they are present on their mission from the Father in obvious ways. The mandate to speak differently about the Son and the Spirit arises directly from Scripture's own way of speaking of them.

The developed doctrines of pneumatology and Christology draw on these different biblical witnesses in diverse ways, and were ramified in the history of doctrine according to different patterns of conflict and clarification: Christology was the focus of major ecumenical councils, while pneumatology was less contested in the disputes that led up to those conciliar judgments. But in the fourth century, and especially in the Niceno-Constantinopolitan Creed of 381, we have one clear indication that the church fathers were intentional about developing distinct vocabularies for the Son and the Spirit. The second article of the Nicene Creed famously describes the Son as *homoousios*, "of the same essence," with the Father. He is true God from true God, light from light, the only-begotten of the Father. When in 381 the Council of Constantinople took up the creed of 325 and expanded the third article, they chose not to apply the same language to the third person of the Trinity. There are numerous historical and even political reasons for this, and the dispute between Gregory of Nazianzus and Basil of Caesarea is well documented. But the final decision reflects a commitment to treat the Holy Spirit in a way that did not simply fold him under Christological categories. Their task was to assert the full divinity of the Spirit, but they sought and found new language for it: he is Lord and giver of life, he is worshipped along with the Father and Son, he proceeds from the Father. This language is strikingly not parallel to the language used of the Son in the second article: the fathers at Constantinople did not affirm that the

Spirit is *homoousios* (though he cannot possibly be of another *ousia*), or even that he is "light from light" (though it is easy to imagine how this language could be applied to the Spirit in an entirely orthodox sense). The Nicene Creed does not even provide us with a common term to apply to the two ways the Son and the Spirit come from the Father: one is begotten, the other proceeds, but we have no Nicene verb for what both do, and no corresponding noun like "procession" to cover them both. This Nicene insistence on recognizing difference, this refusal to enfold Son and Spirit under common vocabularies, is a guideline that two-handed theology attempts to follow. We may call both the Son and the Spirit hands, but the metaphor is so obviously broken that the emphasis can fall on the recognition that the Father has two different hands.

Yet for all this distinction, the action of the two hands is inseparable, and to develop either without attending to the other leads to serious distortion. The inseparability of the work of the Son and the Spirit in the economy of salvation is grounded in their eternal identities as persons of the Trinity. The Son and Spirit do not meet for the first time in the economy of salvation (for instance at Jesus's baptism in the Jordan, or even in his conception by the Spirit in the womb of the virgin), but have known each other from of old. They do not need to work out or achieve the collaboration and correlation of their missions, because their missions into salvation history are grounded in their eternal processions, processions from the Father that constitute the one life of the one living God. In the order of being, the Son and Spirit are eternally distinct and united in the immanent Trinity, "neither confounding the persons nor dividing the substance," and they enact that mysteriously differentiated unity in the economy of salvation. What they carry out here below in their concerted, correlated activity, is the economic correlate of perichoresis, the mutual in-being of the three persons. They are not even theoretically separable, but have their personal being always already in relation to each other, and with an internal and constitutive configuration toward the other and toward the Father. Their united action has a greater unity, a deeper or higher unity, than we can observe among merely created things, for they are one with the unity of God. So theology must do what it can to recognize and describe that sort of unity, and that sort of distinction, in the economy of salvation as it images the immanent being of God.

As two-handed systematic theology undertakes that project, it will be rewarded all along its course because both doctrines, Christology and pneumatology, are integral, pervasive, and structural components of any well-articulated systematic theology. That is, the subject matter of these doctrines informs every other doctrinal locus in Christian dogmatics. For this reason, in two-handed theology the foundational doctrines are those of Christ and the Spirit; the other doctrines are built up from that foundation. John Webster has asserted that "there is only one Christian doctrine, the doctrine of the Holy Trinity in its inward and outward movements. . . . All other doctrines are simply extensions of teaching about God and God's works."[17]

One more methodological observation about this ambidextrous approach to systematic theology. It is an attempt to be more thoroughly and consistently trinitarian in an entire doctrinal system, rather than just in the doctrine of the Trinity proper. It is a strategy for exporting trinitarian values and decisions into the entire system. But in its formulation it may strike some as frustratingly non-triadic. It says "two" more often that it says "three." In particular, it may seem to either promote the Father above the level of his two hands, or it may seem to ignore and marginalize the Father, as if we have nothing to do with him but only his two hands. Those would indeed both be terminal errors of doctrine and of emphasis. But following out the Irenaean image is precisely an attempt to frustrate the overly geometric sense of the importance of triadic structures in doing trinitarian theology. It is certainly true that "these three are one," but the background image of a triangle can work serious mischief in flattening out the revealed differences among the three persons. If the persons of the Trinity are not a man with two hands (and they are, one hopes, self-evidently not), they are also not three points in a geometric plane. The two-hands schema emphasizes the fact that the Father always sends but is never sent, and is not directly present in the economy of salvation. If we have immediate access to the Father, it is a mediated immediacy, a paradoxical presence through Son and Spirit. We have no desire to ignore the first person of the Trinity, but we also refuse to treat the neglected doctrine of the first person (patrology?) as parallel to the doctrines of the co-missioned Son and Spirit. Our position is that of H. C. G. Moule, who said of the doctrine of the Father that

> On this most sacred region of truth much is best said under the Doctrine of the Son, and that of the Spirit. The study of Their revealed glory, always related to that of the Father, who is Their fountain, best illustrates His. And thus, on the other hand, the Christian will always aim, not occasionally, but in deep purpose, in the study of Them, to study Him. All we know of Them is revealed, ultimately, "to the glory of God the Father" (Phil 2:11).[18]

17. Webster, "Principles of Systematic Theology," unpublished essay, 68.
18. H. C. G Moule, *Outlines of Christian Doctrine* (London: Hodder & Stoughton, 1907), 31.

PNEUMATOLOGICAL CHRISTOLOGY AND
CHRISTOLOGICAL PNEUMATOLOGY

If God is ambidextrous, what are we to make of the church's long habit of Christocentrism? It would seem that a God who uses both his hands equally well would have two foci, like an ellipse, rather than one center, like a circle. Does the very notion of Christocentrism compromise the project of two-handed theology; even more, does it suggest a deficient Trinitarian theology, in which the Son gets top billing and the Spirit serves at best as a warm-up act?

Perhaps the elliptical approach is right. Along these lines, we might appeal to the importance of Pentecost, as a coequal moment alongside the incarnation, crucifixion, and resurrection of Christ. In fact, we will do just that in the next section. But we might also insist that to be Christocentric is in no way to detract from the person and work of the Holy Spirit—that in fact the Spirit's role in the economy of salvation involves him drawing our attention to Christ as the center of salvation. We might, that is, underscore the pneumatological character of Christology.

The Holy Spirit signals Jesus's origin from the Father at his baptism. As he began his public career, Jesus submitted to the baptism of John, at which time he heard the Father's acclaiming voice: "This is my beloved Son, with whom I am well pleased." The Father signaled his pleasure in—and claim on—his Son by sending his Spirit "like a dove . . . to rest on him" (Matt 3:17, 16). The Spirit identified Jesus as his Father's Son before the world at his baptism. The one conceived by the Spirit is now anointed by the Spirit and just so called and sent by the Spirit on his mission to the cross. Immediately after his baptism, "Jesus was led by the Spirit into the wilderness to be tempted by the devil" (Matt 4:1). Here, perhaps surprisingly, we see the Spirit as the leader of Jesus's mission, the one who directs, instructs, and empowers him as he faithfully recapitulates Israel's history in himself. Where God led his people out of Egypt, only to watch them career into idolatry, the Spirit led Jesus out of the waters of baptism and throughout his faithful life of self-offering in which he was holy and pleasing to God.

After his time of testing, the incarnate Son announces that the Spirit is upon him, having anointed him to proclaim the good news of the kingdom—the present promise of divine favor for the poor, the captive, the blind and the oppressed (Luke 4:18–19). Because Jesus casts out demons by the Spirit of God, the people can know that God's kingdom has come among them (Matt 12:28). The Spirit is the source, sign, and strength of Jesus's ministry.

While the Gospels are quieter about the Spirit's role as Jesus draws near to the cross, we can borrow from Augustine's description of the Spirit as the "bond of love" between Father and Son and infer the Spirit's work to tether Father and Son as the Son ventures ever further into the far country. Jesus entrusts his life to the Father in the power of the Spirit, and the Spirit enables Jesus to do the work of the Father. Perhaps this forms the backdrop to Jesus's exhortation to the disciples: "When they deliver you over, do not be anxious how you are to speak or what you are to say, for what you are to say will be given to you in that hour. For it is not you who speak, but the Spirit of your Father speaking through you" (Matt 10:19–20).

If the Father always works with his hands, and if one of his hands lies buried in the grave, it is safe to assume that he uses the other hand—the Holy Spirit—to raise the first, the Son from the dead. And we might expect the Spirit of life, the one in whom the incarnate Son was conceived, to be, too, the Spirit of resurrection.

Again, we cannot have Jesus without the Spirit. Without the Spirit, the person and work of Christ are locked into first-century Palestine. This is why, in perhaps the strangest verse in the Bible, Jesus tells his disciples that "it is to your advantage that I go away, for if I do not go away, the Helper will not come to you. But if I go, I will send him to you" (John 16:7). How does he help? By bearing witness about Jesus (John 15:26), by glorifying Jesus and taking what is his and declaring it to those who belong to him (John 16:14–15).

The Holy Spirit does more than tutor us in the way of Jesus. He bears witness to us about Jesus by dwelling in us as the Spirit of Christ. Because we have the Spirit, we have Christ and the promise of life in him. "If the Spirit of him who raised Jesus from the dead dwells in you, he who raised Christ Jesus from the dead will also give life to your mortal bodies through his Spirit who dwells in you" (Rom 8:11). The Spirit's witness to Christ and his indwelling presence unite as the Spirit "bears witness with our spirit that we are children of God, and if children, then heirs—heirs of God and fellows heirs with Christ, provided that we suffer with him in order that we may also be glorified with him" (Rom 8:16–17). The Father makes us sons in the Son by sealing us with the Spirit of adoption by whom we cry out, "Abba! Father!" (Rom 8:15).

As sons, the Son includes us in his Spirit-anointed, Spirit-directed mission to draw all people to himself. This reliance on a community of famously unreliable disciples can only be explained in the light of the power and authority of the Holy Spirit, the one who makes the Son the Son and us sons, too.

Turning to Christological pneumatology, Del Colle called for a Christology whose "dynamism must proceed from a robust pneumatology,"[19] and the

---

19. Del Colle, *Christ and the Spirit*, vii.

logical correlate of that project would be a pneumatology that proceeds from a robust Christology. Such an approach is not as rare as a pneumatological Christology: we have more examples of tethering the Spirit to Christ than of vice versa. The tether is crucial: it is worth rehearsing why we can never have the Spirit without the Son. The Holy Spirit is the Spirit of Christ: the Spirit of the incarnate, crucified, risen Son. His Pentecostal outpouring is the flip side of Christ's ascension and session. No Christian pneumatology can be an end run around, or an alternative to, Christ, and Christ's exclusivity and finality are not dissolved in the freedom of the Spirit. God has spoken in many ways, but in these last days he has spoken through his Son. If we can only hear the Son by means of the Spirit, we nevertheless do not hear another or a different word. The Spirit is not another word of God, but the breath in which the one word is heard. Word articulates breath, breath empowers word (Irenaeus). To put it another way, there is one way to the Father, and that way is Christ. If we can only walk that way by the Spirit, the Spirit is nevertheless not another way.

But that tether is traditionally in place, and having affirmed it we should also explore how the Holy Spirit's economy not only serves the Son's but is also served by the Son's. We can relate the work of the Spirit to the work of the Son not just as salvation accomplished and applied, but also as means to end: the atoning work of the Son is the means to the end of the Spirit's indwelling. If the problem God poses in the Old Testament is, How can the Spirit of the holy God dwell among the sinful people? the answer in the New Testament is, incarnation and atonement. For God to indwell humanity, God will have to take humanity to himself, assume human nature. For the holy to dwell among the sinful, sin will have to be atoned for, purged, purified. Atonement serves indwelling. Christ purifies the temple so that the Spirit can indwell it. The economy of the Spirit serves that of the Son, and the economy of the Son also serves the Spirit. They serve each other, each ministers to the other, they mutually co-minister. There is one economy constituted by two missions, a complex twofold mission, a co-mission: perhaps the Great Co-Mission.

Gospel Ministry with Both Hands

The history of salvation and the order of salvation are, as we have already described, centered on the work of Christ and the Spirit. Galatians 4:4–6 says, "when the fullness of time had come, God sent forth his Son, born of a woman, born under the law, to redeem those who were under the law, so that we might receive adoption as sons. And because you are sons, God has sent the Spirit of his Son into our hearts, crying, 'Abba! Father!'" Turning his attention from the history of salvation to its application in an order of salvation, and even to the personal experience that flows from these objective realities, John Wesley sketched a trinitarian soteriology by saying that "justification implies what God does for us through his Son, sanctification what he works in us by his Spirit."[20] A trinitarian soteriology would be a two-handed doctrine of salvation that attended to the pervasive presence of the Son and the Holy Spirit across this whole span from the *historia salutis*, through the *ordo salutis*, to the shape of a Christian life that follows from them. Though much has been written on the implications of trinitarian soteriology, it continues to be a rich field for exploration.

But look at the two-handedness, the Son-and-Spirit reciprocity, of mission and evangelism. The great Protestant missions movement, especially in its evangelical phase, made much of the great commission, which is the risen Christ's command to go into all the world and make disciples. Jesus commanded his disciples to go and make disciples. And in Matthew's theology, that commission is based on the fact that Jesus, God with us, has been given all authority and is with us to the end. But for most of Christian history, the church's proclamation of the gospel, even across cultural boundaries, was not footnoted to Matthew 28, but to Acts 2. At most times and places, Pentecost drove missions, and if asked why they were going out to testify, Christians would answer that they were equipped by the Spirit to bear witness.[21] Just as Luke and Matthew are both canonical gospels, both rationales for mission are valid. A two-handed, trinitarian approach to mission draws its power from the Spirit poured out on all flesh, who was not given until Christ ascended. The Son and the Spirit are not competing missions agencies; you can't have one without the other, nor the Father without them both, nor them without the Father.[22] For this reason, Christ, who is with us to the end of the age (so Matthew) is present precisely by the agency of the Spirit (so Luke). No wonder, then, that he commanded us to baptize disciples in the one name of the three persons: Father, Son, and Holy Spirit.

Christian discipleship, unsurprisingly, also bears this Son-Spirit character. When Jesus called disciples, they literally followed him down the road, one

20. John Wesley, "Justification by Faith" (Sermon 5), in *John Wesley's Standard Sermons* (Salem, OH: Schmul Publishing, 1988), 45.

21. Harry R. Boer, *Pentecost and Missions* (Grand Rapids: Eerdmans, 1961).

22. See Timothy C. Tennent, *Invitation to World Missions: A Trinitarian Missiology for the Twenty-First Century* (Grand Rapids: Kregel, 2010), for a trinitarian arrangement of the theology of missions.

foot after another. They went where he went. After the ascension, that kind of following is no longer the order of the day: "where I go you cannot go." Since Jesus went up and the Spirit came down, to be led by the Spirit is to follow the Son of God—indeed, so closely as to be conformed to the image of the Son. Tracing this transition between following Jesus before and after the ascension/Pentecost juncture, Allen Coppedge has called Christians "disciples of the Trinity."[23]

This sketch of a two-handed grasp of salvation, mission, and discipleship already gives us the broad outlines of a trinitarian ecclesiology. There is more to say about the being of the church as the body of Christ, the temple of the Spirit, and therefore the people of God. Two voluminous conversations in the twentieth century treated ecclesiology under the headings of communion ecclesiology and *missio Dei* ecclesiology. As we saw above in chapter 4, they are not irreconcilable, nor mutually exclusive. A trinitarian theology that emphasizes the missions of Son and Spirit may tend more obviously toward an ecclesiology that views the church as a creature or instrument of those missions, caught up and carried along by God's own movement in the world. But communion ecclesiology is of course not without its organic connections to the Christological and pneumatological missions. The key point is that both of these major modern ecclesiological motifs are thickly trinitarian, and both require an elaborate account of Son-Spirit reciprocity as the divine work underlying them.

We are describing authentic gospel ministry as never without, but always within, the Trinity by accounting for the two hands of God, and feeling ourselves surrounded by the Trinity. We are only looking at a few key doctrines that make that conspicuous, while hinting that every doctrine repays two-handed analysis. One more doctrine will show us to be fully and truly surrounded, completely held in the Father's two hands. That doctrine is eschatology. The angle of approach should once again be salvation-historical, by way of reflection on the presence of Christ and the Spirit. In the days of Christ's earthly ministry, the Spirit was on him fully, but was not yet given out, that is, was not yet poured out on all flesh in fulfillment of Joel 2, on the basis of his finished work. The Spirit of Pentecost is the unchanging third person of the Trinity, but his coming at Pentecost was an incursion of trinitarian action into the course of salvation history as unique, personal, and time-stamped as the incarnation of the second person. Just as we mark time BC and AD, we could

---

23. Allan Coppedge, *The God Who is Triune: Revisioning the Christian Doctrine of God* (Downers Grove, IL: IVP Academic, 2007), 36–52.

mark it on a pneumatological calendar as before and after Pentecost. The Spirit, who Christ referred to as "another helper," did not come until Christ ascended and sat at the Father's right hand. That is, he did not come until Jesus "went away," in John's idiom. In terms of their epochal personal presences, Christ was personally present first, before the Spirit came. Then after Christ went away, the Spirit came. In this age, Christ is present to us precisely by the Spirit. The Spirit is not his replacement; their reciprocal absences cannot be explained on any sort of modalistic conversion of one into the other (of the sort that would account for Clark Kent and Superman's coordinated absences). What is at work here is a two-handed trinitarian back-and-forth of inaugurated eschatology: the finality of the Messiah's realized eschatological coming is being superintended by the indwelling Pentecostal Spirit who is an earnest of our future inheritance, groaning within us on the way to future eschatology. As Lord of the inaugurated kingdom, the Holy Spirit is the life-giver to our spirits now and to our bodies then, in the consummation. But when Christ returns, he will not "trade places" with the Spirit again. The Helper and the other Helper will both be with us in their properly personal presences. The fulfillment of God's presence in the eschaton will be characterized by a double presence for which the coordinated single presences have prepared us. As Basil of Caesarea said, "Any intelligent man realizes that the work of the Holy Spirit will not cease, as some imagine, when the Lord makes his long-awaited return from heaven. On the contrary, the Holy Spirit will be present with Him on the day of His revelation, when He will judge the universe in righteousness as its only Ruler."[24] With characteristic attention to the theological significance of prepositions, Basil affirmed that Christ rules *by* the Spirit now, but will rule *with* the Spirit then. Basil did not say much more about this, and neither should we. This is not the kind of eschatology that fits well on a chart, or that is subject to detailed narration. But a glorious trinitarian future awaits us, and we would not expect to be able to picture it.

THE DISPOSITION OF EVANGELICAL TRINITARIANISM

I hope the vigor and promise of evangelical trinitarianism, marked by a two-handedness in its integration of Christology and pneumatology, is evident from this brief sketch. I would like to draw out two implications for theological education. The second will concern how the various theological disciplines

24. Basil the Great, *On the Holy Spirit* 16.40.

relate to each other. The first has to do with the arrangement of the material that makes up the biblical doctrine of the Trinity itself. For lack of a better term, I call this the doctrine's *disposition*, meaning thereby to indicate how the material is disposed or arranged (which is what classical rhetoric called an argument's *dispositio*).

In brief presentations of the doctrine of the Trinity, we can observe two different dispositions of the material. On the one hand the main terms can be laid out in a kind of genetic or developmental way, introducing the three persons in a salvation-historical framework that leads with the Father, then adds the Son, and finally (after a brief historical account of the work of the Son) introduces the Holy Spirit. In order to meet all three persons and grasp their unity, the student has to follow the whole exposition. We could call this disposition the Nicene style, because its classic formulation is the Nicene Creed of 381 (though the Apostles' Creed also follows this format). On the other hand the material is sometimes laid out with a kind of static or equilateral disposition, one that offers the word *Trinity* as an advance organizer and then introduces the three persons all in the same line: Father, Son, and Holy Spirit. We could call this style the Quicunquan style, after the so-called Athanasian so-called creed (whose famous opening words are *quicunque vult*, "whoever will"). There is no question of the two dispositions contradicting each other. They are different dispositions of the same doctrine, not two distinct doctrines. The Nicene Creed and the Athanasian Creed do not disagree on the triunity of God. Each delivers the same material, but they pursue different strategies of presentation. The Nicene style is more narrative, the Quicunquan more schematic. And each has its own advantages and disadvantages.

The Nicene style has the advantage of drawing out the natural connections between the persons of the Trinity, which means it jumps off of the history of salvation and then leads with the material content of the relations of origin. "I believe in one God, the Father Almighty, Maker of heaven and earth," it begins, as if that were the whole story. Then it introduces another character who it says has been there the whole time: "one Lord Jesus Christ, the only-begotten Son of God, begotten of the Father before all worlds; God of God, Light of Light, very God of very God; begotten, not made, being of one substance with the Father, by whom all things were made." To understand this, the reader must mentally return to the beginning and rethink what it meant for God the Father to be the maker of heaven and earth. Apparently, God the Father neither made everything by himself nor existed by himself. "Father" must have always implied "Son," as it turns out, though the Nicene style's strategy is not to say so up front. Once it introduces the Son, however, it gives him the lion's share of attention. The center of the creed is a thumbnail sketch of the gospel story, the life of Christ. Finally we meet a third character, the Holy Spirit, who is not only "the Lord" but is also the "Giver of Life," is to be worshiped, and who "proceeds from the Father." The Nicene style demands that you follow the discursive line of exposition to see what emerges, and then mentally go back and insert the conclusion as the presupposition that was silently there all along. Because of this structure, the Nicene style underwrites long-form expositions that are great for rereading. The creed itself (like the Apostles' Creed) functions especially well in liturgical repetition, because it benefits from a synchronic-diachronic dialectic that is best experienced repeatedly. But above all, the Nicene style rehearses biblical history in a way that draws the eternal implications for God's being. That is, it arranges itself around the temporal missions and the eternal processions that ground them.

The Nicene disposition of the material sometimes draws criticism for being inadequately trinitarian, because it does not connect the dots or say the word *Trinity*. Instead of putting the three persons of the Trinity as close together as possible, it intersperses many other words, entire other doctrines, in between the occurrences of the personal names. Even more astonishingly, the Nicene disposition sometimes invites criticism for being subordinationistic, because it leads with the Father and then introduces Son and Spirit in a subordinal sequence (second and third). It is peculiar for anything from Nicaea to be suspected of being too subtle, inadequately trinitarian, or subordinationistic. After all, pro-Nicene theology was and is famously explicit in its trinitarian commitments and rejection of subordinationism. But even though these concerns about the weaknesses of the Nicene disposition as pedagogical arrangement are misplaced, they do throw into relief the Nicene style's characteristic expositional strategy. Perhaps they also show why a supplemental dispositional strategy, the Quicunquan, has emerged with its own role to play.

The Quicunquan style sets the three names as close together as possible and gathers them under the advance organizing title "Trinity," as in: "We worship one God in Trinity, and Trinity in Unity . . . for there is one person of the Father, another of the Son, and another of the Holy Spirit." Having pulled the concepts together tidily, the Quicunquan style can then work back and forth across a three-one dialectic: "The Father eternal, the Son eternal, and the Holy Spirit eternal; and yet they are not three eternals but one eternal." It prompts the reader to seek clarity about what is one (essence) and what is three (persons). In due course, the Quicunquan style will have to appeal to the relations of origin, without which there is no reason to keep rehearsing the three-one data. In the Athanasian Creed itself, the Son's begetting and the Spirit's proceeding are eventually stated in a compact bundle of distinguishing characteristics. Perhaps the relations of origin produce a kind of "Aha!" when they are finally disclosed in the Quicunquan style. But what is striking is that the Quicunquan disposition does not formally require the relations of origin to be made explicit. For example, consider what happens when the logical diagram called the Shield of the Trinity is used as a starting point for teaching the doctrine. It maps certain relations between the persons with great clarity: the Father is God, the Son is God, but the Son is not the Father, and so on. How strange it is to complete the sentence, "The Father _____ the Son" with the verb "is not." Of all the things the Bible affirms about these two persons, and of all the things the Nicene disposition highlights, the bare assertion that these two are not each other seems to be a kind of analytic residue. The Shield of the Trinity, with its bare minimum of relational logic, is the diagrammatic distillation of the Quicunquan disposition of teaching the doctrine of the Trinity. It can support a great deal of solid instructional work. But it does not, in its main outlines, actually require that the relations of origin be made explicit. The title *Trinity*, the rapid juxtaposition of the three names, and the specifying of the kinds of relations ("is" and "is not") that obtain among them, do all of the work.

The point of distinguishing these two dispositions is not to praise one and condemn the other. They can be blended in a wide variety of ways in full-length expositions of trinitarian theology. We can even say that both dispositions have biblical warrant. The risen Lord spoke in something of a Quicunquan idiom when he said to baptize in the name of the Father, the Son, and the Holy Spirit; but he did so in the twenty-eighth chapter of a gospel story with a Nicene plot. Without condemning the Quicunquan style altogether, however, we can say that for all it gains in clarity and simplicity, it loses more in sacrificing the drama of Scripture's own historical unfolding of the Trinity. For my own part, I would press the criticism further. The Quicunquan disposition of trinitarianism makes it possible to under-emphasize the eternal relations of origin, and to do so precisely because it renders their connection to the temporal missions of the Son and Spirit opaque. This marginalization of the missions-processions structure of trinitarian theology is unhealthy for evangelical trinitarianism. The missions and processions, after all, are not so much a matter of mere disposition as a matter of essential content of trinitarianism. The Athanasian Creed does enumerate them, after all; if it did not, it would be inadequately trinitarian. Any attempted trinitarianism that fails to take recourse to the connection between the temporal missions and the eternal processions is by definition bypassing the history of salvation, the evangel. Evangelical trinitarianism, therefore, ought to cultivate the Nicene disposition as much as possible in its explanation of the Trinity. The more the Quicunquan disposition dominates in evangelical catechesis and theological training, the greater the danger that evangelicals will lose the plot.

The Unity of the Theological Disciplines Around the Trinity

The doctrine of the Trinity is important because it is true, and because the gospel and salvation depend upon it, but also for a more particular reason of special interest to teachers and students in the theological disciplines: it provides the essential basis for the unity of the various theological disciplines.

Earlier in this chapter we started as far back as possible with an apprehension of the vastness of the Trinity in order to get a perspective from which we could view the theological lay of the land. Christians read the Bible as the book of the Trinity, or we don't read it at all. If the canon of Scripture is not the coherent book of the Trinity, it is not really itself. The two-testament canon came into being in the church to bear witness that the God of Abraham is the Father of our Lord Jesus Christ. As B. B. Warfield said, the New Testament is "the documentation of the religion of the incarnate Son and of the outpoured Spirit, that is to say, of the religion of the Trinity."[25] That is what the New Testament is, nor does the New Testament make adequate sense without its profound presuppositions in the Old Testament. Without the steady pressure of Old Testament presupposition, what are we to understand by strange terms like *Christ* or the *Spirit*? The two-testament canon, in other words, is wrapped around the salvation-historical advent of the Trinity in the Father's sending of the Son and Spirit.

The Trinity is big: in apprehending the Trinity, we apprehend the primal unity from which all of our academic and theological disciplines descend. Let us speak of divinity: the old-fashioned word for theology, the subject we give master's degrees in. It is not self-evident that all these theological disciplines (Old Testament, New Testament, historical theology, systematic theology, practical theology, ethics, apologetics, etc.) do in fact descend or ramify from a real unity. In fact, the turf currently assigned to each discipline in Western academia was dictated around 1800 on a very different set of presuppositions than the trinitarian set. Our disciplinary boundaries are inherited from

25. B. B. Warfield, "The Biblical Doctrine of the Trinity," in *Works of Benjamin B. Warfield*, vol. 2 (Grand Rapids: Baker Book House, 1981), 35.

a powerful intellectual culture that was culturally Christian but only thinly trinitarian in its doctrinal contours. So it is no surprise that the territory is crisscrossed by boundaries that do not lend themselves to well-grounded or coherent trinitarian doctrine. Division of labor is one thing, and academic specialization is necessary if only because life is too short for many people to learn to read Hebrew and Hegel, Aramaic and Aristotle. Nobody can read all the journals. Expertise is a real thing, and it requires focus. But if you want to learn that the boundaries between our disciplines are not mere dispositions of convenience, try crossing one. If your doctrinal ball rolls into the street, see how the neighborhood responds when you chase it. The boundaries are policed, the divides are enforced. They exist for a reason. Francis Watson describes the boundaries this way: "One line of demarcation divides biblical scholars from theologians; a second absolutizes the division of the Christian Bible into Old Testament and New Testament, by assigning these collections to separate interpretive communities." He goes on,

> In reality the second line of demarcation is simply an extension of the first. The notion of a dialectical unity between two bodies of writing, constituted as "old" and "new" by their relation to the foundation event that they together enclose and attest, only makes sense from a theological standpoint. Where theological concerns are marginalized, the two testaments fall apart automatically.[26]

Minus the Trinity, things fall apart. Minus the Trinity, theological faculties have to go begging for a reason to be. In Berlin in 1800 it was a mix of cultural self-confidence, the emerging history of religions, and the need for civil servants in the state church. In the United States during the twentieth century, some of those were inherited, but the absence of a state church was compensated for by yankee know-how and pragmatism, which added a number of disciplines to the pastor's professional development.

What is next for the unity of the theological disciplines? I am not a prophet or the son of a prophet; just a prof. But for encouragement I look to these words from the late John Webster, who said, "There is no inevitability about these inherited curricular arrangements and their rationale. They are not a fate; they are simply contingent dispositions of the matter whose momentum derives partly

---

26. Francis Watson, *Text and Truth: Redefining Biblical Theology* (Grand Rapids: Eerdmans, 1997), 5–6.

from their establishment in prestigious places of higher learning, partly from the cultural standing of the model of rational activity which undergirds them."[27]

In our current disorder we can pull toward the Trinity and toward each other. We can work for a little revolution every day against the enforced dissolution of our reason for being. One thing we know for certain as we speak of divinity: the Trinity is big. God's triunity is why there is a gospel of grace. Confession of this triunity is why there is a Bible, why there are theological faculties, why the several disciplines taught in those faculties constitute a unity. The triune God put us together in creation, more wonderfully put us back together when we fell, and broke down the dividing wall of hostility between Jew and gentile so we all have access through Christ by one Spirit to the Father. Commitment to the Trinity is the one thing that will hold theological education together in the coming age.

27. John Webster, *Holy Scripture: A Dogmatic Sketch* (Cambridge: Cambridge University Press, 2003), 122.

The Modern Trinity

THE PRECEDING CHAPTERS have described the relation between Trinity and soteriology from a number of angles, and with reference to a cluster of closely related doctrines. The strategy of persuasion in these chapters has characteristically been to offer doctrinal judgments grounded in the dynamics of Scripture's own witness, and to expound these judgments in deeply traditional terms, drawing from a variety of classic witnesses to doctrines widely accepted throughout the history of theology. The argument reaches back, that is, to biblical and patristic trinitarian soteriology. But from the opening pages, there has been constant reference to the modern setting as well; if this book reaches back to the premodern, it does so from a contemporary situation. The modern voices most in evidence have been the leading voices of the trinitarian revival of the late twentieth century. My conviction is that this revival, for all its excesses and errors, brought something to the surface of trinitarian thought that merits close attention. The trinitarian revival of recent decades articulated the link between trinitarian theology and the doctrine of salvation in a way particularly appropriate for the modern mind. If the movement's errors were characteristically modern, so was its vigor, and so were its accurate insights into the fit between God and the gospel. In this chapter and the next, the focus of attention will shift to these modern advocates of radically economic trinitarian soteriology. This chapter carries out a thematic survey of trinitarianism in the long modern period; the next reflects on the nature of retrieving ancient doctrine from our contemporary setting. Together, these chapters clarify the particular construal of theological history presupposed by previous chapters; they make explicit a genealogy of modern errors that has informed the doctrinal judgments I have offered so far. Modern trinitarianism has not been entirely in error, and the theologians examined here are not summoned simply as cautionary tales. In this chapter we will see the deep forces at work in drawing the reality of the Trinity closer to history and experience; in the next we will see the impulse to reach back to the primal truth of salvation grounded in God.

"What Are They Saying About the Trinity?" asked Roman Catholic theologian Anne Hunt in the title of her 1998 book about recent developments in trinitarian theology.[1] Hunt's book was part of Paulist Press's What Are They Saying About series, featuring short volumes that keep readers up to date on topics in theology and biblical studies. It was a replacement volume for Joseph Bracken's 1979 entry in the series, which had also been titled *What Are They Saying About the Trinity?*[2] The point is that theologians keep on talking, and what "they," the theologians, were saying about the Trinity in the late 1970s was not the same as what they were saying in the late 1990s. In fact, the doctrine of the Trinity has been the subject of the most lively and most rapidly developing conversation in modern theology.[3] That such an ancient and established doctrine should be the subject of such vigorous contemporary discussion is striking. It has even become common to talk about the doctrine of the Trinity as having made a comeback from a long period of neglect.

Commentators on modern theology often describe this surge of interest in all things trinitarian as a fairly recent phenomenon. Roger E. Olson, for instance, names "the renaissance of the doctrine of the Trinity" as one of the "triumphs . . . of twentieth century Christian theology," pointing to the years after 1940 in particular as the time of "one of the greatest surprises of twentieth century theology," which was "the resurgence of interest in and renewal of reflection on the doctrine of the Trinity."[4] There has unquestionably been a spike in the number of publications, conferences, and general excitement about the doctrine in the second half of the twentieth century.[5] If the sheer volume of

---

1. Anne Hunt, *What Are They Saying about The Trinity?* (Mahwah, NJ: Paulist Press, 1998).

2. Joseph Bracken, *What Are They Saying About The Trinity?* (Mahwah, NJ: Paulist Press, 1979).

3. The Lutheran journal *Dialog* tracked a particularly active phase of the conversation in a series of articles: Ted Peters, "Trinity Talk," Parts 1 and 2, in *Dialog: A Journal of Theology* 26, no. 1 (Winter 1987): 44-48; and 26, no. 2 (Spring 1987): 133-38; Fred Sanders, "Trinity Talk, Again," in *Dialog* 44, no. 3 (Fall 2004): 264-72.

4. Roger E. Olson, "The Triumphs and Tragedies of Twentieth Century Christian Theology," *Christian Scholars Review* 24, no. 4 (Summer 2000): 665.

5. Good recent summaries of the vast literature can be found in Stanley J. Grenz, *Rediscovering the Triune God: The Trinity in Contemporary Theology* (Minneapolis: Fortress, 2004), and Veli-Matti Kärkkäinen, *The Trinity: Global Perspectives* (Louisville: Westminster John Knox, 2007).

books and articles is the measure of a renaissance, then there has been one since about 1970.[6] "They" are saying more and more about the Trinity.

But if we speak of a renaissance of trinitarianism in modern theology, and especially if we celebrate it, we should be careful to set its starting point accurately. It is not just in the last half-century that the Trinity has been a special focus of concern. Modern interest in the Trinity began about two centuries ago, not two decades ago. If the doctrine suffered a period of neglect, that period was as far back as the seventeenth to eighteenth centuries, when the rationalistic skepticism of the critical Enlightenment reached a high point and had not yet faced the challenge of a constructive response. In that early modern period, anti-trinitarian groups like the Socinians put forth their arguments vigorously. They found a readier reception, because the general intellectual climate of the Enlightenment was opposed to all revealed doctrines. What the Enlightenment considered reasonable was a universally available natural religion that admitted no more content than the existence of a god, duty to others, and justice after death.[7] This was the intellectual climate in which it became possible for public figures like Thomas Jefferson to mock "the incomprehensible jargon of the Trinitarian arithmetic." The charge was that the modern age had arrived, and the Trinity seemed like a very pre-modern doctrine, ready to be jettisoned.

By about 1800, though, around the time of the Romantic reaction to the Enlightenment, the doctrine had been recast in distinctively modern ways. Romanticism resists precise definition, but it has been called an international cultural force that "began as a cluster of movements and became the spirit of an age," and it arose between 1789 and 1815.[8] It was a rather Romantic doctrine of the Trinity that made its way into the modern age. The Trinity, that is, had been reinterpreted in light of three epochal Romantic ideas: world history, human experience, and the retrieval of the past. These are the major intellectual forces that would shape modern trinitarianism down to our own time. This chapter will survey modern trinitarianism under these three headings: history, experience, and retrieval.

---

6. As early as 1952, however, a prescient observer like Claude Welch could see a resurgence underway. See his thorough survey *In This Name: The Doctrine of the Trinity in Contemporary Theology* (New York: Scribner's, 1952), 3–122.

7. For the major figures in "The Critical Enlightenment," such as Reimarus, Semler, and Lessing, see the chapter with that name in Samuel L. Powell, *The Trinity in German Thought* (Cambridge: Cambridge University Press, 2001), 60–96. For the British scene, see the chapter "The Rise, Growth, and Danger of Socinianism" in Philip Dixon's *Nice and Hot Disputes: The Doctrine of the Trinity in the Seventeenth Century* (London: T&T Clark, 2003), 34–65.

8. Jacques Barzun, *From Dawn to Decadence: 500 Years of Western Cultural Life* (New York: HarperCollins, 2000), 465.

THE TRINITY AND HISTORY

The leading thinkers of the critical Enlightenment were committed to reason, by which they meant a set of necessary truths in a realm above historical flux, best typified by mathematical and logical relations. Truths of reason were contrasted with mere matters of fact: facts might happen to be true in this world, but the truths of reason were necessarily true for all possible worlds. The rationality of the Enlightenment had a pristine, ahistorical character, which made for great gains in clarity, but also opened a gap between rationality and worldly reality.[9] G. E. Lessing (1729–1781) felt the crisis keenly, and stated it as an axiom: "Accidental truths of history can never become the proofs of necessary truths of reason." Especially in matters of religion, it seemed that no events taking place in world history could ever be more than historically probable, and thus could never succeed in carrying metaphysical significance. Faced with the Christian claim that God was definitively revealed in the historical life of Christ, Lessing spoke for the crisis of Enlightenment rationality when he admitted that even if Christ had risen from the dead, "to jump from that historical truth to a quite different class of truths" was impossible. "That, then, is the ugly, broad ditch which I cannot get across."[10] With the historical Jesus on one side of the divide, and divinity on the other side, the Trinity was strictly unthinkable. Some sort of supreme being might be compatible with Enlightenment reason, but not the Father, Son, and Spirit of traditional Christian faith.

Hegel: The Trinity as Absolute Spirit Coming to Itself

It was G. W. F. Hegel (1770–1831) who took up the task of reconciling reason and history, in a grand philosophical synthesis that he habitually elaborated in trinitarian terms. For philosophical reasons of his own, Hegel set out to broaden the very definition of reason to encompass the historical. "Reason," he declared, "is the law of the world, and . . . therefore, in world history, things have come about rationally."[11] The historical flux in which all real things have

9. For all their differences, the rationalists (following Descartes) and the empiricists (following Locke, but most explicitly Hume) shared this characteristic inability to reckon with history. For a nuanced argument about the Enlightenment's ahistorical tendencies, see Ernst Cassirer, *The Philosophy of the Enlightenment* (Boston: Beacon Press, 1951), 197–209.

10. "On the Proof of the Spirit and of Power," in *Lessing's Theological Writings*, ed. Henry Chadwick (Stanford: Stanford University Press, 1956), 53–55.

11. G. W. F. Hegel, *Reason in History: A General Introduction to the Philosophy of History*, trans. Robert S. Hartman (New York: Macmillan), 11.

their being was not an obstacle to reason according to Hegel, but was the very place where the philosopher could trace the path of reason as it made its way from abstract ideals to concrete realities. "The time has finally come," said Hegel, with confidence that his own system was a step forward in the progress of philosophy, "to understand also the rich product of creative Reason which is world history."[12]

Hegel was an idealist, basing his entire system on the ultimate reality of mental entities and cultivating metaphysical speculation in a grand style. But where previous varieties of idealism had been subjective, Hegel's was absolute and objective: the crucial thing for him was that the ideal was not one thought among others, nor was it merely a thought at all. The ideal, for Hegel, was ultimately the real. That is, the ideal became concrete reality in the course of world history, giving rise to cultures and epochs and philosophies, art and music and languages, as it developed and elaborated itself. Hegel's system, in other words, can be categorized as a form of absolute, objective idealism.

Hegel's thought defies brief summaries, but one way of thinking about world history according to Hegel is that it is the ultimate coming-of-age story. His masterpiece, the *Phenomenology of Spirit*, has been called "a kind of *Bildungsroman* (a novel that portrays a character's growth, acculturation, and philosophical development), but one where the protagonist is 'consciousness.'"[13] Coming of age is no straight or easy path for this hero who we can call consciousness, or spirit, or thought, or the real, or the absolute and objective ideal. To develop its potential and unfold its powers, it has to pass through an ordeal in which it seems in danger of losing itself. Pure thought is something that emerges from abstraction, posits itself in the form of something actual, and reintegrates abstraction and actuality into one living whole called Spirit. Absolute reality undergoes what Hegel called diremption (*Entzweiung*), affirming itself by positing an other and then overcoming the estrangement.

What this dialectic of diremption and reconciliation has to do with the Trinity seemed obvious to Hegel. The doctrine of the Trinity is a kind of pictorial representation, at the level of religious myth, of the structure of the ultimate spiritual reality that encompasses absolutely everything. It was Hegel's task to make that structure explicit. Charles Taylor claims that "the dogma of the Trinity is ideal for Hegel's purposes." It is a system in which

---

12. Hegel, *Reason in History*, 18.

13. Craig B. Matarrese, *Starting with Hegel* (London: Continuum, 2010), 52. See *The Phenomenology of Spirit*, trans. A. V. Miller (Oxford: Oxford University Press, 1977).

The Universal goes out of itself, undergoes self-diremption and engenders the particular (the Father begets the Son before all ages); and the particular nevertheless returns to unity with the Universal in a common life (the Holy Spirit proceeds from Father and Son and unites them). Thus Hegel sees deep speculative meaning in the notion of an eternal Trinity, a play of love in the absolute itself.[14]

Instead of being a doctrine hung on the horns of the Enlightenment dilemma between universal truths and contingent facts, for Hegel, the Trinity became the principle of the unity between the two and the grammar of universal truth's self-communication in history. To make his case for a trinitarianism that had metaphysical implications, Hegel sometimes availed himself of the traditional religious language of trinitarianism, and sometimes paraphrased it into his increasingly idiosyncratic metaphysical jargon. "When the time was fulfilled, God sent his Son," he quoted from Galatians 4:4, and then offered the Hegelian paraphrase: "When the need for Spirit came into existence, Spirit manifested the reconciliation."[15]

Hegel's own intentions are hard to discern: Was he a Christian apologist claiming ultimate truth for the church's doctrine of the Trinity, or an atheist who pillaged trinitarian terminology to say something altogether different? Interpreters are divided. But Hegel's influence on modern trinitarianism has been so pervasive as to be nearly inescapable. His work established a style for modern trinitarianism, according to which the doctrine is grounded in the dynamics of world process.

Moltmann: The Suffering, Open Trinity

The way this Hegelian heritage has played out in more recent trinitarian theology is obvious if we turn to one of its most creative and influential advocates, Jürgen Moltmann. Moltmann's starting point was an intentionally radical account of the cross of Christ, which he described as the event of God's self-abandonment in history. As he worked out this fundamental commitment, Moltmann recognized that it demanded a robust, and thoroughly historicized, doctrine of the Trinity: "The doctrine of the Trinity is the conceptual frame-

---

14. Charles Taylor, *Hegel* (Cambridge: Cambridge University Press, 1975), 489.

15. Cited in Stephen Crites, "The Gospel According to Hegel," *Journal of Religion* 46, no. 2 (April 1966), 252.

work that is necessary if we are to understand this history of Christ as being the history of God."[16] Classical, premodern theology had consistently argued that God in his own divine nature is impassible and incapable of falling into suffering. The incarnation, on the traditional view, was God the Son participating in human suffering, but not experiencing suffering in the divine nature. Moltmann self-consciously sets himself against the tradition and teaches "the pathos of God," a doctrine of divine suffering. In order to describe the death of Christ as the saving work of "the human, crucified God," Moltmann asserted that "the theology of the cross must be the doctrine of the Trinity and the doctrine of the Trinity must be the theology of the cross."[17]

What this entailed for an overall theology became clear with Moltmann's 1981 book *The Trinity and the Kingdom*. In that book, he declared that "the history of the world is the history of God's suffering." "If a person once feels the infinite passion of God's love," said Moltmann, "then he understands the mystery of the triune God. God suffers with us—God suffers from us—God suffers for us."[18] In Moltmann's hands, the doctrine of the Trinity becomes a theology of the redemptive suffering of God in human history. In order to heal his creatures, God has opened himself up to their suffering and made it his own, internalizing it so that only by delivering himself from the exile of history will he deliver them also. "The theology of God's passion leads to the idea of God's self-subjection to suffering. It therefore also has to arrive at the idea of God's eschatological self-deliverance."[19] This account of salvation has the Hegelian family likeness; it is another version of redemption by diremption.

History obviously matters for this sort of doctrine of the Trinity, and Moltmann emphasizes its importance strikingly, portraying the entire Western metaphysical tradition from Plato to Barth as a series of efforts to contrast the realm of being with the realm of becoming, keeping God on one side of the divide and the world on the other.[20] Moltmann thinks that this divide makes it impossible to confess the Christian God—God with us—since it begins with the eternal, immanent Trinity located safely in the realm of being, and sees only a ghostly reflection of that real Trinity down here with us under conditions of finitude and in the processes of becoming. Such a God would be closed off from real fellowship with creatures, and Moltmann takes the doctrine of the Trinity to be a declaration of God's openness to the world, openness for real relationship.

16. Moltmann, *The Future of Creation: Collected Essays* (Minneapolis: Fortress, 1979), 81.
17. Moltmann, *The Crucified God* (New York: Harper & Row, 1974), 241.
18. Moltmann, *The Trinity and the Kingdom* (New York: Harper & Row, 1981), 4.
19. Moltmann, *Trinity and the Kingdom*, 60.
20. Moltmann, *Trinity and the Kingdom*, 158–159.

Moltmann even rejects the classic descriptions of God's unity as being too one-sided, because they are biased against history. If God is one because he is the supreme substance, or if he is one because he is the absolute subject, then his unity is already established before the doctrine of the Trinity is taken into account. Instead, Moltmann describes God's unity as a perichoretic unity of the fellowship of the three persons in the history of salvation. God is one, in other words, because "the unity of the Father, the Son and the Spirit is . . . the eschatological question about the consummation of the trinitarian history of God."[21] Moltmann obviously has an instinct for finding the edges of traditional doctrines, and his treatment of the unity of the Trinity leads him to innovations like an unprecedentedly social doctrine of the Trinity, a rejection of a metaphysical-political construct he identifies as monotheism, and a panentheistic account of God's relationship to the world. Some of these positions are idiosyncratic to Moltmann's maverick temperament, no doubt, but most of them are driven by his decision "to develop a historical doctrine of the Trinity" from "the history of Jesus the Son."[22]

Pannenberg: The Historical Self-Actualization of the Trinity

Moltmann's trinitarianism is not just historical but eschatological. Yet ever since his breakout book *Theology of Hope*, Moltmann tried to find a balance between two different meanings of eschatology: an orientation toward an open future on the one hand, and an orientation toward a definitively ultimate conclusion on the other. Moltmann's contemporary Wolfhart Pannenberg is much more decisively invested in the priority of the latter orientation. For Pannenberg, the whole point of biblical eschatology is that it brings all things to definitive completion. Eschatology is temporal holism (more on this below). Pannenberg views being itself as historical, but only because it is truly on its way to a definite state of completion.

The doctrine of the Trinity is central to Pannenberg's thought precisely because it is a working out of the tensions of his eschatological ontology. Early in his career, Pannenberg framed this idea in a famously controversial way. Having argued that the concept of God's being was bound up with the concept of God as the all-determining power, Pannenberg pointed out that during the course of history, God does not appear to be determining all things. Therefore until the coming of God's kingdom, his very existence remains dubious be-

21. Moltmann, *Trinity and the Kingdom*, 149.
22. Moltmann, *Trinity and the Kingdom*, 19.

cause it is not enacted. God without his kingdom is not God. For this reason, as Pannenberg put it, "it is necessary to say that, in a restricted but important sense, God does not yet exist."[23] Pannenberg could state this claim more expansively, as he did in his *Systematic Theology*, where he argued that "Only with the consummation of the world in the kingdom of God does God's love reach its goal and the doctrine of God reach its conclusion."[24] The realization that God rules with love and power will only occur when time is taken up into and included in eternity; which is to say, when the kingdom of God comes.[25] At this point the temporal whole will be fully present, and the events of history, having passed through judgment, will become eternal. But Pannenberg only elaborates his full position when he brings the doctrine of the Trinity to the task. The missions of the Son and the Spirit into world history, he claims, are the central events of God establishing his kingdom. So the fullness of the being of God the Trinity apparently waits on the course of world history, the consummation of salvation history in the eschatological work of the Son and Spirit, and the coming of the kingdom in the future.

Pannenberg seems to be quite aware of the doctrinal and metaphysical dangers involved in linking the being of the Triune God to history so directly. Integrating the divine life into the historical reality of the world tends toward pantheism, and Pannenberg is eager to ward off that danger. He argues, "refuted herewith is the idea of a divine becoming in history, as though the trinitarian God were the result of history and achieved reality only with its eschatological consummation."[26] Although such divine becoming might appear to be taking place from our point of view, what actually happens is that "the eschatological consummation is only the locus of the decision that the trinitarian God is always the true God from eternity to eternity."[27]

Whenever Pannenberg talks from two points of view, he shows some comfort with a broadly Platonic ontology in which an eternal reality is manifested under the changing conditions of history. In Pannenberg's case, that eternal reality lies in a real future rather than in a strictly atemporal world above. But once Pannenberg admits a stable eternity, how can he square it with the notion of a divine reality fully engaged in the process of history, a God for whom history really counts? Pannenberg admits that this can only

23. Wolfhart Pannenberg, *Theology and the Kingdom of God* (Philadelphia: Westminster, 1969), 56.

24. Pannenberg, *Systematic Theology*, vol. 1 (Grand Rapids: Eerdmans, 1991), 447.

25. Pannenberg, *Systematic Theology*, vol. 3 (Grand Rapids: Eerdmans, 1998), 595.

26. Pannenberg, *Systematic Theology*, 1:331.

27. Pannenberg, *Systematic Theology*, 1:331.

come about if we develop "a concept of God which can grasp" in one unified conceptual framework "not only the transcendence of the divine being and his immanence in the world but also the eternal self-identity of God and the debatability of his truth in the process of history, along with the decision made concerning it by the consummation of history."[28] Pannenberg piles up a lot of ideas in sentences like this, but the main thing to notice is that he piles them up in the ultimate future, which is the locus of God's decision that determines reality.

Another way Pannenberg makes this point is to talk about God's self-actualization. "God actualizes himself in the world by his coming into it," he says.[29] Only God is capable of self-actualization, since in order to actualize oneself, one would have to already be somebody who is identical with the somebody who is to be actualized. This is what the eternal God does in the course of world history: "The idea of self-actualization transcends our measure as finite beings. . . . Nevertheless, the relation of the immanent to the economic Trinity, of God's inner trinitarian life to his acts in salvation history inasmuch as these are not external to his deity but express his presence in the world, may very well be described as self-actualization. For here the subject and result are the same, as the expression demands."[30] Once again, it is the historical action of the Son and Spirit in the world that enables Pannenberg to think of God's very being as intimately connected to the outcome of world history. But much more clearly than Moltmann, Pannenberg also succeeds in using trinitarian categories to recognize the antecedent reality of God:

> It is certainly true that the trinitarian God in the history of salvation is the same God as in His eternal life. But there is also a necessary distinction that maintains the priority of the eternal communion of the triune God over that communion's explication in the history of salvation. Without that distinction, the reality of the one God tends to be dissolved into the process of the world.[31]

If this futurist metaphysic is convincing, the doctrine of the Trinity lets Pannenberg have his historical-ontological cake and eat it too.

28. Pannenberg, *Systematic Theology*, 1:333.
29. Pannenberg, *Systematic Theology*, 1:390.
30. Pannenberg, *Systematic Theology*, 1:392.
31. Pannenberg, "Books in Review: Robert W. Jenson, *Systematic Theology: Volumes I & II*," *First Things* 103 (May 2000): 49–53.

Jenson: Three Characters in the Story of God

One other trinitarian theologian who has given priority to history is the American Lutheran Robert W. Jenson, whose work is a kind of narrative theology that rises to the level of making metaphysical claims. Jenson's early book *The Triune Identity* argued that "Father, Son, and Holy Spirit" is the name of God.[32] In his later work he argues that "the primal systematic function of trinitarian teaching is to *identify* the *theos* in 'theology.'"[33] This God-given tool for identifying God becomes, for Jenson, the basic equipment for a revisionist metaphysic, an ontology in which the central role is played by narrativity. Identity, according to Jenson, is something that is narrated in a history, and a history is something that has closure. This narrative closure applies also to God: "Since the biblical God can truly be identified by narrative, his hypostatic being, his self-identity, is constituted in dramatic coherence."[34] It is the death and resurrection of Christ that provide the dramatically coherent narrative of the identity of God. The doctrine of the Trinity is what specifies the content of that narrative and picks out its three characters: "It is the very function of trinitarian propositions to say that the relations that appear in the biblical narrative between Father, Son, and Spirit are the truth about God himself."[35] Jenson has much in common with Moltmann and Pannenberg, but his emphasis on the narrative character of revelation sets him apart. It is important to note that Jenson is not simply ignoring metaphysics or seeking to change the subject from being to stories. Instead, he is installing story as the central ontological category. Jenson claims that narrativity is ontological, because in its highest form it is the identity of Trinity.

The theologians considered above share a commitment to history that shapes their trinitarianism. It is instructive to contrast their approaches with a group of modern theologians who made an opposite decision about the role of history for the Christian faith. Emerging from the historical-critical fires of the nineteenth century, theologians like Wilhelm Herrmann were concerned to minimize history's claim by arguing that faith must not be thought of as mere assent to historical data but must be grounded in the inner life of Jesus as pictured in the New Testament. Paul Tillich shared that desire to secure a

32. Robert W. Jenson, *The Triune Identity: God according to the Gospel* (Philadelphia: Fortress, 1982).

33. Robert W. Jenson, *Systematic Theology*, vol. 1 (New York: Oxford University Press, 1997), 60. Emphasis in the original.

34. Jenson, *Systematic Theology*, 1:64.

35. Jenson, *Systematic Theology*, 1:150.

historical safe zone for Christian faith. He joked with his classes, "I do not wish the telephone in my office to ring and to hear from some New Testament colleague: 'Paulus, our research has now finally removed the object of your ultimate concern; we cannot find your Jesus anywhere.'"[36] Tillich (like Bultmann in this regard) made use of certain existential motifs to remove Christian commitment from a merely historical foundation, basing faith instead on resources that faith itself could guarantee. For Tillich, the biblical picture of Christ is true, whether it corresponded to anything historical or not. Modern theologies that made this basic decision about history tended to find themselves cut off from the motive that impelled serious reflection on the Trinity in other sectors of modern theology. Tillich has a theology of religious symbolism that permits some rather thin reflection on trinitarian dynamics; Bultmann can make almost nothing of the doctrine. This underdevelopment of the doctrine among thinkers who made a different choice about how to handle the challenge of history simply underlines how history exerts formative influence on the shape of modern trinitarianism. A complete survey of the way the doctrine of the Trinity was enlivened in the modern period by reflection on history, movement, and the world process would have to include many more figures and schools of thought. The work of process theology, open theism, and the revival of panentheism in philosophical theology deserve to be considered under this heading, as do numerous theologians who are less influenced by Hegelian patterns of thought but are nevertheless committed to history.[37]

THE TRINITY AND EXPERIENCE

The second major category that enlivened trinitarianism and gave it a modern form is the category of experience. Around the time of the rise of Romanticism, it began to seem to many people that truths had to come within the range of personal experience before they could be meaningful. Once again, this was in reaction against the Enlightenment depiction of truth as an objective body of facts that were true whether they were experienced or not. Though the requirement that truth be a matter of experience did not immediately favor the doctrine of the Trinity, it soon became a key element of how the doctrine was to be stated in the modern period.

36. As quoted by Langdon Gilkey in *Gilkey on Tillich* (New York: Crossroad, 1990), 151.
37. See, for instance, Bruno Forte, *The Trinity as History: Saga of the Christian God* (New York: Alba House, 1989).

Schleiermacher: The Capstone of the Christian Consciousness

Friedrich Schleiermacher (1768–1834) stands at the head of the category of experience. Schleiermacher had a pietistic upbringing, but developed into the first great modern theologian. In standard accounts of how the Trinity came to be neglected in modern thought, Schleiermacher typically receives much of the blame. He famously placed the doctrine in the last few pages of his influential work *The Christian Faith*, making it something of an appendix to the main work.[38] To understand why the doctrine would be located there, we must understand how Schleiermacher constructed his system. For him, Christianity is "essentially distinguished from other faiths by the fact that in it everything is related to the redemption accomplished by Jesus of Nazareth."[39] Schleiermacher's theology was entirely centered on that redemption, or rather on the knowledge of that redemption, the contents of the self-consciousness of the redeemed. The theologian's task was to unpack and articulate the Christian's self-consciousness of being redeemed: "We shall exhaust the whole compass of Christian doctrine if we consider the facts of the religious self-consciousness, first, as they are presupposed by the antithesis expressed in the concept of redemption, and secondly, as they are determined by that antithesis."[40]

To "exhaust the whole compass of Christian doctrine" by analyzing redemption (what redemption presupposes, and what it brings about) may seem to run the risk of reducing theology to a study of salvation. But Schleiermacher's method was expansive enough to include much besides salvation. The Christian consciousness of redemption presupposes concepts such as God's holiness, righteousness, love, and wisdom; the opposing negative states of evil and sin; and the transition between them by way of Christ and the church through rebirth and sanctification. These concepts, further, presuppose others: creation and preservation, an original state of human perfection, and the divine attributes of eternity, omnipresence, omnipotence, and omniscience. Even angels and devils can be given a place within the redemption-centered project of *The Christian Faith*, although only a bit tentatively, since their alleged operations are so far at the periphery of the Christian conscious-

---

38. Friedrich Schleiermacher, *The Christian Faith*, 2nd ed. (Edinburgh: T&T Clark, 1928), 738–51.

39. Schleiermacher, *The Christian Faith*, 52.

40. Schleiermacher, *The Christian Faith*, 123.

ness of redemption that angelology "never enters into the sphere of Christian doctrine proper."[41]

The Trinity, however, could not be admitted to the doctrinal system proper, because it is not directly implicated in redemption. "It is not an immediate utterance concerning the Christian self-consciousness but only a combination of several such utterances." Piecing together doctrines to construct more elaborate doctrines was something Schleiermacher regarded with horror, because it led out from the living center of the faith to the arid regions of theological formulations, where dogmaticians do their deadening work. Schleiermacher had long since rejected that approach in his *Speeches* on religion: "Among those systematizers there is less than anywhere, a devout watching and listening to discover in their own hearts what they are to describe. They would rather reckon with symbols."[42] The young Romantic may have grown up to write a big book of doctrine, but he continued his "devout watching and listening" and never betrayed his basic insight or became one of "those systematizers" content to "reckon with symbols."

Because the Trinity could not be directly connected to redemption, Schleiermacher placed it well outside the life-giving core of the *Christian Faith*. In the heading of the section where he finally treated it, Schleiermacher pointed out that the doctrine of the Trinity could not be considered an issue that was "finally settled," because after all it "did not receive any fresh treatment when the Protestant Church was set up; and so there must still be in store for it a transformation which will go back to its very beginnings."[43] Schleiermacher considered it obvious that if the Trinity were implicated in the *evangel*, the *evangelisch* (that is, Protestant) awakening of the sixteenth century would have transformed and deepened it as it had everything central to Christian redemption.

For these reasons, Schleiermacher is not usually reckoned among the champions of the modern doctrine of the Trinity. He did in fact push it to the margin of his system for reasons that were very important to him. But he also set the terms and declared the conditions under which the doctrine could reemerge in the modern period, with a "transformation which will go back to its very beginnings." For well over a century, the doctrine remained dormant

41. Schleiermacher, *The Christian Faith*, 156.
42. *On Religion: Speeches to Its Cultured Despisers* (New York: Harper & Brothers, 1958), 52.
43. Schleiermacher, *The Christian Faith*, 747. I have changed the standard translation here at the word *Evangelical*, which Schleiermacher manifestly meant in the sense of Protestant.

CHAPTER 9

wherever Schleiermacher's influence was felt. But when it reemerged from hibernation, it would be as a doctrine of Christian experience.

LaCugna: The Trinity as Mystery of Salvation

In her influential book *God for Us: The Trinity and the Christian Life*, Catherine Mowry LaCugna's opening thesis is that "the doctrine of the Trinity is ultimately a practical doctrine with radical consequences for the Christian life."[44] LaCugna argues that the history of trinitarian theology is the history of an increasing alienation from the doctrine's original soteriological and doxological position; it is the story of "the emergence and defeat of the doctrine of the Trinity." The doctrine emerged in the first place as an explanation of how God's relationship to us in salvation history (*oikonomia*) reveals and is grounded in the eternal being of God (*theologia*). As it increasingly came to be a description of God *in se*, however, trinitarian theology grew speculative and unrelated to Christian experience, and finally issued in a doctrine of God that had no internal links to the doctrine of salvation. She traces this nonsoteriological doctrine of God to its underlying "metaphysics of substance; the pursuit of what God is 'in se,' what God is 'in Godself' or 'by Godself'" (3). According to LaCugna, the central challenge faced by trinitarian theology in the modern period is reconnecting the doctrine of God to the doctrine of salvation. The doctrine of the Trinity is the place to demonstrate that "theology is inseparable from soteriology, and vice versa" (211).

LaCugna attempted to carry out this agenda by transcending the distinction between God in himself and God in salvation. She described a larger view of God's ways with the world, a view in which "there is neither an economic nor an immanent Trinity; there is only the *oikonomia* that is the concrete realization of the mystery of *theologia* in time, space, history, and personality" (223). The book *God for Us* is aptly titled, since on LaCugna's view of the Trinity, God is for us, without remainder. The opening page has the suggestive sentence, "The life of God—precisely because God is triune—does not belong to God alone" (1). One of the things this turns out to mean is that, doctrinally speaking, "The doctrine of the Trinity is not ultimately a teaching about 'God' but a teaching about God's life with us and our life with each other" (228).

LaCugna's development of trinitarian theology in light of the experience of salvation seems to some critics to be a complete conflation, a collapsing of the

---

44. Catherine Mowry LaCugna, *God for Us: The Trinity and Christian Life* (San Francisco: HarperSanFrancisco, 1991), 1. Hereafter, page references from this work will be given in parentheses in the text.

being of God into the experience of salvation in the economy. But whether she succeeded or not, LaCugna at least intended to safeguard God's mystery and eternity. "Trinitarian theology is not merely a summary of our experience of God," she cautions. "It is this, but it also is a statement, however partial, about the mystery of God's eternal being" (4). For LaCugna, there simply is no option to think about "God in himself," so what is often called the immanent Trinity can only be discerned as the divine mystery inherent in the economic Trinity. LaCugna declares that in a well-ordered trinitarian theology, "divine self sufficiency is exposed as a philosophical myth," and that "the God conceived as a self enclosed, exclusively self-related triad of persons does not exist" (397). Finally, sounding a feminist note not often heard in her publications, LaCugna argues that the notion of a self-contained Trinity is a projection, an idolatrous self-enlargement of "the idea of person as self-sufficient, self-possessing individual, which is perhaps the ultimate male fantasy" (398).

Johnson: Naming Toward the Triune God from Women's Experience

Feminist theology was not, for several decades, a likely quarter in which to seek dialogue on trinitarian theology. The first generations of feminist theologians tended to identify this doctrine as self-evidently problematic. Ranging from Mary Daly's 1973 *Beyond God the Father*[45] to Rosemary Radford Ruether's 1983 *Sexism and God-Talk: Toward a Feminist Theology*, the bare fact of language about Father and Son seemed to mark the doctrine as a boys' club; it was viewed as a provocation to feminists, and they responded to it with subversion and parody. But the category of experience has been crucial for feminist theology, and this eventually brought the experiential Trinity of modern theology within range of the feminist project. Ruether, for example, declares experience to be the bedrock of all theological reflection, with the supposedly objective sources like Scripture and tradition being nothing more than codified experience. Feminist theology, on this account, uses women's experience as the criterion of what counts as "usable tradition" in the larger Christian tradition. When it comes to the Trinity, the question is essentially Schleiermacher's, with a feminist turn: Are women conscious of an experience of the triune God?

The most mature and fruitful affirmative answer is Elizabeth Johnson's *SHE WHO IS: The Mystery of God in Feminist Theological Discourse*. Johnson views the Christian community's religious language as formative and instrumental. "The symbol of God functions," she repeats: our concept of God shapes our

45. Mary Daly, *Beyond God the Father* (Boston: Beacon Press, 1973).

worldview and our conduct.[46] Johnson does not object to the use of male metaphors for God altogether, but she does object to them being used "exclusively, literally, and patriarchally," as they have been in the Christian church.[47] Her goal in *SHE WHO IS* is to supplement that masculine imagery with feminine imagery, "to speak a good word about the mystery of God recognizable within the contours of Christian faith that will serve the emancipatory praxis of women and men, to the benefit of all creation, both human beings and the earth."[48]

Though Johnson's project is intentionally revisionist, her work is deeply informed by the traditional trinitarian categories. She takes up each of the three persons and expounds them in feminine imagery, using the wisdom terminology of Sophia as a kind of master metaphor. The first person, accordingly, is Mother-Sophia (who mothers the universe, establishes the mercy of justice, and nurtures growth toward maturity); the second person is Jesus-Sophia (who is not just a human savior but a cosmic deliverer, is in solidarity with the oppressed, and whose incarnation affirms the body and sacramentality); and the third is Spirit-Sophia (who gives life, empowers, graces, and befriends). But Johnson actually reverses the traditional order and begins her exposition with the Spirit, precisely because the work of the third person is the point of deepest experiential contact, and thus the best starting point. Theology, on Johnson's account, is a project of "naming toward God," that is, starting analogically from a basis in human experience and predicating things about God from there.[49] "The God of inexhaustible mystery who is inexpressibly other is also with the world in the flesh of history, and is furthermore closer to us than we are to ourselves. Sophia-God is beyond, with and within the world; behind, with, and ahead of us; above, alongside, and around us."[50] As Johnson moves through the three persons and considers the one triune God in experiential, feminist-Sophia categories, she arrives at many of the same positions we have seen in Moltmann and others: a panentheistic relation of God to the world and a strong stance on God as a fellow-sufferer in the pain of the oppressed.

46. Elizabeth Johnson, *SHE WHO IS: The Mystery of God in Feminist Theological Discourse* (New York: Crossroad, 1992), 4, 5, 36, etc.

47. Johnson, *SHE WHO IS*, 33.

48. Johnson, *SHE WHO IS*, 8.

49. There is an extensive discussion internal to feminist theology about the legitimacy of essentializing "women's experience." For an analysis of Johnson and essentialism, see Kathryn Greene-McCreight, *Feminist Reconstructions of Christian Doctrine: Narrative Analysis and Appraisal* (New York: Oxford University Press, 2000), 112.

50. Johnson, *SHE WHO IS*, 191.

The result of Johnson's feminist investigation of trinitarian theology is a Trinity deeply resonant with the experience of women. This refashioning of the doctrine was made possible by the modern turn to experience, the same turn that also brought the doctrine of the Trinity within range of a number of other liberationist theological projects. Leonardo Boff, for example, describes the Trinity as the perfect society and appeals to it as a model and a critique of human order: "Society offends the Trinity by organizing itself on a basis of inequality."[51] The turn to experience has also been an invitation to theologians from many cultures to explore the doctrine afresh: Indian, African, and Asian Christian authors have made connections between Trinitarian theology and their cultural backgrounds.[52] Another obvious extension of the project of applying the Trinity to human experience is the recent rush to relevance in Trinitarian theology. The most sophisticated and promising approach to the Trinity in experiential terms is the work of Sarah Coakley, whose investigations of contemplative prayer in the church fathers and in contemporary spirituality have found an "ineluctably tri-faceted" component of religious experience. Coakley has been answering the question "Can God be experienced as Trinity?" with a nuanced "yes," and claiming that this experience is actually the "soft underbelly" of the origin of the doctrine of the Trinity,[53] as well as an important resource for contemporary faith and thought.

Rahner: A Synthesis of Experience and History

Karl Rahner is one of the most important thinkers in the doctrine of the Trinity's modern career. It would be possible to tell the whole story of trinitarian theology from 1960 on as the story of how Rahner's work was accepted, rejected, or modified.[54] We have already had to gloss over his influence on several figures in this thematic survey (an influence that is especially marked in

51. Leonardo Boff, *Trinity and Society* (London: Burns and Oates, 1988), 236.
52. For a survey that intentionally highlights cultural diversity, see Veli-Matti Kärkkäinen, *The Trinity: Global Perspectives* (Louisville: Westminster John Knox, 2007). Kärkkäinen devotes chapters to Leonardo Boff, Justo Gonzalez (Latin American and Hispanic authors), Jung Young Lee and Raimundo Panikkar (Asian theologians), and C. Nyamiti and A. O. Ogbonnaya (African theologians).
53. A great early essay is Sarah Coakley, "Can God Be Experienced as Trinity?" *Modern Churchman* 28, no. 2 (1986): 11–23. See her more recent, systematic treatment in *God, Sexuality, and the Self: An Essay 'On the Trinity'* (Cambridge: Cambridge University Press, 2013).
54. I have done this in *The Image of the Immanent Trinity: Rahner's Rule and the Theological Interpretation of Scripture* (New York: Lang, 2001).

Pannenberg and LaCugna) in order to reserve him for this key role synthesizing both streams, history and experience. Rahner's lament over the doctrine of the Trinity's neglect in "the catechism of head and heart" is the classic starting point of dozens of books on the Trinity. Rahner warned that if the doctrine were to be deleted from the textbooks and the histories of doctrine, there would be little change in the life or thoughts of the average Christian, and that much of Christian literature, sadly sub-trinitarian as it was, would remain unaltered. In systematic theology, the doctrine had shrunk to an obligatory short chapter safely contained within the much more important treatise on the one God, where it is dutifully discussed and then "never brought up again," giving no shape or power to the rest of the doctrines.

But for this thematic survey, we consider Rahner not as the chronological source of certain lines of influence, but as the synthesis of the two major themes studied so far. Karl Rahner's overall theological project, which can be called transcendental Thomism, is devoted to synthesizing experience and history. He taught that ultimate truth manifests itself in two ways to humans: first as the transcendent condition of all possible experience, and second as an actual historical entity to be encountered. The first claim is very abstract, but Rahner considers it his central message as a theologian: Summarizing his masterpiece, *Foundations of Christian Faith*, Rahner said, "I really only want to tell the reader something very simple: Human persons in every age, always and everywhere, whether they realize it and reflect on it or not, are in relationship with the unutterable mystery of human life that we call God."[55] But because humanity is also physically and historically actual, this transcendental openness to grace will be matched to a historical entity that presents itself to us concretely in world history. That entity is the man Jesus Christ, whose ministry is present in an ongoing way in the church and sacraments. So on the one hand there is human openness to transcendent grace, and on the other hand there is the historical occurrence of grace in the person of Jesus Christ. When these two meet, salvation is present. God communicates himself in experience as such and in a particular history.

These categories come to life in Rahner's trinitarian theology, where they are roughly correlated with the omnipresent Spirit and the incarnate Son. It is the proper office of the Holy Spirit to pervade all human experience as its horizon and term, and it is the proper office of the Son to become incarnate

---

55. *Karl Rahner in Dialogue: Conversations and Interviews 1965–1982* (New York: Crossroad, 1986), 147. He is describing his own book *Foundations of Christian Faith: An Introduction to the Idea of Christianity* (London: Darton, Longman & Todd, 1978).

and stand among us as the presence of God in a particular. Where Augustine started a tradition of mapping the Son and the Spirit onto the psychological categories of knowledge and love, Rahner intentionally mapped them onto salvation history and existential experience, respectively.

Rahner's theology is highly philosophical in character, and its main elements can only be described in detail by taking up his major philosophical influences: Thomas Aquinas, Kant, Heidegger, and more. But in line with this synthesis of history and experience, Rahner also proposed a methodological approach to trinitarianism that has been his greatest legacy for the doctrine. When we consider the Trinity in itself, he argued, we must always begin with the manifestations of the Son and Spirit in the economy of salvation. These two missions are ultimate, because in them the Trinity appears in the history of the world, and they are revelations of the eternal Trinity in itself.

Together on their mission from the Father, the Son and Spirit constitute the economic Trinity. But there is no discrepancy, and hardly even a distinction, between the Trinity we meet here in the gospel story (the economic Trinity) and the eternal Trinity in itself (the immanent Trinity). There is no gap, no inconsistency, between the Trinity in itself and the Trinity in salvation history. Rahner summed this up in what he called his fundamental axiom (*Grundaxiom*), and which interpreters have called Rahner's Rule: "*The economic Trinity is the immanent Trinity, and the immanent Trinity is the economic Trinity.*"

Applying this axiom consistently, Rahner was led to insist that the person of the Trinity who became incarnate was not only the eternal Son, but was necessarily the Son. No other person of the Trinity could have become incarnate. This is not just because, as voices in the tradition have long argued, it is appropriate to the Son's character to be sent and to become incarnate, but because, in Rahner's terms, the economic Logos is the immanent Logos, and vice versa. Applying the axiom to the Holy Spirit, Rahner argued that the presence of the Holy Spirit in the economy of salvation (whether as the Spirit of Pentecost binding the church together, or the indwelling of God in the faithful heart as uncreated grace) is a clear and direct extension of the inner-divine role of the Spirit in the immanent Trinity. Rahner's use of his own Rule pulls together the economic Trinity and the immanent Trinity, but also pulls together the modern emphases on history and experience, the *historia salutis* and the *ordo salutis*. In Rahner's theology, it also becomes apparent that the approaches to the Trinity through history and experience converge in focusing attention so much on the economic Trinity, that it becomes somewhat difficult to talk about the immanent Trinity.

The Trinity and Retrieval

The standard account of the trinitarian renaissance of the twentieth century is a tale of two Karls: Karl Rahner, the Jesuit theologian whose trinitarian thought we have just met, and Karl Barth, the Swiss Protestant theologian whose work we come to now. Barth's influence in trinitarian theology is certainly vast, and did make a major difference on the theological scene. When Barth announced programmatically in 1931 that the doctrine of the Trinity would be foundational and central to his *Church Dogmatics*, he was intentionally moving against the un-trinitarian tide of liberal Protestantism. The doctrine of the Trinity was widely considered to have outlived any usefulness it might have ever had, and a strategy of polite neglect was moving it to the very margin of Christian discourse. When Barth brandished the teaching as his starting point, he was accused of having taken counsel with reactionary confessionalists and the most entrenched, conservative sorts of Roman Catholics. In the preface to the first volume of the *Dogmatics*, he admitted that he was open to "the charge . . . that historically, formally and materially, I am now going the way of scholasticism. . . . I obviously regard the doctrine of the early Church as in some sense normative. I deal explicitly with the doctrine of the Trinity, and even with that of the Virgin Birth. The last-named alone is obviously enough to lead many contemporaries to suspect me of crypto-Catholicism. What am I to say?"[56] The question "What am I to say?" was rhetorical, because Barth was certainly not at a loss for words. The tens of thousands of pages of *Dogmatics* he would generate in the coming decades were themselves a demonstration that turning to the Trinity gave theology everything it needed to keep talking with confidence. As Hans Frei and John Webster have pointed out, "Barth was reinstating a theological language which had fallen into disrepair, and doing so by using the language in a lengthy and leisurely fashion."[57] Retrieving and elaborating the ancient doctrine of the Trinity in late modernity, Barth was insisting that "not merely the most important but also the most relevant and beautiful problems in dogmatics begin at the very point where the fable of 'unprofitable scholasticism' and the slogan about the 'Greek thinking of the fathers' persuade us that we ought to stop."[58] Losing interest in this central Christian doctrine (along with other

---

56. Karl Barth, *CD*, 1/1, xiii.

57. John Webster, *Karl Barth* (London: Continuum, 2000), 50. Webster is paraphrasing Frei's insight.

58. *CD*, 1/1, xiv.

unfashionable doctrines like the virgin birth) was one of the chief symptoms of the disease of theological liberalism:

> Shall I . . . bemoan the constantly increasing confusion, tedium and irrelevance of modern Protestantism, which, probably along with the Trinity and the Virgin Birth, has lost an entire third dimension—the dimension of what for once, though not confusing it with religious and moral earnestness, we may describe as mystery—with the result that it has been punished with all kinds of worthless substitutes.[59]

In other words, Barth's championing of the doctrine of the Trinity was self-consciously a form of theology as retrieval of the endangered past. As such it represents the third major trend giving modern trinitarianism its particular shape.

Retrieval, says John Webster, is "a *mode* of theology, an attitude of mind and a way of approaching theological tasks," rather than a distinct school of thought. Various kinds of modern theologians have turned to projects of retrieval for a whole range of different reasons:

> These theologies are differently occasioned: some are generated by dissatisfaction with the commanding role played by critical philosophy or by historical and hermeneutical theory in mainstream modern theology; some derive more directly from captivation by the object of doctrinal reflection as unsurpassably true, good, and beautiful. All, however, tend to agree that mainstream theological response to seventeenth- and eighteenth-century critiques of the Christian religion and Christian religious reflection needlessly distanced theology both from its given object and from the legacies of its past.[60]

Considered in light of the broader cultural reaction of Romanticism against the critical Enlightenment, the motif of retrieval can be seen in any of the creative arts that found inspiration in repristinating medieval resources. The revival of trinitarian thought, especially as we see it in someone like Barth, cannot be reduced to a Romantic urge to return to the Middle Ages. But it shares in the spirit of protest against the thinness of critical modernism.

---

59. *CD*, 1/1, xiv.

60. John Webster, "Theologies of Retrieval" in *The Oxford Handbook of Systematic Theology*, ed. John Webster, Kathryn Tanner, Iain Torrance (Oxford: Oxford University Press, 2007), 584. Webster briefly discusses the Trinity in the project of retrieval at 594–95.

Barth's own deployment of the doctrine of the Trinity can be summarized briefly. He linked the doctrine closely to all his other characteristic themes, especially Christology and revelation. Barth begins with the fundamental assertion that taking Christian faith seriously demands that we base our understanding of God on the revelation in Jesus Christ; in other words, that God must be as we see him revealed in Christ. There can be no "revelation gap" between God and Jesus, such that somewhere in the unrevealed mystery behind the God of Jesus Christ lurks the "real, absolute God." Barth then unfolds his doctrine of the Trinity from the fact of the revelation in Jesus Christ: God is Trinity in himself, and no less so in his revelation, and then once again equally so in the effect of his revelation. To put it in the densest form: "God reveals himself as Lord." God himself, through himself, reveals himself, as Lord. Stated thus briefly, Barth's Trinity doctrine can seem to be unfolded analytically from the structure of the concept of revelation. But Barth filled out this schema richly with abundant Scriptural material drawn, not from the concept of "revealer, revelation, and revealedness," but from the actions of God in the history of salvation. And by moving the doctrine of the Trinity to the front of his system, engaging it with his central ideas, Barth restored the doctrine to its original place in the structure of Christian faith: as the hermeneutical key to theological discourse rather than as one more problematic puzzle in need of explanation and justification.

Of Barth's three major contributions (closing the revelation gap, unfolding the doctrine of the Trinity from the concept of revelation, and using the Trinity as hermeneutical key), the first and last have been widely influential and have set the tone of the ensuing conversation. Fewer people have been able to follow Barth in treating the doctrine as an immediate implication of the fact of revelation. But the most important legacy of Karl Barth for modern trinitarianism is the confidence and consistency with which he carried out the remarkable act of retrieval.

Great as was Barth's achievement, it would be too much to say, as is often said, that Karl Barth simply brought back the doctrine of the Trinity. First of all, that would be insulting to the various theological communities who never lost track of the doctrine in the first place, and therefore could never have it brought back. As Colin Gunton has pointed out with reference to modern theology, "in all periods there have been competent theologians, Catholic and Protestant alike, who have continued to work with traditional trinitarian categories while being aware of the reasons that have led others to question, modify or reject traditional orthodoxy."[61] Or as John Webster says, "It is not

---

61. Colin Gunton, "The Trinity in Modern Theology," in *Companion Encyclopedia of Theology*, ed. Peter Byrne and Leslie Houlden (London: Routledge, 1995), 937.

that the doctrine ever disappeared from view (it is basic to Roman Catholic school dogmatics and massively present in, for example, Protestant dogmaticians like Dorner and Bavinck)."[62] Barth put the Trinity back on the agenda of self-consciously modern theology, specifically among the liberal mainstream of academic theology in Europe and America, and in particular among those for whom history and experience were decisive modern categories dictating the conditions of Christian thought. What Barth accomplished was to leverage his own credibility as a decidedly modern theologian, in touch with all the right academic interlocutors and able to draw the attention of academic practitioners, to put the classic doctrine of the Trinity in terms that could engage that subculture. He scored such a direct hit that it has become common to say that he revived the doctrine altogether.

A good index of how well Barth succeeded in drawing attention to this retrieved doctrine is the way liberal theologians of the time responded. The German-American theologian Wilhelm Pauck published in 1931 an interpretation of what Barth was up to, under the title *Karl Barth: Prophet of a New Christianity?* To Pauck's mind, Barth was almost, but not quite, the prophet of something new. Pauck applauded Barth's existential interpretation of revelation (though he described it in terms that would be more comfortable for Tillich than for Barth). What Pauck could not accept was the large amount of traditional material that kept cropping up in the Dogmatics.

> Barth . . . throws himself with all the intellectual passion that he can command into these old doctrines of the Church, desiring to think them through from the point of view of the revelation of God. He does not, however, do his task well. He acts altogether too often in a way which hides his real interest. The impression which every unprejudiced reader must derive from his discussion on revelation, is that a clever and exceedingly eloquent theologian has applied himself to the old forms of theological thought with a profound emotional intellectualism, trying almost beyond the power of his capacity to understand them. As if it were really a matter of life and death, that as members of the church of the Twentieth Century—we should accept the dogma of the Trinity![63]

For this kind of academic theological culture, Barth's retrieval of the doctrine of the Trinity was epochal. It would be possible to show how Barth employed the categories of history and experience in giving his trinitarian the-

62. Webster, "Theologies of Retrieval," 595.
63. Wilhelm Pauck, *Karl Barth: Prophet of a New Christianity?* (New York: Harper, 1931), 189.

ology a distinctively modern contour, and we could have considered Barth's work instructively under each of those categories. But it is worth remembering that Barth's trinitarianism shook up the modern theological world simply by being a retrieval of a classic central theme of the Bible and the Christian tradition. Theologians like Pauck dug in and resisted: "We deny that it is necessary that, in our efforts for a new expression of the Christian faith, we occupy ourselves with the Trinity and Christology. We would then commit the same mistake that Barth makes in his *Dogmatics*."[64] Whatever mistakes Barth made in his *Dogmatics*, his retrieval of the Trinity has turned out to be the most forward-looking of his major decisions.

As for the "competent theologians" whom Colin Gunton alluded to, "Catholic and Protestant alike, who have continued to work with traditional trinitarian categories" all throughout the modern period, it is hard to say what they failed to provide in their trinitarian theology. Everything that is routinely praised as belonging to the excitement of the trinitarian revival of recent times is fairly easy to find in those older sources, and there does not seem to be any chronological gap during which serious theological voices were not holding forth on the doctrine of the Trinity with faithfulness and creativity. If we are looking for a treatment of the Trinity that recognizes it as the core content of the continuity of the Christian faith, we can find it in the British Methodist William Burt Pope (1822–1903):

> The doctrine of the ever-blessed Trinity is essential to Christianity; there is no Theology, there is no Christology without it. . . . This has been the catholic belief, as the catholic interpretation of Scripture. Whatever exception may be taken to dogmatic definitions, the eternal underlying truth is the life of the Christian revelation.[65]

If we are looking for a recognition that the doctrine is eminently practical, and is not just a revealed mystery cobbled together in propositional form, we can find it in the American Presbyterian Charles Hodge (1797–1878):

> Truth is in order to holiness. God does not make known his being and attributes to teach men science, but to bring them to the saving knowledge

64. Pauck, *Karl Barth*, 201.
65. William Burt Pope, *Compendium of Christian Theology*, vol. 1 (New York: Phillips & Hunt, 1881), 284.

of Himself. The doctrines of the Bible are, therefore, intimately connected with religion, or the life of God in the soul. . . . This is specially true of the doctrine of the Trinity. It is a great mistake to regard that doctrine as a mere speculative or abstract truth, concerning the constitution of the Godhead, with which we have no practical concern, or which we are required to believe simply because it is revealed.[66]

If we are looking for a recognition that the doctrine is organic and integral, revealed progressively in divine actions in history but also emerging directly from Christian experience, we can find it in Dutch Calvinist Herman Bavinck (1854–1921):

> The doctrine of the Trinity makes God known to us as the truly living God, over against the cold abstractions of Deism and the confusions of pantheism. A doctrine of creation—God related to but not identified with the cosmos—can only be maintained on a trinitarian basis. In fact, the entire Christian belief system stands or falls with the confession of God's Trinity. It is the core of the Christian faith, the root of all its dogmas, the basic content of the new covenant. The development of trinitarian dogma was never primarily a metaphysical question but a religious one. It is in the doctrine of the Trinity that we feel the heartbeat of God's entire revelation for the redemption of humanity.[67]

And if we are looking for the doctrine of the Trinity as the theological factor that identifies Christian doctrine as Christian, that specifies who the God of the Bible is and therefore what is biblical about any of the individual doctrines, we can find it in the American Episcopalian Francis J. Hall (who published from 1908–1922):

> The doctrine of the Trinity is the interpretive principle of all Christian doctrine, the ultimate basis of Christian ideals and hopes, and the most vital and inspiring of all the truths which human minds can contemplate. . . . The doctrine of the Trinity must occupy the central place in any sound or adequate conception of spiritual realities. It constitutes the postulate of the doctrines of the Incarnation, of the Atonement, of the Church, of justifi-

66. Charles Hodge, *Systematic Theology*, vol. 1 (Grand Rapids: Eerdmans, 1995), 443.
67. Herman Bavinck, *Reformed Dogmatics*, vol. 2 (Grand Rapids: Baker Academic), 260.

cation and salvation, and of the coming kingdom of God. If it were shown to be false, these doctrines would have to be modified beyond recognition, and Christianity would become something quite other than it actually is.[68]

In light of these and many other voices that were speaking throughout the entire period under question, we should be careful how we talk about retrieval when it comes to the Trinity. There is an oft-told tale of how the doctrine of the Trinity was marginalized in the modern period, until a heroic rescue was performed by one of the Karls (Barth or Rahner). But for theologians like Pope, Hodge, Bavinck, and Hall, as for most Christians, there was no need for an absolute retrieval of a completely lost doctrine. Retrieval is a normal part of responsible theological method, and theologians were actively engaged in a kind of low-level, ordinary retrieval throughout the modern period, a retrieval so incremental as to be indistinguishable from conservation.

Jaroslav Pelikan has said that "the modern period in the history of Christian doctrine may be defined as the time when doctrines that had been assumed more than debated for most of Christian history were themselves called into question: the idea of revelation, the uniqueness of Christ, the authority of Scripture, the expectation of life after death, even the very transcendence of God."[69] Defined in this way, of course, the doctrine of the Trinity faced major challenges in the modern period. But as we have seen, its crisis point was near the end of the critical phase of the Enlightenment, and by the dawn of the nineteenth century Christian theology had begun to transpose the traditional doctrine into modern categories like history and experience. Those modern categories often had a distorting influence on the doctrine, pressing the content of the doctrine of the Trinity into new forms that did not succeed in maintaining continuity with the great tradition or faithfulness to the revelation in Scripture. It was especially difficult to confess the freedom of God over creation and salvation, for example, when the motifs of world history and human experience came to dominate the expression of the doctrine of God. But the modern categories also provided a great opportunity for an unforeseen development and elaboration of the doctrine of the Trinity. Premodern theology simply had not pondered its trinitarian resources in the suggestive terms of history and experience, and the modern forms of trinitarianism brought to light new resources previously unglimpsed. At the very least, the level of wide-

68. Francis J. Hall, *Dogmatic Theology*, vol. 4 (London: Longmans, Green & Co., 1910), 2–3.
69. Jaroslav Pelikan, *Christian Doctrine and Modern Culture (Since 1700)* (Chicago: University of Chicago Press, 1989), viii.

spread doctrinal excitement over the Trinity became a new and invigorating element of late twentieth-century discourse, and it shows no signs of abating. As trinitarian theology continues to be discussed and developed, theologians will do well to carry on the modern trinitarian project by articulating this classic Christian doctrine in such a way that the doctrine is not an opaque monolith of inherited terminology, but is transparent to history, transparent to human experience, and transparent to its biblical foundation

Retrieval and the Doctrine of the Trinity

T HE PREVIOUS CHAPTER treated retrieval as one of the characteristic modern modes of pursuing trinitarian theology. But the concept of retrieval proved difficult to work with, since any notion of retrieval presupposes some genealogical account of loss or forgetting, and, as we saw, it is not self-evident that the doctrine of the Trinity was uniformly lost or forgotten. Nevertheless, there is something particularly appropriate about treating the doctrine of the Trinity under the heading of retrieval, and especially when what is at issue is the question of the doctrine's relevance for soteriology. This chapter revisits the theme of retrieval more comprehensively, recommending close attention to the way trinitarian theology is inherently retrospective in its deep structures.

The doctrine of the Trinity always seems to be making a comeback. Its most recent return was probably its best-publicized and most widely heralded. In the explosion of academic publications on trinitarian theology in the late twentieth century, participants frequently congratulated each other and themselves for recovering "the Forgotten Trinity."[1] As we have already seen, there is ample reason for skepticism about the attendant hype. The main lines of the recent trinitarian revival have to be judged so inadequate as retrievals of the doctrine as to be counterproductive; in many cases the main lines of the movement are more about revision than retrieval. Yet the modern movement's note of retrieval rang true, partly because it resonated deeply with something that has always accompanied trinitarian theology: a retrospective element, a gesture of reaching back, a return to deep sources.

The retrospective tone can be heard in all the classic documents of trinitarianism. The Nicene Creed itself (that is, the Nicene-Constantinopolitan

---

1. *The Forgotten Trinity: Report of the BCC Study Commission* (London: British Council of Churches, 1989).

Creed of 381) was already an exercise in resolutely reclaiming the theological achievement of 325's Council of Nicaea.[2] Even the prologue of John's gospel, so influential for the main lines of patristic thought,[3] framed its teaching not as a sheer *novum* but as an enriched rereading of Moses, one that found more persons present "in the beginning" than had originally been imagined by readers of Genesis. Trinitarianism appears to be not just a doctrine that is frequently subject to retrieval, but perhaps a dogmatic case of retrieval all the way down. The triune God is the fountain of salvation, and *ad fontes* may be the most telling motto for the doctrine of the *fons salutis Trinitas*.[4]

Likewise, this chapter's exposition will move backward, starting with recent theology and peeling off layers of history and historiography from there. We begin with a look at the various mythological accounts of trinitarianism's fall and recovery, work back through a variety of purported great divides among types of trinitarianism through history, and finally describe the sort of structural retrospection that is properly inherent to trinitarian theology itself.

Revival versus Retrieval

If the twentieth century witnessed a revolution in Trinitarian projects in systematic theology, it was a revolution followed rapidly by a counter-revolution in historical theology. Almost anywhere that modern systematic theologians claimed to find ancient warrant for the claims they wanted to make, modern historical scholars returned a negative assessment. More was at stake than a mere "strife of faculties," though; both systematic and historical theologians have a stake in assessing the continuity or discontinuity in what the church has taught in its doctrine of God. Stephen Holmes's 2012 book *The Holy Trinity: Understanding God's Life* provided a helpful summary of the issues involved, with a sharpness that is clarifying. Holmes describes himself as a theologian much influenced by the "new trinitarianism" of the late twentieth century, who

2. Lewis Ayres, *Nicaea and Its Legacy: An Approach to Fourth-Century Trinitarian Theology* (New York: Oxford University Press, 2004), 244–69; Khaled Anatolios, *Retrieving Nicaea: The Development and Meaning of Trinitarian Doctrine* (Grand Rapids: Baker Academic, 2011), 20–27.

3. T. E. Pollard, *Johannine Christology and the Early Church* (Cambridge: Cambridge University Press, 1970).

4. See the introduction to this volume: "*Fons salutis Trinitas*" is from Venantius Fortunatus's sixth-century hymn *Vexilla regis*.

eventually had to rethink the movement's own claims, evidences, and conventional wisdom. In *The Holy Trinity*, Holmes argues that "the explosion of theological work claiming to recapture the doctrine of the Trinity that we have witnessed in recent decades in fact misunderstands and distorts the traditional doctrine so badly that it is unrecognizable."[5] What is usually told as a story of exciting discovery and renewal, Holmes re-narrates as "a catastrophic story of loss."[6] He lists three areas in which the modern trinitarian revival parted ways with the traditional view: it tended to entangle the being of the triune God with the world's history; to describe the life of the Trinity as continuous with, or extended into, the life of the church; and to subject trinitarian terminology to an analytic treatment that closed the analogical gap between creator and creature. In these ways, "the twentieth century renewal of trinitarian theology" depended "in large part on concepts and ideas that cannot be found in patristic, medieval, or Reformation accounts of the doctrine of the Trinity"; in fact, it depended on concepts and ideas that were "explicitly and energetically repudiated as erroneous"[7] by the earlier consensus. Writing mainly in a historical mode for this project, Holmes reserves judgment about whether the truth about the Trinity is on the side of the ancients or the moderns. His point is simply that the two differ, and if the moderns are right, "we need to conclude that the majority of the Christian tradition has been wrong in what it has claimed about the eternal life of God."[8] Even allowing for a bit of rhetorical overstatement, we have to acknowledge that Holmes draws a sharp dividing line here, calling into question recent trinitarianism's appeal to the past. In a perceptive review of Holmes's work, Scott Swain summed up the modern revival of interest in the doctrine of the Trinity as a case of "renewal without retrieval." For twentieth-century theology, in Swain's words, "the path to trinitarian renewal required bypassing rather than retrieving the classical trinitarian consensus."[9]

Holmes's assessment may seem stark, and Swain's summary of "renewal without retrieval" may not sound like the kind of judgment that the participants in the trinitarian revival would accept as a fair description of what they were undertaking. Certainly there were many motivations and agendas at work

5. Stephen Holmes, *The Holy Trinity: Understanding God's Life* (Milton Keynes: Paternoster, 2012), xv.

6. Holmes, *Holy Trinity*, xviii.

7. Holmes, *Holy Trinity*, 2.

8. Holmes, *Holy Trinity*, 2.

9. "The Quest for the Trinity," The Gospel Coalition, https://www.thegospelcoalition.org/reviews/quest-trinity/.

across the range of writings on the Trinity in this period. But it is interesting to note how often "renewal without retrieval" actually fits the self-understanding of the movement. Theologians who contributed to the surge of publications on the doctrine of the Trinity in the late twentieth century understood themselves to be participants in a revival of interest in trinitarianism, but not always a return to the actual content of trinitarianism. In fact, many of the most vigorous and influential promoters of the new work on the doctrine of the Trinity in the 1990s were quite aggressive in positioning themselves over against a major historical figure, or even to the dominant tradition of classical trinitarian theology.

Two examples, one Protestant and one Catholic, are illustrative. Colin Gunton's *The Promise of Trinitarian Theology* was published in 1991, and began with the programmatic essay "Trinitarian Theology Today." In that chapter he celebrated the centrality of the doctrine of the Trinity, but lamented "the unfortunate fact" that "the shape of the Western tradition has not always enabled believers to rejoice in the triune being of God."[10] Famously, Gunton identified Augustine as the supreme culprit for the defects of the West's spiritual history, and equally famously, Gunton's historical case has been found wanting.[11] But even if we pardon his rough handling of Augustine and overlook the defects of Gunton as historical theologian in order to focus on the benefits of Gunton the constructive systematician, there is a consistent tone of novelty or of fresh discovery in his presentation. He intends to say something about the Trinity that has not been said before, or at least has not been said in Latin or English.[12] Gunton's contagious excitement about the prospect of a refreshed trinitarianism comes through clearly in this essay: "Because God is triune, we must respond to him in a particular way, or set of ways, corresponding to the richness of his being. . . . In turn that means that everything looks—and, indeed, is—different in the light of the Trinity."[13]

Something very similar was found in contemporaneous Roman Catholic theology, such as Catherine Mowry LaCugna's 1993 *God for Us: The Trinity and*

---

10. Gunton, *The Promise of Trinitarian Theology* (Edinburgh: T&T Clark, 1991), 2.

11. A detailed critical examination of Gunton's treatment of Augustine can be found in Brad Green, *Colin Gunton and the Failure of Augustine: The Theology of Colin Gunton in Light of Augustine* (Eugene, OR: Pickwick Publications, 2011).

12. Gunton does use a rhetoric of retrieval with regard to the Cappadocians and succeeded in transmitting to many readers an excitement about retrieving their thought. However, his reception of Cappadocian trinitarianism is fraught and may be inextricable from an East-versus-West schema, which we will discuss below.

13. Gunton, *Promise*, 4.

the Christian Life. The same tone of new prospects opening up can be heard in its opening pages: "The doctrine of the Trinity is ultimately a practical doctrine with radical consequences for the Christian life. That is the thesis of this book."[14] But as with Gunton, LaCugna's programmatic sense that an important theological project was now underway was dependent on the claim that something had previously gone awry, and that it must now be set right. But for LaCugna, the problems were not just localized to Augustine, or to Western theology in his wake. She diagnosed the problems as more widespread in the West (unrepaired by Aquinas and other scholastics) and also at work in the East (unresolved by simple appeal to the Cappadocians, whose legacy was also problematic). For LaCugna, the trinitarian dysfunction had to be stated more broadly as well: the ultimate problem was that the doctrine of the Trinity had become a "nonsoteriological doctrine of God," a merely cognitive statement about God's nature. On the contrary, in the new trinitarianism she championed, "the doctrine of the Trinity is not ultimately a teaching about 'God' but a teaching about God's life with us and our life with each other."[15] The crucial thing for LaCugna's project was that it oriented the doctrine of the Trinity proper toward practice and experience; her work inspired theologians to articulate trinitarian theology toward making a difference for the Christian life and church practice.

But as with Gunton's project, the affirmation of something new required the negation of something old; the project's forward thrust was only achieved by kicking off from something traditional. The later reception of the work of both Gunton and LaCugna inevitably posed the question of whether their contributions (everything "looking different in light of the Trinity," a "practical doctrine with radical consequences") could be maintained without the negative judgment about vast tracts of theological tradition.[16] Was the revisionist rhetoric marginal or essential to their constructive task? Was the revival necessarily opposed to retrieval? In many ways, the task of trinitarian theology in the succeeding years has been to disentangle the remarkable sense of the revival's prospects and projects on the one hand from its counter-traditional articulations on the other.

14. Catherine Mowry LaCugna, *God for Us: The Trinity and Christian Life* (San Francisco: HarperSanFrancisco, 1991), 1.

15. LaCugna, *God for Us*, 228.

16. Both authors died in the middle of carrying out their own projects, LaCugna at age forty-four in 1997, and Gunton at age sixty-two in 2003. The fact that they did not live to extend and revise their own lines of thinking adds a poignancy to the question of the ends toward which their ideas were tending.

Decontextualized Critiques

In journalistic accounts of the trinitarian revival, it has become conventional to trace its origins to the work of Barth and Rahner. Bibliographically, this origin story has considerable plausibility. The trail of footnotes indeed tends to lead back from current discussions to one Karl or another. But as we attend to the way Barth and Rahner put trinitarian theology on the twentieth-century agenda, it is worth noting how the particular, local stories both of them told about the doctrine's decline were rapidly appropriated and extended to other contexts. The way these origin stories were stretched to cover new situations reveals much about the motives and preoccupations of the trinitarian revival.

Karl Barth knew what he was doing when he brandished the doctrine of the Trinity in the opening pages of the *Church Dogmatics*. His primary intention was doctrinal in good earnest, as he had found in trinitarian theology a way to draw together the form and the content of revealed theology under the sign of God's self-revelation as Lord. But he was also being provocative on purpose, deliberately baiting the leading practitioners of the academic Protestant theology that was enshrined in the universities and divinity schools of a regnant high liberalism. To take recourse to the doctrine of the Trinity was to invite the charge of being positively medieval. "Historically, formally and materially," Barth admitted, "I am now going the way of scholasticism," volunteering for his opponents the easily available evidence: "I obviously regard the doctrine of the early Church as in some sense normative. I deal explicitly with the doctrine of the Trinity."[17] As we have seen, the provocation was as deliberate as it was effective, evoking from Wilhelm Pauck the blustering response: "As if it were really a matter of life and death, that as members of the church of the Twentieth Century—we should accept the dogma of the Trinity!"[18] Pauck considered Barth an inconsistent prophet of a new age for Christian theology, one who kept trying to reach forward to the truly modern, fully existentialist mode of teaching that was appropriate to the twentieth century, but who kept lapsing back into antiquated modes of thought. For theologians like Pauck, it was clear that the doctrine of the Trinity belonged not to the emerging new age but to the irretrievable dark ages: "We deny that it is necessary that, in our efforts for a new expression of the Christian faith, we occupy ourselves with the Trinity and Christology. We would then commit the same mistake that Barth makes in

---

17. Karl Barth, *CD* 1/1, xiii.
18. Wilhelm Pauck, *Karl Barth: Prophet of a New Christianity?* (New York: Harper, 1931), 189.

his *Dogmatics*."[19] Using the terms then current to describe theological trends, we might say that for Pauck, Barth's articulation of neo-orthodoxy entailed too much orthodoxy and not enough neo. In recent years, John Webster has observed that a particular combination of the new and the old, with strategic emphasis on the old, was what set Barth apart from his neo-orthodox cobelligerents: "What was original to Barth was not his Christological concentration so much as his combination of it with classical conciliar incarnational dogma and Reformed teaching about the hypostatic union."[20] We might say the same about his appeal to the doctrine of the Trinity throughout the entire scope of the *Church Dogmatics*. What is novel, or distinctively modern, in it will fade away sooner than the relatively classical lines on which he developed his trinitarianism.

Without diminishing Barth's achievement in his own culture and context, we can nevertheless marvel that later thinkers in widely divergent traditions have written as if they, too, were shaking off the scholarly antitrinitarianism of high liberalism. Conservative Protestants and Roman Catholics have acted as if Barth's voice led them out of similar dead ends, when in fact Barth's voice was calling German Protestant theology to be, in respect of received dogma at least, more like these other communities. In context, his task was to "bemoan the constantly increasing confusion of modern Protestantism, which, probably along with the Trinity and the Virgin Birth, has lost an entire third dimension . . . which . . . we may describe as mystery."[21] To overcome liberal dismissiveness and reengage academic Protestant theology with trinitarianism, Barth was willing to risk sounding like some kind of Roman Catholic, or even a fundamentalist evangelical!

Speaking of Roman Catholic theology, Karl Rahner's book *The Trinity* has been so influential that during the Trinitarian revival it seemed *de rigueur* to begin every essay by quoting his opening laments: that "despite their orthodox confession of the Trinity, Christians are, in their practical life, almost mere 'monotheists,'" and that the situation is so dire that "should the doctrine of the Trinity have to be dropped as false, the major part of religious literature could well remain virtually unchanged."[22] Even for theological reflection on

19. Pauck, *Prophet?*, 201.

20. John Webster, "Christology, Theology, Economy," in *God without Measure: Working Papers in Christian Theology*, vol. 1, *God and the Works of God* (London: Bloomsbury T&T Clark, 2016), 56.

21. Barth, *Church Dogmatics* 1/1, xiii.

22. Karl Rahner, *The Trinity*, trans. Joseph Donceel (New York: Crossroad, 1997), 10–11.

the incarnation, Rahner says, there is almost nothing Trinitarian informing "the catechism of head and heart (as contrasted with the printed catechism)."[23] So deep is the "anti-trinitarian timidity"[24] that the doctrine in theological treatments has become systemically inert, meaning that "when the treatise is concluded, its subject is never brought up again" in relation to other doctrines. The mystery seems to have been "revealed for its own sake" such that "we make statements about it, but as a reality it has nothing to do with us at all."[25]

These complaints are stinging. But the most curious thing about them is their subsequent usage. They have been cited and echoed in such a vast literature, in provinces so widely different from their context of origin, that they serve as an all-purpose lament against every kind of neglect of the doctrine of the Trinity.[26] In context, what Rahner was railing against was Trinitarian doctrine's isolation in "textbook theology," and in particular in Roman Catholic dogmatics of the neoscholastic period. Whether Rahner was fair or not in his critique of the style, or simply the hegemony, of the neo-Thomism that flourished after 1879's *Aeterni Patris*, his complaints would seem to have been brought against such a specific school of thought that they might not have been transferable.[27] To take one example, when Rahner complained that the treatise *De Deo Uno* ought not to be separated from the treatise *De Deo Trino*, or at least ought not be handled in such a way that it solves in advance all the problems of trinitarianism and thus renders the second treatise superfluous, he was offering a criticism that could only apply to a very disciplined tradition of inquiry. When that complaint was echoed in theological traditions lacking the kind of formal precision and traditioned structures of neo-Thomism, it made less sense. Consider the parallel warning passed on by students of Bernard Lonergan, who quipped that Thomist trinitarianism was in danger of being "five

23. Rahner, *The Trinity*, 11.

24. Rahner, *The Trinity*, 13.

25. Rahner, *The Trinity*, 14.

26. It would be impossible to show how widely diffused Rahner's lament is in Trinitarian literature of the revival period. In retrospect it seems custom designed to be quotable on the opening pages of any book about the Trinity, since it carries with it the justification for writing any book about the Trinity.

27. For a survey of the broader issues at stake in engaging neo-Thomism, including a dispute about "classical theism," see Derrick Peterson, "A Sacred Monster: On the Secret Fears of Some Recent Trinitarianism," *Cultural Encounters* 12, no. 1 (2016): 3–36; especially part 3, on "Rahner's Rule as Historiography." Peterson's essay is also available in *The Lord Is One: Reclaiming Divine Simplicity*, ed. Joseph Minich and Onsi A. Kamel (Leesburg, VA: Davenant Press, 2019), 174–213.

notions, four relations, three persons, two processions, one nature, and zero comprehension." The complaint is as stinging as Rahner's. But unlike Rahner's it is so obviously focused on a particular tradition that it is not transferable. Neo-Thomism seemed, for some of its inheritors, to threaten Trinitarian vitality by an overabundance of formal precision. It seems ironic that Rahner's lament against it has been found serviceable in theological traditions with considerably less concern for formal precision or elaborate distinctions in their stated theological positions.

Alongside Barth and Rahner, a third force contributed to the modern trinitarian revival. That force was the influx of Eastern Orthodox theology, and constructive dialogue with it, in Western centers of theological discourse in the early twentieth century. The literature produced especially by Russian expatriates working in Paris was vast and vibrant, and the writings of Georges Florovsky, Sergei Bulgakov, and Vladimir Lossky are major contributions to twentieth-century theology at large. But in the doctrine of the Trinity, these theologians and their students frequently adopted an oppositional stance to all things Western. In part this can be accounted for by the revival and extension of polemics against the theology of the *filioque*, which occupied a key position in distinguishing East from West. One would expect Russians working in Paris to feel the need for a ready answer to the question of what distinguishes the two traditions, and theologians as profound as these would necessarily develop more than an ad hoc answer. But as was the case with Barth and Rahner, the arguments and diagnoses put into circulation by these Orthodox critics of Western trinitarianism took on a life of their own.[28] Criticisms that made a certain sense as strategic projections in their original setting came to sound increasingly bizarre as young Western theologians adopted them as if they were an accurate self-description of their own traditions. But again, what worked for Russian expatriates writing in Paris in the 1930s made one kind of sense; for Western theologians to accept this projection as their own self-understanding is bizarre.

Surely it is an optical illusion when modern evangelical Protestants in the United States, whose actual narrative is one of outgrowing the constrained horizons of fundamentalism, see themselves somehow implicated in Barth's reaction against high liberalism, and claim to be recovering the doctrine of

---

28. See the very helpful survey of waves of reception of the Orthodox argument, and especially to their complex interactions with Rahner's work, in Travis E. Ables, "The Decline and Fall of the West? Debates about the Trinity in Contemporary Christian Theology," *Religion Compass* 6, no. 3 (2012): 163–73.

the Trinity for reasons similar to his. Surely some unconscious alienation is at work when Presbyterians with Turretin or Bavinck in their intellectual heritage see themselves and their ancestors somehow reflected in the mirror of Rahner's lament that neoscholastic textbook theology has made them "almost mere monotheists." Surely some signals have become crossed when Western theologians in the lineage of Thomas and Bonaventure appropriate as their own self-descriptions the accounts projected onto them by Eastern Orthodox critics, and think of themselves as accidental modalists who have started with the one divine nature and tried in vain to derive the three persons from it. The analyses must ring true, or they would not be so widely redeployed. In some cases, those who retail these criticisms may be using them to draw analogous connections, fully aware of the differences between the situations. There must be some background pressure at work to dislodge these criticisms from their contexts of origin, putting them into circulation throughout the theological world. What capacity for receiving such critiques, apparently any critiques that came along, motivated theologians in such different contexts to apply them to themselves, to their own traditions, to the tradition of Trinitarian theology as a whole?

The Idea of a New Trinitarianism

There is something built into the modern epoch that tends in the direction of a readiness to subject the past to limitless critique. Recall Jaroslav Pelikan's summary comment that "the modern period in the history of Christian doctrine may be defined as the time when doctrines that had been assumed more than debated for most of Christian history were themselves called into question: the idea of revelation, the uniqueness of Christ, the authority of Scripture, the expectation of life after death, even the very transcendence of God."[29] It is also the period when old forms and structures were aggressively reinterpreted, or assigned brand new content. Whatever tensions began to be felt by theologians under the conditions of modernism, they apparently rendered the doctrine of the Trinity a uniquely vulnerable field for exploitation.

Friedrich Schleiermacher is a curious case study in this regard. His *Christian Faith* was a remarkable reframing of Christian doctrine in modern categories, consolidating all of theology around the Christian consciousness of the

---

29. Jaroslav Pelikan, *Christian Doctrine and Modern Culture (Since 1700)* (Chicago: University of Chicago Press, 1989), viii.

redemption achieved by Jesus Christ. He crafted every doctrine as a presupposition or an implication of that redemption. This method, which sounds so restrictive or even reductive, in fact yields a remarkably full system of Christian doctrine, and certainly one with a striking order and clear connections. But the doctrine of the Trinity fits poorly into the system, partly because it includes a statement about God absolutely in the divine self, which by its nature is not something that can be derived from the Christian consciousness of redemption (a consciousness that is only possible in relation to a God who has stepped out of absolute aseity and crossed over into relation with fallen creatures). As a result, the doctrine of the Trinity, in Schleiermacher's judgment, "is not an immediate utterance concerning the Christian self-consciousness but only a combination of several such utterances."[30] This is the reason the doctrine was assigned a place, notoriously, at the very end of the Christian Faith, on the border of what could be said about God within the constraints of the *Glaubenslehre*'s logic: a "doctrine of the faith" needs to be a statement of what faith itself apprehends.

But there is another reason the doctrine of the Trinity fit poorly into Schleiermacher's new account of the Christian faith. The problem with the doctrine is that it had not changed. Schleiermacher begins his account of the doctrine in the *Christian Faith* by saying that the doctrine cannot be considered one of the doctrines that is "finally settled." The reason it cannot be considered settled is that it did not change at the Reformation; it "did not receive any fresh treatment when the Evangelical [Protestant] Church was set up; and so there must still be in store for it a transformation which will go back to its very beginnings."[31] Schleiermacher is not moved here by a mere presupposition that progress or doctrinal development is the only reliable sign of life. Instead, he is so committed to the centrality of redemption, including the Protestant recovery of teaching on it, that he expects that redemption to throw a new light on every aspect of Christian doctrine. It simply follows that any doctrine that did not receive a fresh formulation in the sixteenth century must be destined either for imminent reformulation or oblivion; it either leans toward the future or the past. Schleiermacher himself, as we have seen, did not find a way to reinterpret the doctrine in line with his own principles, at least not in a way that moved it to the center of his concerns. Later in the nineteenth century, theologians working in the *Glaubenslehre* tradition, and theologians attempting to mediate between that method and more traditional ones, would find ways to make the

---

30. Schleiermacher, *The Christian Faith*, 2nd ed. (Edinburgh: T&T Clark, 1928), 156.
31. Schleiermacher, *Christian Faith*, 747.

Trinity more central, but its role in Schleiermacher's own carefully articulated system was peripheral. It had all the marks of a doctrine that could wither and fade without affecting the overall scope of Christian doctrine.

The tone set by Schleiermacher has become a pervasive feature of modern theological culture. The notion that the doctrine of the Trinity had fallen into disuse and is ripe for recovery has become such a widespread assumption that it can be found across the spectrum of theological and pastoral writers. Some especially clear phrasing of the attitude can be found in James Morris Whiton, a New England Congregationalist pastor and theologian, who published in 1892 *Gloria Patri: Our Talks about the Trinity*. In the preface he expresses his hope that "sooner or later it must be, that the Church will reap rich harvests of spiritual thought and life from this now weed-grown field, so long left fallow. It cannot be that this fundamental and all comprehending truth of Christianity will always be left in the cloud which barren scholastic controversy has raised about it."[32] The harvest he hopes to reap is to use the Trinitarian form of church confession to teach that "the immanent is one with the transcendent Power; the Filial Stream is one with its Paternal Fount."[33] Whiton plays loose with the language of "Filial Stream," exploiting its traditional sound but in fact assigning it a novel meaning. What is filial about the Filial Stream is that it is creation; its oneness with the Paternal Fount signifies that God and creation are one. The eternal Son is replaced by an eternal world, with filial categories covering the switch:

> The Living Father, Maker of heaven and earth, does not live apart from His creation, but lives in it from the beginning, as its Begotten or Filial Life. And this universal Life, whether existing or pre-existing, whether before the world or in the world, through all its myriad ranks from the highest to the lowest, whether in angels or in amoebas, in men or in the Christ, is His coeternal Word, or Son—His utterance, His offspring.[34]

The world, according to Whiton, slumbers in unconscious sonship except when it wakes in Christ to know itself as being one with the Father. The Spirit, in his scheme, is an even deeper immanence, if that is possible in a system that is all dialectical immanence.

32. James Morris Whiton, *Gloria Patri: Our Talks about the Trinity* (New York: Thomas Whittaker, 1892), 4.
33. Whiton, *Gloria Patri*, 92.
34. Whiton, *Gloria Patri*, 91.

In the down-market Unitarianism represented by Whiton, it is easy to recognize earlier forms of thought; Schleiermacher's influence is less evident than certain arguments given currency by David Friedrich Strauss. The replacement of the second person of the Trinity by the created world is a sure sign of left-wing Hegelianism at work, and in Whiton it predictably results in the dogma of an incarnation of God in humanity rather than in one particular human. What is crucial for the story of modern appropriations of trinitarianism, however, is not whatever content the modern thinker may choose to pour into the inherited forms and terms of Trinitarian doctrine; what is crucial is the whole idea that the doctrine of the Trinity requires new content. Whiton's own doctrines have rarely been revived and taught explicitly, but his revisionist maneuver is strikingly common. Whiton offered this prophecy for the future of the doctrine: "Doubtless, many will move on into the larger Trinitarianism which modern thinking requires. But quite as many will stay within the narrower lines of the past, and will imitate the Greek church in calling themselves 'the orthodox.'" But he was confident that the old view would be utterly replaced by the inevitable logic of the new view: "There is too much of the Holy Spirit now in the church to permit the new Trinitarianism to be again excommunicated by the old."[35] Whiton's phrase "the larger Trinitarianism" did not catch on, but one still hears about a "new Trinitarianism" from time to time.

Trinitarianism Since Jane Austen

There have by this time been enough new trinitarianisms in succession that it might be profitable to construct a typology of their varieties. It would be interesting to see what they have in common with each other and where they differ. But the net result of so many modern theologians adopting the tropes of revival and novelty, of bringing back something old and simultaneously brandishing it as something new, is that the doctrine of the Trinity itself has begun to seem unstable and indeterminate for several generations of theology students and church leaders. There is a constant harassment by bright new ideas, and a relentless production of new schemas by which to distinguish the latest trinitarianism from the errors that have gone before.

One of the requirements for anybody narrating a revival is to specify some historical coordinates that make the revival a possibility. The main coordinates are a rise and a fall; a time of initial flourishing in the distant past, and a time

---

35. Whiton, *Gloria Patri*, 128.

of deadening at some point thereafter, setting up the revival as the third step in the sequence. There has not been great agreement among the participants in the Trinitarian revival about when these earlier demarcations ought to fall. Some theologians look back to a golden age of Nicene theology followed by an Augustinian fall (Gunton); others think of Nicaea itself as the beginning of fatal missteps (LaCugna). Some might extend the golden age all the way into the early Middle Ages and find the culprits as late as a sclerotic Scholasticism; others could restrict the golden age of trinitarianism to the early strata of the New Testament itself, and find the decline setting in already in those New Testament documents that show greatest signs of acute Hellenization. Wherever the lines are drawn, the revival story won't work unless they are in place.

A related strategy is to subdivide by region. The notion of an Eastern version of trinitarianism standing in opposition to a Western version of trinitarianism has become firmly entrenched in the literature of the Trinitarian revival.[36] It is a fairly elaborate schema, typically involving the following cluster of themes:

> East and West differ so sharply as to have different theologies of the Trinity. The East is personalistic; the West is essentialist.
> The East starts with threeness and seeks oneness; the West does the opposite.
> The East is social Trinitarian; the West is psychological-analogy Trinitarian.

Some version of this contrast is operative in a great deal of the literature. Sarah Coakley has lamented that it "has obtained the unfortunate status of a truism in much systematic theological work of the later twentieth century," and that "generations of students have been pedagogically formed by this misleading narrative."[37] Indeed, the present moment is an awkward one for theological instruction. This construal of East and West has been problematized quite effectively by a couple decades worth of historical and descriptive work, especially Michel Barnes's exploration of its surprising genealogy.[38] But the schema was so pervasive for the most productive decades of late twentieth-century trinitarianism that it is very difficult to assign introductory books that are not infected by it in some way. Students can be counted on to pick up this facile simplification, because its strengths lie precisely in providing a broad

36. For some documentation, see Ayres, *Nicaea and Its Legacy*, 385.

37. Sarah Coakley, "Introduction: Disputed Questions in Patristic Trinitarianism," *Harvard Theological Review* 100, no. 2 (2007): 131.

38. Michel René Barnes, "De Régnon Reconsidered," *Augustinian Studies* 26 (1995): 51–79. For good reporting and analysis, see Ables, "The Decline and Fall of the West?"

organizing category for vast tracts of literature. Nevertheless, it is, as David Bentley Hart points out, self-doomed:

> The notion that, from the patristic period to the present, the Trinitarian theologies of the Eastern and Western catholic traditions have obeyed contrary logics and have in consequence arrived at conclusions inimical each to the other—a particularly tedious, persistent, and pernicious falsehood—will no doubt one day fade away from want of documentary evidence.[39]

It is indeed the documentary evidence that will banish this divisive schema, because whatever help it may appear to give in organizing a field of study, it provides no help in navigating any actual primary texts from any period of historical theology. Even as a guide to late polemics about the *filioque*, the East-versus-West schema is of limited help. Sarah Coakley likewise looks forward to being able to teach fourth- and fifth-century theology without the distorting paradigm in place: "Once the false wedge between East and West in this early period is removed, certain sorts of polemicizing about the innate superiority of one approach over the other become suspect, and we are returned to the texts themselves with fresh eyes, and—by implication—with fresh possibilities for ecumenical engagement."[40] Just as each chronological period requires more precise definition, if we were to use geographical zones to trace differences in the theological cultures of patristic thought, we would have to zoom in much closer than East and West; we would have to consider actual locations with traditions of inquiry like North Africa, Rome, Palestine, Asia Minor, Constantinople, and Antioch.

One of the ironies of the Trinitarian revival literature is that as it drew much of its energy from attempting to inscribe divisions like this, it actually divided itself from the great, consensual tradition of trinitarianism that, with admitted variations of time and place, nevertheless spans Christendom in a striking way. The doctrine of the Trinity simply has not been the site of marked disagreement among the churches, relatively speaking. The modern tendency to draw dividing lines through the history of the doctrine in fact is one of the eccentricities of modernism; it marks modern trinitarianism itself off as being divided from all that went before.

---

39. David B. Hart, "The Mirror of the Infinite: Gregory of Nyssa on the *Vestigia Trinitatis*," *Modern Theology* 18 (2002): 541.
40. Coakley, "Introduction," 134.

Much is at stake in sorting out falsified historiographies. When C. S. Lewis moved to Cambridge University to occupy a new chair, he took up the title of Professor of Medieval and Renaissance Literature. In his inaugural lecture for that chair, he argued at length that the "and" in the title was significant, and that what it signified was a real unity: medieval literature and renaissance literature belonged together as a single field of study. Lewis devoted most of his inaugural lecture, entitled "*De Descriptione Temporum*," to delegitimizing and relativizing the distinction between the two periods, a distinction that he identifies as "a figment of humanist propaganda."[41] By this he means that the distinction between the periods was calculated by Renaissance scholars to cast the Middle Ages as the Dark Ages (a period of baneful Christian influence), and to congratulate the Renaissance for being a new birth of wisdom. How did Lewis attack this false division between periods? By examining the details of the actual record.

There is a striking parallel to the deconstruction of the East-West paradigm, and other bedeviling subdivisions of the field of historical trinitarianism. What is needed now in systematic theology's appeal to historical theology is the elaboration of a trinitarianism that is both Eastern and Western, with the "and" signifying real unity. Of course there are many differences to mark, and the descriptive tools of academic historians will always excel at marking those differences. But they are differences within a striking unity and coherence from the earliest to the latest period.

Or not quite to the latest. For his part, though he disagreed with the inherited periodization of his field, Lewis realized he could not simply abolish all periodization. While recognizing the provisional and heuristic character of periodization, he did propose a new way of dividing the times and epochs. Lewis proposed that we should think of everything from antiquity through the Middle Ages and the Renaissance as belonging to one major period, and mark the great transition at an idiosyncratic point: Jane Austen. Western literature could be divided between pre-Jane and post-Jane. No doubt Lewis was being puckish in proposing Austen as the point of division of the ages of Western thought. But the point is striking, and a similar point needs to be made in the doctrine of the Trinity. A history of the doctrine of the Trinity that treated everything down to the time of Jane Austen as one kind of trinitarianism, and everything after as an-

---

41. C. S. Lewis, "De Descriptione Temporum," in *Selected Literary Essays* (Cambridge: Cambridge University Press, 1969), 2.

other kind, would be instructive.[42] Such a history would run the risk of smoothing out too many differences, and telling the story of the doctrine's development without enough dramatic conflict. But for this doctrine, the light of continuity would be more revealing than the light of discontinuity. Such a history would be able to make the most of Richard Muller's careful work on the lines of continuity that connect Protestant thought to the great tradition; and to appreciate Colin Gunton's perceptive remark that during the times normally considered periods of decline and neglect by the revivalists, nevertheless "in all periods there have been competent theologians, Catholic and Protestant alike, who have continued to work with traditional trinitarian categories while being aware of the reasons that have led others to question, modify, or reject traditional orthodoxy."[43]

RETROSPECTION AND INHERENT RETRIEVAL

We began this chapter with the claim that Trinitarian theology has something retrospective built into its deep structure, and suggested that trinitarianism may be a doctrinal case of retrieval all the way down. To deliver the doctrine from movements that claim to revive it but actually revise it, or at their worst strip out its essential content and fill its form with something new, it may be helpful to sketch three ways in which trinitarianism is constituted by retrospection.

First, trinitarian theology is inherently a matter of retrieval because it has the structure of praise. Biblical praise is a creaturely response to divine initiative and action, offering thanks for something that God has done. But praise does not terminate on the thing that has been done; it aspires to offer praise of the giver as well as the gift. Doxology takes its stand on a divine action in history and thinks back from the action into the being of the actor. Praise is always provoked by a concrete and categorical act of deliverance or blessing, but it is not true to itself unless it reasons its way back to something behind that action. This structure of biblical praise can be seen in the microcosm of

---

42. Jason Vickers, *Invocation and Assent: The Making and the Remaking of Trinitarian Theology* (Grand Rapids: Eerdmans, 2008), comes very close, putting the dividing line around the seventeenth century, but drawing a lot of the right lessons about how the torsions of early modernism distorted the doctrine.

43. Colin Gunton, "The Trinity in Modern Theology," in *Companion Encyclopedia of Theology* (London: Routledge, 1995), 937.

every deliverance, and in the macrocosm of the entire scope of God's story of keeping covenant with his people. Trinitarian theology is a pan-biblical summarizing doctrine that reads the entire economy of salvation as one integrated act of God for which he is to be praised. As such, it looks back along the lines of salvation history *pro nobis* to who God is *in se*. Trinitarian theology is a confession that in the fullness of time, the Father sent the Son and the Holy Spirit because in the fullness of eternity God is the Father, Son, and Holy Spirit. It retrieves divine identity from the divine economy.

Second, trinitarian theology is inherently retrieval-oriented because at the level of an exegetical undertaking it takes the form of rereading, or of construing the earlier phases of a progressive revelation in light of the later phases. Rereading in light of fuller awareness is a fundamental hermeneutical maneuver, without which the church would never have been able to confess the doctrine of the Trinity at all. The Gospels themselves are constructed as inspired rereadings of the life of Jesus Christ in light of his death and resurrection; the retrospective act of understanding more is built into them. The total canon of Scripture is a body of texts to be reread sequentially so that God is disclosed as the one who made promises and then fulfilled them, and his initial, mysterious disclosures lean forward to a future time of greater disclosure. Theological readers of Scripture come to understand God's identity by revisiting prior sites of revelation, hearing with greater clarity the referents of old words, as God who spoke in many ways and many portions long ago speaks at last in his Son.

Third, trinitarian theology has the character of retrieval because it is a mystery. It is a mystery because it is an articulation of what the entire biblical witness to the divine economy discloses about God. Scripture is a two-part revelation, with an Old Testament corresponding to a New Testament, and the forward pressure of the Old pushing into the greater clarity of the New. Though "mystery" can properly signify many things, and is always associated with the Trinity, in the New Testament the primary meaning of *mystery* is something that was once kept secret but has now been revealed. Built into the structure of God's self-revelation is a duality in which the second half derives its meaning from revisiting the first half. Knowledge of God comes to us from a biblical act of retrieving God's identity from the first half of the Bible in a way that is faithful to his revelation in the second half of the Bible.

The doctrine of the Trinity thus has a retrospective character built into it, and fruitful work in the field of trinitarian theology ought to be aligned with that retrograde motion. It ought to be more conspicuously centered on biblical reflection than it typically has been. But even in the misguided phases of the trinitarian revival, which so often seemed more like raids on the history of theology or exploitations of the external form of the doctrine, there was frequently some awareness that going back to the Trinity was the right thing to do. We can hope that the way forward in trinitarian theology will also follow this path back to the deeply retrospective trinitarianism of Scripture.

Acknowledgments

Chapter 1, "The Trinity as the Norm of Soteriology," revises "What Trinitarian Theology Is For: Placing the Doctrine of the Trinity in Christian Theology and Life," in *Advancing Trinitarian Theology: Essays in Constructive Dogmatics*, ed. Oliver D. Crisp and Fred Sanders (Grand Rapids: Zondervan, 2014), 21–41.

Chapter 2, "The Doctrine of the Trinity and the Scope of God's Economy," revises "The Trinity," in *The Oxford Handbook of Systematic Theology*, ed. John Webster, Kathryn Tanner, and Iain Torrance (Oxford: Oxford University Press, 2007), 35–53.

Chapter 3, "Trinity and Atonement," revises "These Three Atone: Atonement and the Trinity," in *The T&T Clark Companion to the Atonement*, ed. Adam Johnson (London: Bloomsbury T&T Clark, 2017), 19–34.

Chapter 4, "Trinity and Ecclesiology," revises "Ecclesiology and the Doctrine of the Trinity," in *The T&T Clark Companion to Ecclesiology*, ed. Kimlyn J. Bender and D. Stephen Long (London: Bloomsbury T&T Clark, 2020), 311–22.

Chapter 5, "Trinity and the Christian Life," revises "The Triune God," in *Sanctified by Grace: A Theology of the Christian Life*, ed. Kent Eilers and Kyle Strobel (London: Bloomsbury T&T Clark, 2014), 21–32.

Chapter 6, "Salvation and the Eternal Generation of the Son," revises "Eternal Generation and Soteriology," in *Retrieving Eternal Generation*, ed. Fred Sanders and Scott R. Swain (Grand Rapids: Zondervan, 2017), 260–70.

Chapter 7, "Salvation and the Eternal Procession of the Spirit," revises "The Spirit Who Is from God: The Pneumatology of Procession and Mission," in

The Third Person of the Trinity: Explorations in Constructive Dogmatics, ed. Oliver D. Crisp and Fred Sanders (Grand Rapids: Zondervan, 2020), 23–42.

Chapter 8, "Trinitarian Theology, Gospel Ministry, and Theological Education," revises "Evangelical Trinitarianism and the Unity of the Theological Disciplines," in *Journal of the Evangelical Theological Society* 60, no. 1 (2017): 65–80. It was originally delivered as a plenary address at the sixty-eighth annual meeting of the Evangelical Theological Society in San Antonio, Texas, on November 15, 2016. In this revised form, the chapter also includes several paragraphs from a paper copresented with Matt Jenson at a 2015 regional ETS meeting. The paper was entitled "Two-Handed Theology" and was never published. Matt may be the author of several of the sentences; we collaborated so closely that it is hard to be certain. But as a long-term theological confidante, Matt is in some larger sense a coauthor for the shape of the chapter.

Chapter 9, "The Story of the Modern Trinity," revises "The Trinity," in *Mapping Modern Theology: A Thematic History of Recent Theological Reflection*, ed. Kelly M. Kapic and Bruce L. McCormack (Grand Rapids: Baker Academic, 2012), 21–44.

Chapter 10, "Retrieval and the Doctrine of the Trinity," revises "Back to the Trinity," in *Theologies of Retrieval: An Exploration and Appraisal*, ed. Darren Sarisky (London: Bloomsbury T&T Clark, 2017), 213–28.

Select Bibliography

Ables, Travis E. "The Decline and Fall of the West? Debates about the Trinity in Contemporary Christian Theology." *Religion Compass* 6, no. 3 (2012): 163–73.

Anatolios, Khaled. *Retrieving Nicaea: The Development and Meaning of Trinitarian Doctrine.* Grand Rapids: Baker Academic, 2011.

Aquinas, Thomas. *Summa Theologiae.* Translated by the Fathers of the English Dominican Province. Westminster, MD: Christian Classics, 1981.

Athanasius. *Orations Against the Arians*, 2nd ser. Vol. 4, *The Nicene and Post-Nicene Fathers.* Edited by Henry Wace and Philip Schaff. Peabody, MA: Hendrickson Publishers, 1999.

Augustine. *The Trinity.* Vol. 5, *The Works of Augustine.* Translated by Edmund Hill, OP. Hyde Park, NY: New City Press, 1991.

Ayres, Lewis. *Nicaea and Its Legacy: An Approach to Fourth-Century Trinitarian Theology.* New York: Oxford University Press, 2004.

Badcock, Gary D. *Light of Truth and Fire of Love: A Theology of the Holy Spirit.* Grand Rapids: Eerdmans, 1997.

Balthasar, Hans Urs von. *Mysterium Paschale: The Mystery of Easter.* Grand Rapids: Eerdmans, 1993.

Barnes, Michel René. "De Régnon Reconsidered." *Augustinian Studies* 26 (1995): 51–79.

Barth, Karl. *Church Dogmatics.* Edited by G. W. Bromiley and T. F. Torrance, translated by G. W. Bromiley. Four volumes in thirteen. Edinburgh: T&T Clark, 1975.

Basil of Caesarea. *On the Holy Spirit.* Crestwood, NY: St. Vladimir's Seminary Press, 1980.

Bavinck, Herman. *Reformed Dogmatics.* Vol. 2, *God and Creation.* Edited by John Bolt, translated by John Vriend. Grand Rapids: Baker Academic, 2004.

Behr, John. "The Paschal Foundation of Christian Theology." *St Vladimir's Theological Quarterly* 45, no. 2 (2001): 116.

Boer, Harry R. *Pentecost and Missions.* Grand Rapids: Eerdmans, 1961.

Boff, Leonardo. *Trinity and Society.* London: Burns and Oates, 1988.

Bosch, David. *Transforming Mission: Paradigm Shifts in Theology of Mission.* Maryknoll, NY: Orbis Books, 2011.

Bray, Gerald. "Out of the Box: The Christian Experience of God in Trinity." Pages 37–56 in *God the Holy Trinity: Reflections on Christian Faith and Practice*, edited by Timothy George. Grand Rapids: Baker Academic, 2006.

Calvin, John. *Institutes of the Christian Religion.* Edited by John T. McNeill, translated by Ford Lewis Battles. Philadelphia: Westminster, 1960.

Coakley, Sarah. *God, Sexuality, and the Self: An Essay 'On the Trinity.'* Cambridge: Cambridge University Press, 2013.

Coffey, David. *Deus Trinitas: The Doctrine of the Triune God.* New York: Oxford University Press, 1999.

Congar, Yves. *I Believe in the Holy Spirit.* 3 vols. New York: Crossroad Herder, 1997.

Dale, R. W. *Christian Doctrine: A Series of Discourses.* London: Hodder and Stoughton, 1894.

Davidson, Ivor J. "Introduction: God of Salvation." Pages 1–14 in *God of Salvation: Soteriology in Theological Perspective*, edited by Ivor J. Davidson and Murray A. Rae. Burlington, VT: Ashgate, 2011.

———. "Salvation's Destiny: Heirs of God." Pages 155–75 in *God of Salvation: Soteriology in Theological Perspective*, edited by Ivor J. Davidson and Murray A. Rae. Burlington, VT: Ashgate, 2011.

Del Colle, Ralph. *Christ and the Spirit: Spirit Christology in Trinitarian Perspective.* Oxford: Oxford University Press, 1994.

Denney, James. *Studies in Theology.* London: Hodder and Stoughton, 1895.

Didymus the Blind. "On the Holy Spirit." Pages 143–227 in *Works on the Spirit: Athanasius and Didymus*, translated by Mark DelCogliano et al. Yonkers, NY: St. Vladimir's Seminary Press, 2011.

Dolezal, James. *All That Is in God: Evangelical Theology and the Challenge of Classical Christian Theism.* Grand Rapids: Reformation Heritage Books, 2017.

Doyle, Brian M. "Social Doctrine of the Trinity and Communion Ecclesiology in Leonardo Boff and Gisbert Greshake." *Horizons* 33, no. 2 (2006): 239–55.

Driel, Edwin Chr. Van. *Incarnation Anyway: Arguments for Supralapsarian Christology.* Oxford: Oxford University Press, 2008.

Duby, Steven J. *God in Himself: Scripture, Metaphysics, and the Task of Christian Theology.* Downers Grove, IL: InterVarsity Press, 2019.

Dupré, Louis. *The Common Life: The Origins of Trinitarian Mysticism and its Development by Jan Ruusbroec.* New York: Crossroad, 1984.

Emery, Gilles. *The Trinity: An Introduction to Catholic Doctrine on the Triune God.* Washington, DC: Catholic University Press, 2011.

———. "The Personal Mode of Trinitarian Action in Saint Thomas Aquinas." *Thomist* 69 (2005): 31–77.

Feiner, Johannes, and Magnua Löhrer, eds. *Mysterium Salutis: Grundriss Heilsgeschichtlicher Dogmatik.* Vol. 2. Einsiedeln: Benziger Verlag, 1965.

Flett, John. *The Witness of God: The Trinity, Missio Dei, Karl Barth, and the Nature of Christian Community.* Grand Rapids: Eerdmans, 2010.

Gerhard, Johann. *Theological Commonplaces: On the Nature of God and On the Trinity.* St. Louis: Concordia, 2008.

Green, Brad. *Colin Gunton and the Failure of Augustine: The Theology of Colin Gunton in Light of Augustine.* Eugene, OR: Pickwick Publications, 2011.

Gregory of Nazianzus. *On God and Christ: The Five Theological Orations and Two Letters to Cledonius.* Popular Patristics 23. Yonkers, NY: Saint Vladimir's Seminary Press, 2002.

Gunton, Colin. *Father, Son, and Holy Spirit: Essays toward a Fully Trinitarian Theology.* Edinburgh: T&T Clark, 2003.

———. *The Promise of Trinitarian Theology.* Edinburgh: T&T Clark, 1991.

———. "The Trinity in Modern Theology." Pages 937–57 in *Companion Encyclopedia of Theology*, edited by Peter Byrne and Leslie Houlden. London: Routledge, 1995.

Hall, Francis J. *Dogmatic Theology.* Vol. 4. London: Longmans, Green, & Co., 1910.

Harvey, Lincoln. "Essays on the Trinity: Introduction." Pages 1–13 in *Essays on the Trinity*, edited by Lincoln Harvey. Eugene, OR: Cascade Books, 2018.

Haudel, Matthias. "The Relation between Trinity and Ecclesiology as an Ecumenical Challenge and Its Consequences for the Understanding of Mission." *International Review of Mission* 90 (2001): 401–8.

Hegel, G. W. F. *Reason in History: A General Introduction to the Philosophy of History.* Translated by Robert S. Hartman. New York: Macmillan, 1995.

Hilary of Poitiers. *The Trinity.* Translated by Stephen McKenna. Washington, DC: Catholic University of America Press, 1954.

Hodge, Charles. *Systematic Theology.* Vol. 1. Grand Rapids: Eerdmans, 1995.

Holmes, Stephen R. *The Quest for the Trinity: The Doctrine of God in Scripture, History, and Modernity.* Downers Grove, IL: IVP Academic, 2012.

Irenaeus of Lyon. *Against Heresies.* Edited by Alexander Roberts, James Donaldson, and A. Cleveland Coxe. N.p.: Ex Fontibus, 2010.

Iwand, Hans Joachim. "Wider den Mißbrauch des 'pro me' als methodisches Prinzip in der Theologie." *Evangelische Theologie* 14 (1954): 120–24.

Jenson, Robert W. *Systematic Theology.* Vol. 1. New York: Oxford University Press, 1997.

———. *The Triune Identity: God according to the Gospel.* Philadelphia: Fortress Press, 1982.

John of Damascus. *An Exact Exposition of the Orthodox Faith.* In *Saint John of Damascus: Writings,* translated by Frederic H. Chase Jr. New York: Fathers of the Church, 1958.

Johnson, Adam J. *Atonement: A Guide for the Perplexed.* London: Bloomsbury T&T Clark, 2015.

Johnson, Elizabeth. *SHE WHO IS: The Mystery of God in Feminist Theological Discourse.* New York: Crossroad, 1992.

Kärkkäinen, Veli-Matti. *The Trinity: Global Perspectives.* Louisville: Westminster John Knox, 2007.

Kasper, Walter. *The God of Jesus Christ.* New York: Crossroad, 1984.

Keating, Daniel. "Trinity and Salvation." In *The Oxford Handbook of the Trinity,* edited by Gilles Emery, OP, and Matthew Levering, 442–53. Oxford: Oxford University Press, 2012.

Kimel, Alvin F., Jr, ed. *Speaking the Christian God: The Holy Trinity and the Challenge of Feminism.* Grand Rapids: Eerdmans, 1992.

LaCugna, Catherine Mowry. *God for Us: The Trinity and Christian Life.* San Francisco: HarperSanFrancisco, 1991.

Louth, Andrew. *Discerning the Mystery: An Essay on the Nature of Theology.* Oxford: Clarendon Press, 1983.

Marshall, Bruce D. "The Trinity." Pages 183–203 in *The Blackwell Companion to Modern Theology,* edited by Gareth Jones. Oxford: Blackwell, 2004.

———. "'Ex Occidente Lux? Aquinas and Eastern Orthodox Theology." Pages 19–46 in *Aquinas in Dialogue: Thomas for the Twenty-First Century,* edited by Jim Fodor and Frederick Christian Bauerschmidt. Oxford: Blackwell, 2004.

Mastricht, Petrus van. *Theoretical-Practical Theology.* Vol. 2, *Faith in the Triune God.* Grand Rapids: Reformation Heritage Books, 2019.

Molnar, Paul D. *Divine Freedom and the Doctrine of the Immanent Trinity: In Dialogue with Karl Barth and Contemporary Theology.* 2nd ed. London: Bloomsbury T&T Clark, 2017.

Moltmann, Jürgen. *The Crucified God: The Cross of Christ as the Foundation and Criticism of Christian Theology.* Minneapolis: Fortress, 1974.

———. *The Future of Creation.* Philadelphia: Fortress, 1979.

———. "Theological Proposals towards the Resolution of the Filioque Controversy." Pages 164–73 in *Spirit of God, Spirit of Christ: Ecumenical Reflections on the Filioque Controversy*, edited by Lukas Vischer. World Council of Churches Faith and Order Paper No. 103. London: SPCK.

———. *The Trinity and the Kingdom: The Doctrine of God*. Minneapolis: Fortress, 1981.

Muller, Richard. *Post-Reformation Reformed Dogmatics: The Rise and Development of Reformed Orthodoxy, ca. 1520 to ca. 1725*. Vol. 4, *The Triunity of God*. Grand Rapids: Baker Academic, 2003.

Newbigin, Lesslie. *The Relevance of Trinitarian Doctrine for Today's Mission*. Edinburgh: Edinburgh House Press, for the World Council of Churches Commission on World Mission and Evangelism, 1963.

Oakes, Edward T. S. J. "Diastasis in the Trinity." Pages 125–47 in *A Man of the Church: Honoring the Theology, Life, and Witness of Ralph Del Colle*, edited by Michel Rene Barnes, 125–47. Eugene, OR: Pickwick, 2012.

Packer, J. I. *Knowing God*. Downers Grove, IL: InterVarsity Press, 1993.

Pannenberg, Wolfhart. "Books in Review: Robert W. Jenson, *Systematic Theology: Volumes I & II.*" *First Things* 103 (May 2000): 51.

———. *Systematic Theology*. 3 vols. Grand Rapids: Eerdmans, 1991–1997.

———. *Theology and the Kingdom of God*. Philadelphia: Westminster, 1969.

Pelikan, Jaroslav. *Christian Doctrine and Modern Culture (Since 1700)*. Chicago: University of Chicago Press, 1989.

Peters, Ted. "Trinity Talk, Part 1." *Dialog: A Journal of Theology* 26, no. 1 (Winter 1987): 44–48.

———. "Trinity Talk, Part 2." *Dialog: A Journal of Theology* 26, no. 2 (Spring 1987): 133–38.

Peterson, Derrick. "A Sacred Monster: On the Secret Fears of Some Recent Trinitarianism." Pages 174–213 in *The Lord Is One: Reclaiming Divine Simplicity*, edited by Joseph Minich and Onsi A. Kamel. Leesburg, VA: Davenant Press, 2019.

Pollard, T. E. *Johannine Christology and the Early Church*. Cambridge: Cambridge University Press, 1970.

Pope, William Burt. *A Compendium of Christian Theology: Being Analytical Outlines of a Course of Theological Study, Biblical, Dogmatic, Historical*. 3 vols. London: Wesleyan Conference Office, 1879.

Rahner, Karl. *The Trinity*. Translated by Joseph Donceel. New York: Crossroad, 1997.

———. "Trinity in Theology." Pages 1755–71 in *Encyclopedia of Theology: The Concise Sacramentum Mundi*. New York: Crossroad, 1986.

Sanders, Fred. *The Deep Things of God: How the Trinity Changes Everything*. Wheaton, IL: Crossway, 2010.

———. *The Image of the Immanent Trinity: Rahner's Rule and the Theological Interpretation of Scripture*. New York: Lang, 2005.

———. *The Triune God*. Grand Rapids: Zondervan, 2016.

———. "Trinity Talk, Again." *Dialog* 44, no. 3 (Fall 2004): 264–72.

Schleiermacher, Friedrich. *The Christian Faith*. 2nd ed. Edinburgh: T&T Clark, 1928.

———. *On Religion: Speeches to Its Cultured Despisers*. New York: Harper & Brothers, 1958.

Schmid, Heinrich. *The Doctrinal Theology of the Evangelical Lutheran Church*. Minneapolis: Augsburg, 1889.

Shedd, William G. T. *Dogmatic Theology*. 3rd ed. Edited by Alan W. Gomes. Phillipsburg, NJ: P&R Publishing, 2003,

Smail, Thomas A. *The Giving Gift: The Holy Spirit in Person*. London: Hodder and Stoughton, 2002.

Sokolowski, Robert. *The God of Faith and Reason: Foundations of Christian Theology*. Washington, DC: Catholic University of America Press, 1995.

Sonderegger, Katherine. *Systematic Theology: The Doctrine of God*. Minneapolis: Augsburg Fortress, 2015.

Soulen, Kendall. *The Divine Name(s) and the Holy Trinity*. Philadelphia: Westminster, 2011.

Swain, Scott R. "Divine Trinity." Pages 78–106 in *Christian Dogmatics: Reformed Theology for the Church Catholic*, edited by Michael Allen and Scott R. Swain. Grand Rapids: Baker Academic, 2016.

———. *The God of the Gospel: Robert Jenson's Trinitarian Theology*. Downers Grove, IL: IVP Academic, 2013.

Taylor, Charles. *Hegel*. Cambridge: Cambridge University Press, 1975.

Tennent, Timothy C. *Invitation to World Missions: A Trinitarian Missiology for the Twenty-First Century*. Grand Rapids: Kregel, 2010.

Tillard, J.-M. R., OP. *Church of Churches: The Ecclesiology of Communion*. Collegeville, MN: Liturgical Press, 1992.

Torrance, Thomas F. *The Christian Doctrine of God: One Being Three Persons*. Edinburgh: T&T Clark, 1996.

Turretin, Francis. *Institutes of Elenctic Theology*. Vol. 3. Phillipsburg: P&R Publishing, 1997.

Vanhoozer, Kevin J. *The Drama of Doctrine: A Canonical-Linguistic Approach to Christian Theology*. Louisville: Westminster John Knox, 2005.

———. *Remytholoizing Theology: Divine Action, Passion, and Authorship*. Cambridge: Cambridge University Press, 2010.

Vickers, Jason. *Invocation and Assent: The Making and the Remaking of Trinitarian Theology*. Grand Rapids: Eerdmans, 2008.

Volf, Miroslav. *After Our Likeness: The Church as the Image of the Trinity*. Grand Rapids: Eerdmans, 1997.

Warfield, B. B. "The Biblical Doctrine of the Trinity." Pages 133–72 in *Works of Benjamin B. Warfield*. Vol. 2. Grand Rapids: Baker Book House, 1981.

Webster, John. *The Domain of the Word: Scripture and Theological Reason*. London: Bloomsbury T&T Clark, 2012.

———. *God without Measure: Working Papers in Christian Theology*. Vol. 1, *God and the Works of God*. Edinburgh: T&T Clark, 2016.

———. *Holy Scripture: A Dogmatic Sketch*. Cambridge: Cambridge University Press, 2003.

———. *Karl Barth*. London: Continuum, 2000.

———. "Reading Theology." *Toronto Journal of Theology* 13, no. 1 (1997): 53–63.

———. "Theologies of Retrieval." Pages 583–99 in *The Oxford Handbook of Systematic Theology*, edited by John Webster, Kathryn Tanner, and Iain Torrance. Oxford: Oxford University Press, 2007.

Welch, Claude. *In This Name: The Doctrine of the Trinity in Contemporary Theology*. New York: Scribner's, 1952.

Whiton, James Morris. *Gloria Patri: Our Talks about the Trinity*. New York: Thomas Whittaker, 1892.

Wilken, Robert Louis. "Is Pentecost a Peer of Easter? Scripture, Liturgy, and the Proprium of the Holy Spirit." Pages 158–77 in *Trinity, Time, and Church: A Response to the Theology of Robert W. Jenson*, edited by Colin E. Gunton. Grand Rapids: Eerdmans, 2000.

Williams, A. N. *The Ground of Union: Deification in Aquinas and Palamas*. Oxford: Oxford University Press, 1999.

Witsius, Herman. *Sacred Dissertations on What Is Commonly Called the Apostles' Creed*. Edinburgh: Fullarton & Co., 1823.

Wolterstorff, Nicholas. "Is There Justice in the Trinity?" Pages 177–87 in *God's Life in Trinity*, edited by Miroslav Volf and Michael Welker. Minneapolis: Fortress, 2006.

Index of Authors

Ables, Travis E., 190n28, 195n38
Allen, Michael, 108n20
Anatolios, Khaled, 183n2
Aquinas, Thomas, 35, 37, 42, 70, 96, 100, 102, 173, 191
Athanasius, 25, 89–90, 91, 93, 107, 125
Augustine, 36n15, 37, 42, 121, 122–23, 135, 142–43, 185
Austen, Jane, 197–98
Ayres, Lewis, 138n16, 183n2, 195n36

Badcock, Gary D., 43
Balthasar, Hans Urs von, 57n5, 64
Barnes, Michel René, 64n25, 195
Barth, Karl, 2, 20, 34, 36, 40, 42–43, 78, 80, 97n8, 107n18, 119, 174–78, 187–88
Barzun, Jacques, 156n8
Basil of Caesarea, 7, 119–20, 139, 147
Bauerschmidt, Frederick Christian, 51n44
Bavinck, Herman, 177, 179, 191
Beckwith, Carl L., 137n11
Behr, John, 58–59
Blocher, Henri, 138n15
Blount, Walter Kirkham, 5n10
Boer, Harry R., 145n21
Boff, Leonardo, 77, 171
Bosch, David, 78–79
Bracken, Joseph, 155
Bray, Gerald, 108n21, 135–36
Bromiley, G. W., 2n3, 119n12
Bulgakov, Sergei, 190
Bultmann, Rudolf, 165
Butner, D. Glenn, 25n9
Byrne, Peter, 176n61

Calvin, John, 1, 21, 31, 51–52, 98, 125
Carson, D. A., 131
Cassirer, Ernst, 157n9
Chadwick, Henry, 157n10
Chase, Frederic H., Jr., 44n32, 101n1
Clark, J. O. A., 105n11
Coakley, Sarah, 171, 195, 196
Coffey, David, 39
Congar, Yves, 51
Conti, Charles C., 22n7
Coppedge, Allan, 146
Crites, Stephen, 159n15

Dale, R. W., 18–19
Daly, Mary, 169
Davenant, John, 136
Davidson, Ivor J., 2, 91, 106
Del Colle, Ralph, 138, 143–44
Denney, James, 33n2
Didymus the Blind, 112, 137–38
Dixon, Philip, 156n7
Dolezal, James, 3
Dorner, Isaak A., 177
Doyle, Brian M., 77–78
Driel, Edwin Chr. van, 57–58n5
Duby, Steven J., 3
Dupré, Louis, 32n1

Emery, Gilles, 50n43, 88n1, 93, 97–98

Fangmeier, Jürgen, 119n12
Farrer, Austin, 22
Feiner, Johannes, 38n16, 41n26
Flett, John, 80
Florovsky, Georges, 190

Compendium of Systematic Theology
(Pope), 65–69
consubstantiality, 37, 89–90, 95, 125
Councils: of Constantinople (381), 125,
139–40 (*see also* Nicene-Constantinopolitan Creed [381]); of Florence (1431–
1449), 117; of Nicaea (325), 125, 183 (*see
also* Nicene-Constantinopolitan Creed
[381]); of Trent (1545–1563), 51
created grace, doctrine of, 50–52
creation, doctrine of, 60–62
creator-creature distinction, 21, 60, 72, 107
cultural diversity, 30, 35, 171
Cyril of Alexandria, 112

Daly, Mary, 169
"De Descriptione Temporum" (Lewis
lecture), 197
Deep Things of God, The (Sanders), 9
deism, 31, 179
Dei verbum (Vatican II), 24, 46
Didymus the Blind, 112, 137–38
discipleship, Christian, 145–46
disposition of the doctrine of the Trinity:
implications for evangelical theological
education, 147–51; Nicene style, 148–51;
Quicunquan style and the (so-called)
Athanasian Creed, 148, 149–51
divine impassibility, doctrine of, 62–63,
160
Divine Name(s) and the Holy Trinity, The
(Soulen), 29–30
divine self-revelation, 16, 18–27, 39, 46,
60, 99, 129, 187, 199; and incarnation, 21;
inferences about God's eternal life from
the economy of salvation, 23–27, 46; in
the Son of God as human being, 21–23;
three limitations to divine self-communication, 20–21
divine suffering, doctrine of, 62–63, 159–61;
Johnson's feminist theology and Sophia
categories, 170; Moltmann's trinitarian
theology, 26, 62–63, 159–61; theopaschitism, 26, 63
doxology, 19–20, 42, 65–69, 129, 198–99;

and doctrine of atonement/doctrine of
Trinity, 65–69; doctrine of Trinity as, 129;
Pope's *Compendium of Systematic Theology*, 65–69; and retrospective character
of trinitarian theology, 198–99

Eastern Orthodoxy: and doctrine of created grace, 51; and doctrine of uncreated
energies, 45, 50–51; *filioque* question, 43,
83, 190, 196; trinitarian revival, 190–91,
195–96
ecclesiology and Trinity, 70–86, 146;
communion and mission, 76–81, 146;
communion ecclesiology, 76–81, 146;
and evangelical gospel ministry with
both hands, 144–47; *koinōnia*, 70, 77, 78,
80–81; *missio Dei* ecclesiology, 76–81,
146; structural analogies, 81–85; Webster
and trinitarian deduction of ecclesiology,
72–76, 79, 85–86
economic-immanent axis, 28–29, 38,
42–49
economy of salvation, 32–53; economic-immanent axis, 28–29, 38, 42–49;
inferences about God's eternal life from,
23–27; "real presences," 49–53; re-centering trinitarianism on, 38–42, 52
ecumenism: *communio* and *missio Dei*
ecclesiologies, 70, 76–81; convergence on
doctrine of the Trinity, 52; dialogue over
the *filioque*, 44, 83, 117, 196
Eilbertus of Cologne, workshop of, 11–14
Enlightenment, critical: Hegel's task of
reconciling reason and history, 157–59;
Lessing and, 157; rationalism and inability to reckon with history, 157n9;
Romantic reaction against, 156, 165–68,
175; and trinitarian revival, 156, 157–59,
165–68, 175, 180
epideictic rhetoric, 130
eschatology, doctrine of, 36, 56, 71, 146–47;
Moltmann on unity of the Trinity, 161;
Pannenberg and the historical self-actualization of the Trinity, 161–63; salvation

66–67; and retrieval through reading Scripture, 199; and trinitarian reading of salvation history, 16

God for Us: The Trinity and Christian Life (LaCugna), 3–4, 40, 168–69, 185–86

God in Himself (Duby), 3

gospel and Trinity, 52

gospel ministry and theological education, evangelical, 129–53; and disposition of evangelical trinitarianism, 147–51; epideictic rhetoric, 130; and God's internal self-relatedness (speaking of divinity "relation-wise"), 134–36; gospel ministry with both hands, 144–47; missteps evangelical theologians make in teaching on the Trinity, 130–33; persuasion for deeper commitment to, 130–33; pneumatological Christology and christological pneumatology, 142–44; scope and place of teaching on doctrine of the Trinity, 133–36; "two-handed" systematic theology and internal approach to gospel ministry, 136–41; unity of theological disciplines around the Trinity, 151–53

great commission, 46, 144, 145

Hegel, G. W. F., 23–24, 157–59; metaphysical implications of the Trinity for, 159; reconciliation of reason and history, 157–59

Hegelianism, 23–24, 63, 157–59, 165, 194

Heidelberg Catechism, 101, 104–5

Herrmann, Wilhelm, 164

historical-critical biblical research, 48–49, 103

history and the Trinity, 157–65, 180–81, 183, 197; Hegel's reconciliation of reason and history, 157–59; Jenson and the narrative of the Trinity, 29, 34, 59–60, 71, 164; modern historical trinitarianism, 157–65, 180–81, 183, 197; modern theologians who minimize role of history, 164–65; Moltmann and theology of divine suffering, 62–63, 159–61; Pannenberg and eschatological self-actualization of the

Trinity, 161–63; reactions against Enlightenment rationality, 156, 157–59, 180

history of religions, 152

Holy Spirit: Athanasius and the Arian crisis, 125; biblical pattern of naming the "third person of the Trinity," 110–16; and Calvin's *Institutes*, 125; and doctrine of eternal procession, 25, 57, 87, 88–98, 100, 110–28; dove imagery of Eilbertus of Cologne, 13; and the economic-immanent axis, 42–49; eternal spiration, 92, 95–96, 98, 118; and *filioque* question, 43–44; gift as name for third person of the Trinity, 121–24; Greek *pneuma* and Greek-language theology, 124; Gregory of Nazianzus on Jesus and, 115–16; John of Damascus on, 44; Johnson's feminist theological project and the Spirit-Sophia, 170–71; Newman on, 127–28; New Testament consolidation of names for, 113; New Testament gospels, 125–26; and Nicene Creed, 125; Old Testament names for, 112–13; Paul on, 127, 128; pneumatology and Christology, 27, 49–50, 139–41, 142–44; and Rahner's Rule, 173; tethered to Christ (as the Spirit of Christ), 144; thirdness and the Spirit who was always already there, 124–28; Webster on pneumatological illumination, 128. *See also* eternal procession of the Spirit, doctrine of; Pentecost and the Spirit

Holy Trinity: Understanding God's Life, The (Holmes), 183–85

homoousios, 139–40

hospitality and God, 64

idealism, Hegelian, 158

Image of the Immanent Trinity, The (Sanders), 9

immanent Trinity, doctrine of, 2, 4, 8–9, 17, 24–25; and doctrine of Trinity in Bible, 17; and economic-immanent axis, 28–29, 38, 42–49; Rahner's Rule, 38–40, 68–69, 173; and salvation history, 39–41; and social trinitarianism, 45

incarnation, 49, 57–58; and God's self-rev-

pantheism, 162, 179

Paulist Press's What Are They Saying series, 155

Pentecost and the Spirit, 25, 43, 50, 71, 92, 100, 121–22, 139, 142, 145–47, 173

perichōrēsis, 37, 44, 54, 70, 77, 82–83, 140, 161

Phenomenology of Spirit (Hegel), 158

Pietism, 52

pluralism, doctrinal, 30, 35

pneumatology and Christology, 27, 49–50, 139–41, 142–44. *See also* Holy Spirit

Pope, William Burt, 65–69, 105, 178

positivism, historical, 19, 42

process theology, 24, 165

Promise of Trinitarian Theology, The (Gunton), 185

Protestant missions movement, 145

Protestant theology: distinction between God considered absolutely and God considered relatively, 108; liberalism and Barth's retrieval of doctrine of the Trinity, 174–75, 187–88; Reformation, 48, 184, 192; Reformed, 45, 52, 62, 135; Schleiermacher, 35–36, 166–68, 191–94; Trinity and indwelling of the Holy Spirit in the believer, 51–52

Pseudo-Dionysius, 21

Quicunquan style of disposition of the doctrine of the Trinity, 148, 149–51

Rahner, Karl, 3, 9, 31, 35, 38–40, 68–69, 171–73, 174, 187–91; *Grundaxiom* (Rahner's Rule) on the economic and immanent Trinity, 38–40, 68–69, 173; methodological approach to trinitarianism, 173; Rahner's lament and the trinitarian revival, 172, 187, 188–91; synthesis of the themes of experience and history, 171–73; and trinitarian revival, 171–73, 187, 188–91

redemption, Christian consciousness of, 166–68, 191–93

Reformation, 48, 184, 192

Reformed Protestant theology, 45, 52, 62, 135

relevance and the doctrine of the Trinity, 88–89

Remythologizing Theology (Vanhoozer), 3

resurrection of Christ, 12, 57–59, 71, 90, 142, 143, 164, 199

retrieval, theological method of, 174–81, 182–200; Barth, 174–78, 187–88; and doxology, 198–99; Gunton, 185; and Holmes's critique of the revival, 183–85; and LaCugna, 185–86; and mystery, 199; and Rahner's lament, 172, 187, 188–91; reasons for turning to, 175; and rereading, 199; and retrospective tone of trinitarian theology, 182–83, 198–200; Swain on "renewal without retrieval," 184–85; theologians positioned against historical retrieval, 185–86; three ways in which trinitarian theology is constituted by retrospection, 198–200; and the trinitarian revival, 174–81, 182–200; Webster on, 175. *See also* trinitarian revival

revelation, doctrine of, 27, 176. *See also* divine self-revelation

rhetoric: Aristotelian, 103; epideictic, 130

Rhineland mystics, 31, 97

Roman Catholic theology: and Barth's retrieval of the doctrine of the Trinity, 174, 188; doctrine of created grace, 51; LaCugna on doctrine of Trinity, 185–86; *Mysterium Salutis* group and Vatican II, 38–39, 41; and neo-Thomist trinitarianism, 189–90; Rahner's lament and the trinitarian revival, 188–90

Romantic reaction against the critical Enlightenment, 156, 165–68, 175

Ruether, Rosemary Radford, 169

salvation, doctrine of: connection to doctrine of Trinity, 1–4, 30–31, 32, 154; and doctrine of creation, 62; and doctrine of eternal generation, 99, 100; and doctrine of the Christian life, 97; error of deficiency, 30–31; error of excess, 30–31; and nonsoteriological doctrine of